Ratting

The Use and Abuse of Informants in the American Justice System

Robert M. Bloom

Westport, Connecticut
London

Library of Congress Cataloging-in-Publication Data

Bloom, Robert M., 1946–
    Ratting : the use and abuse of informants in the American justice system /
    Robert M. Bloom.
        p. cm.
    Includes bibliographical references and index.
    ISBN 0-275-96818-9 (alk. paper)
        1. State's evidence—United States.   2. Informers—Legal status, laws, etc.—
    United States.   I. Title.
KF9665 .B58   2002
345.73'06—dc21   2001058037

British Library Cataloguing in Publication Data is available.

Library of Congress Catalog Card Number: 2001058037
ISBN: 0-275-96818-9

First published in 2002

Praeger Publishers, 88 Post Road West, Westport, CT 06881
An imprint of Greenwood Publishing Group, Inc.
www.praeger.com

Printed in the United States of America

∞™

The paper used in this book complies with the
Permanent Paper Standard issued by the National
Information Standards Organization (Z39.48-1984).

10   9   8   7   6   5   4   3   2   1

Contents

Acknowledgments

I wish to thank Dean John Garvey of the Boston College Law School and the Walter Weckstein Research Grant for their support of this project. I also thank my research assistants Sharon Leifer and Nicholas Kenney for their valuable contribution. Special thanks go to Theresa Kachmar and Alice Lyons for their ability to translate my vague instructions into an end product. As always I thank my wife Christina Jameson for her editorial assistance.

Preface

At this late date in the annals of law enforcement, it seems to me that we cannot say either that every use of informers and under-cover agents is proper or, on the other hand, that no uses are. There are some situations where the law could not adequately be enforced without the employment of some guile or misrepresenta-tion or identity. A law enforcement officer performing his official duties cannot be required always to be in uniform or to wear his badge of authority on the lapel of his civilian clothing. Nor need he be required in all situations to proclaim himself an arm of the law. It blinks the realities of sophisticated, modern-day criminal activity and legitimate law enforcement practices to argue the contrary. However, one of the important duties of this Court is to give careful scrutiny to practices of government agents when they are challenged in cases before us, in order to insure that the pro-tections of the Constitution are respected and to maintain the integrity of federal law enforcement.
—United States v. Hoffa, 385 U.S. 293, 315 (1966),
Chief Justice Earl Warren, dissenting

As the words of the late chief justice of the Supreme Court indicate, in our society today in order to investigate a great many wrongful acts in-formants have become a necessary evil. With many crimes involving willing participants, it is often necessary for the government to utilize in-dividuals with nefarious motives to investigate these crimes. This book will explore the use and, for that matter, the abuse, of informants in a variety of settings and with diverse motivations. Each of the informants has one salient feature: They provide information to the government, which in some way helps the government to investigate people whom they wish to prosecute.

My approach will be to introduce the informants in a narrative format. I have chosen actual informants who provide good illustrations of the roles of informants in different contexts. In Chapter 1 we will look at the history of the use of informants and focus briefly on perhaps the most infamous informant—Judas Iscariot. In Chapter 2 we look at Linda Tripp who was used to investigate the President of the United States. In Chapter 3 we look at an imaginary informant who is fabricated by a police officer in order to justify his investigatory activity. In Chapter 4 we look at Leslie White and Anthony Sarivola who were used to gather evidence within a prison or jailhouse context. In Chapter 5 we will look at James J. "Whitey" Bulger and Stephen "The Rifleman" Flemmi who were used to infiltrate and destroy an organized crime operation. In Chapter 6 I will summarize and suggest ways to use informants without incurring high costs.

In looking at these informants we will explore their motivations. We will see that informants do what they do for a variety of reasons, including financial gain, political power, attention, elimination of competitors, and the avoidance of criminal punishment. We will also explore how the law intersects with the activities of these informants.

Chapter 1

A Historical Overview of Informants

From the dawn of our history, internal law and order has had to depend in greater or less measure on the informer.
                                                        —Police Manual[1]

Informers date as far back as the first records of governing institutions. As long as states have existed, they have needed information about challengers to their authority. In fact, the words "informer" and "informant" derive from the informer's role as supplier of information. This information is usually given to the state for its prosecution of crime.[2]

There are two basic types of informers: the "incidental" informer and the "recruited" (or "confidential") informer. Incidental informers supply information to the authorities about one particular incident; they might receive a one-time reward, but they are not "on the payroll." Incidental informers often act out of a sense of civic duty. They do not have repeated contact with the authorities but rather supply information about one incident or from one meeting. In contrast, confidential informants provide information for ongoing investigations during the course of repeated meetings with police. Because this type of informer receives ongoing compensation, the government considers them "on the payroll."[3]

Confidential informers began to play a larger role as our governing institutions developed more complex policing systems and formalized investigative techniques. From ancient Greece through the early nineteenth century, there was little widespread or systematic use of confidential informers. Most informers played a minimal role in the criminal justice system. When police forces in western Europe began to professionalize, informant use became much more prevalent. Although this reflects the general pattern of informer history, there are examples of extensive use of confidential informants in ancient Rome and during the Middle Ages.[4]

INFORMANTS IN ANCIENT CIVILIZATIONS

The laws of antiquity did not draw a distinction between criminal acts and private wrongs, as most legal systems do today. Rather, all violations against private individuals were categorized as *delicts* (a broader term than our "tort," although by and large *delicts* are what we would today call torts). Victims could bring private actions against their perpetrators, but the state played no role in gathering evidence or prosecution. For example, in a homicide case, the victim's estate would have the burden of initiating, funding, and prosecuting the murderer. Consequently, informers as we understand them today, people who give information about a crime to the government or police, were not widely known or used in these types of cases.[5]

Informers were vigorously employed, however, in cases of treason. The birthplace of democracy, classical Athens (425–322 B.C.), had a rich tradition of encouraging the reports of planned and already committed treasonous acts.[6] Termed *menutai* in Greek, any person could come forward, whether it be man or woman, slave or free person, citizen or foreigner.[7] The informer would report to the *Boule* or *Ekklesia*, courts of capital crimes in Athenian society. As for the system of rewards and punishment, a 415 B.C. law provided that an informer be given impunity if his information was true, but he would be put to death if it was not. Often, an informer was a member of the conspiracy to commit treason and would come forward on condition of impunity.[8]

Andocides was the most renowned Greek informer. In 415 B.C., he conspired in the desecration of sacred Athenian statues called the Hermae, which were "sacred pillars topped by busts of the gods."[9] Andocides was acquitted in exchange for informing on his fellow conspirators, including his own father, Legoras. All the named culprits were executed except for Legoras, who like his son, informed on other criminals to gain his freedom.[10]

Similarly, in ancient Roman society, the ruling authority used informers chiefly to combat subversion. Functioning as modern-day spies, private entrepreneurs, known as *delatores*, brought information to the urban magistrate and the emperor. These *delatores* are the closest historical example of what is now considered a confidential informer. In fact, in the second century A.D., emperors used a group of *delatores* called the *frumentarii* to gain information about subversive activity. These officials were uniquely suited to observe activity across the empire because they supplied grain to the legions and thus could provide contacts across the Mediterranean on a regular basis.[11]

In conclusion, classical history exhibits the use of informers to extend the reach of state-sponsored law enforcement. Greek and Roman governments were primarily concerned with crimes against the state's power and stability, not with crimes against individuals. Consequently, informers in ancient times were key players only in cases of treason and subversion.

JUDAS ISCARIOT: THE MOST FAMOUS INFORMANT

Judas Iscariot, one of Jesus' twelve apostles, was the "one who betrayed him" (Matt. 10:4). His name has become "synonymous with betrayal"[12] and likened to Benedict Arnold.[13] Therefore, we regard Judas as one of the early informants.

According to biblical accounts, Judas was an informer for the Romans, the ruling government, against Jesus. In 33 A.D., the local authorities wished to arrest Jesus and hand him over to the Romans, who planned to execute him for sedition. However, as Jesus' popularity was great, leaders feared that a public arrest might result in a riot. During the Passover feast, Judas guided the Roman soldiers to Gethsemane, a remote grove outside Jerusalem where Jesus was celebrating the feast. When Judas and the Romans arrived, Judas identified Jesus under the torchlight by giving him a kiss. Thus, Judas supplied the information needed to arrest Jesus quietly and thus avoided an uprising. In exchange for his role as an informant, Judas received thirty pieces of silver. Without Judas's role as an informer, the arrest might have had to be made more publicly and resulted in an insurrection, which, in turn, might have brought the Roman army down on all Jerusalem.[14]

The New Testament contains little information about Judas's history prior to his betrayal of Jesus.[15] Folklore holds that Judas was born to Reuben and Cyborea, a Jewish couple.[16] When Cyborea was pregnant, she dreamed that Judas would grow up to destroy the entire Jewish people.

Fearing this prophecy, Cyborea put the baby Judas into a chest and sent him out to sea. The childless queen of the island Skariot discovered the infant and raised him as her own. She later gave birth to a son, whom Judas eventually killed upon learning of his own origin. Judas then left Skariot and landed in his birthplace. There, not knowing him to be his father, Judas entered into a fight with Reuben and killed him. Now a member of Pilate's entourage, Judas married Reuben's wife, unaware that she was actually his mother.[17] When he and Cyborea uncovered the truth about their familial relations, Judas went to Jesus for forgiveness and became one of his favorite disciples (John 12:6). Judas became a member of Jesus' inner circle, known as the twelve apostles. In this group, Judas was the treasurer and carrier of the common purse. In search of the motivation for Judas's act of betrayal, the Book of John attributes this position to Judas's being a thief.[18] Some scholars see Judas's connection with money as having corrupted him and thus made his turn to evil and betrayal more comprehensible. However, this money theory could be interpreted in another way. Since Judas was keeper of the purse and had ready access to money, then it is unlikely that money motivated his betrayal. Further, given that Jesus gave him this important and responsible position, Jesus probably regarded Judas as being honest and not a thief.

Another theory of motivation focuses on Judas's possible altruistic motives. Judas had great faith that Jesus was indeed the Son of God. He hoped that when Jesus was seized by the authorities he would manifest his power for all the world to see. Of course, one could also argue that this reflects Judas's impatience and concern with an earthly manifestation of divinity rather than a heavenly one.[19]

Still another theory of Judas's motivation might be his personal animus toward Jesus. There are two reasons for this feeling. First, Judas was the only apostle from Judea in the south; the rest were from Galilee in the north. Although he had a trusted position, Judas was not part of Jesus' inner circle. Second, Judas expected Jesus to become a ruler of an earthly kingdom and himself to have an important role in this regime. Since this never happened, Judas felt disappointed in his own personal advancement and began to resent Jesus (Matt. 27:3–5). Clearly, the truth of any of these theories is only speculative. Judas Iscariot, the informer, could have been motivated by greed, hate, altruism, or a combination of factors. These same factors continue to influence and motivate informants in their actions today.

According to the Book of Matthew (27:3–5), Judas repented for his notorious act of betrayal and returned the thirty pieces of silver to the Romans. He then hanged himself. The chief priests used the money (which at this point was blood money and could not be put back into the treasury) to buy a field in which to bury foreigners. To this day, the field is still called the Field of Blood.

Members of the early Christian Church used the Judas story to discourage informing among its persecuted members. Vilification of Judas in the tradition fluctuated with the level of Roman persecution of Christians.[20] In contemporary times, Judas has been associated with such infamous informants as Linda Tripp[21] and others considered to have betrayed or informed on someone. Debate about the exact motives of Judas continues today. Additionally, some disagreement continues regarding the proper translation of the words describing Judas's acts in informing on Jesus. However, because the story of Judas's betrayal is so well-known, Judas Iscariot remains the epitome of betrayal and informing to many.[22]

INFORMANTS FROM THE MIDDLE AGES THROUGH THE ENLIGHTENMENT

By 1275, informant use in England had broadened to include felony prosecutions.[23] The "approver system," as it was termed, set up procedural incentives for informers to come forward. To become an approver, a person accused of treason or a felony could confess and inform on any remaining accused persons. A successful approver would be fully pardoned and exiled, but if the approver's testimony was proved false, the approver risked execution.

The system was rife with flaws.[24] There was nothing to lose by appealing to approve. If an accused murderer stood trial, he could lose and face execution. If he appealed to "approve" against his fellow conspirators, he could likewise lose and face execution.[25] Either way the accused risked execution, so he might as well inform. Furthermore, the system provided an incentive to blackmail innocent parties. A person could threaten to appeal for approval against an innocent person unless the innocent person handed over money. Law enforcement officials sometimes compelled prisoners to inform on innocent parties in order to extort ransom. Ultimately, the system succumbed to its long history of abuse and was gradually replaced by the common informer system.

A common informer was "a person who brought certain transgressions to the notice of the authorities and instituted proceedings, not because he, personally, had been aggrieved or wished to see justice done, but because under the law he was entitled to a part of any fine which might be imposed."[26] This system, too, was subject to widespread abuse.[27] For instance, in the eighteenth century, poachers learned to have a friend come forward as the informer so they would have rights to the fine. "Five pounds sterling went from the poacher to the JP [Justice of the Peace], then to the friend (as informer) and back again to the poacher over a pint in the alehouse."[28] Thus, the common informer system proved too costly and vulnerable to corruption for the small benefits of justice it produced.[29]

THE RISE OF PROFESSIONAL POLICE AND INFORMANTS IN THE NINETEENTH CENTURY

Western European states began to develop more sophisticated police forces in the early nineteenth century.[30] In France, François Vidocq, imprisoned for a minor crime, agreed to provide information to the police about other prisoners.[31] He was later released in exchange for having given this information and went on to found the Paris Sûreté, a criminal investigation division of the Paris police. From 1810 to 1827, Vidocq set up a network of informers, hired former criminals as detectives, and pioneered systematic use of police surveillance and investigation.

In 1877 an English barrister, Howard Vincent, emulated Vidocq's work and established the Criminal Investigation Department (CID). Much like the approver and common informer systems, CID informers provided new opportunities for police corruption. By the 1920s the metropolitan CID "had become a thoroughly venal private army."[32]

Despite the failures and abuses of this method of criminal investigation and prosecution, England developed a deep tradition of using informants effectively. This early informant system, though imperfect, laid the foundation for the establishment of improved information-gathering systems, particularly in the policing of colonies such as Ireland and America. English imperial history is full of examples of the Crown forces skillfully using an informer to subvert its enemies.[33]

For instance, in America, the British used informers to enforce the unpopular Navigation Acts and other similar legislation.[34] Because distrusting informers was a large part of American colonials' distrust of British rule, after the Revolution the new government refrained from employing these same policing techniques. In fact, informers did not come back into use until American cities developed professional police forces in the mid-nineteenth century. By this time, even private enterprises, such as Allan Pinkerton's private detective agency, used a network of informers to carry out the assignments of its corporate clients.

INFORMANTS IN THE TWENTIETH CENTURY

Prohibition and communism increased the demand for informer activity. Confronted with the threat of Bolshevism from Russia at the end of World War I, American citizens and law enforcement officials alike supported the use of informers to combat crime.[35] The Federal Bureau of Investigation (FBI), established during the presidency of Theodore Roosevelt in 1908, developed and cultivated informers across the country who were essentially domestic spies. From the 1920s to the 1970s, the FBI infiltrated and investigated what it considered to be radical groups, such as the Black Panthers, the Students for a Democratic Society, the Progressive Labor Party, and Vietnam Veterans against the War.[36] The informers not only investigated crimes, but also sabotaged the work of these groups. For the most part, the informants were political operatives, harkening back to ancient Greek and Roman civilizations when informers were primarily used to undermine subversive activity.

The FBI has also used informers in criminal investigations. It has distinguished between people with legitimate occupations, whom it calls "confidential sources," and those in close contact with criminal elements, whom it classifies as "informants." The FBI is infamous for its use of informers in investigating organized crime. Recently, the FBI Law Enforcement Bulletin (November 1998) addressed the informer issue directly. This bulletin focused on the failures and abuses that have plagued informer systems since their inception. The bulletin also discussed how to recruit reliable informants, how to document and assess the value of informant information, how to identify false or misleading information, and how "to handle" informants.

Since much of the crime in America today involves willing participants, the need for informants has increased substantially. In order for law enforcement authorities to solve crimes such as drug dealing, gambling, loan-sharking, money laundering, and political corruption, they need information from individuals who are either closely aligned with the participants or are participants themselves.

Chapter 2

The Political Informant

"A Certain Fair-Weather Friend"[1]—The Story of Linda Tripp

INTRODUCTION

The story of Monica S. Lewinsky's sexual liaison with President William J. Clinton is known throughout the world. The president's efforts to conceal the affair eventually led to his impeachment proceedings and consumed the United States government's attention and energies for many months. This sordid tale would not have seen the light of day but for the involvement of a career government employee named Linda R. Tripp. Tripp befriended Lewinsky, a young woman nearly half her age, while they were coworkers at the Pentagon. She gained her trust and then betrayed her. Not only did she share Lewinsky's secrets with others, but she taped their conversations and ultimately shared the tapes with Kenneth W. Starr, the special prosecutor investigating the president. She turned a private affair into a scandal that threatened the President of the United States. This well-known story finds its way into this book because once Tripp started to work for the government (through the office of Kenneth Starr) she became an informant, a political informant.

LINDA: THE EARLY YEARS

Linda R. Carotenuto was born in 1949 to a middle-class family in suburban New Jersey. Her father taught high school math and science, while her mother stayed home to raise Linda and her younger sister. In

1967, when she was a senior in high school, Linda and her family were shaken by her father's scandalous affair with another teacher. Soon after his affair was exposed, he abandoned the family. Upon graduating from high school, Linda, while living at home, attended Katharine Gibbs School. In 1971, less than a year after her parents' divorce, she married Lieutenant Bruce Tripp, a career army officer. They had two children: a son Ryan in 1975 and a daughter Allison in 1979. As a military wife, Tripp accompanied her husband to numerous places, including Germany, the Netherlands, North Carolina, and Maryland. Tripp cared for her children at home until they were of school age. She then began working at various jobs for the Department of the Army, depending on where her husband was stationed.[2] Tripp and her husband separated in 1990 and divorced in 1992.[3]

In April 1991, Tripp entered the Bush administration White House secretarial pool. She was carried over to the Clinton administration and eventually worked in White House Counsel Bernard Nussbaum's office. Tripp was working in Nussbaum's office in July 1993 when Deputy Counsel Vincent W. Foster Jr. committed suicide. Her claim to fame at the White House was that she served Foster his last meal before he allegedly shot himself.[4] In November 1993, Tripp also witnessed Kathleen Willey emerging from the Oval Office with her blouse disheveled and her lipstick off.[5] Linda Tripp had given Willey's name to Paula Jones's lawyers, who later subpoenaed Willey to testify in Jones's sexual harassment case against President Clinton. On March 15, 1998, five days after testifying before the Starr Grand Jury, Willey appeared on *60 Minutes* to publicly accuse the president of sexual harassment.

While at the White House, Tripp was an informal career counselor to several young women on the staff. Although she encouraged young women to share their problems with her, she never discussed her own problems.[6] "According to one former co-worker, Tripp was the kind of person others confided in, and she often befriended younger women on the staff, soliciting confidences and offering career advice."[7]

After Lloyd Cutler replaced Nussbaum in the spring of 1994, Tripp was reassigned within the White House but found herself with little to do. With the help of Joel Klein, Cutler's deputy, she obtained a Pentagon job with a substantial pay increase.[8] On August 22, 1994, Tripp began working in the Pentagon's Office of Public Affairs for the Secretary of Defense. In April 1996, she met Monica Lewinsky, a young intern recently transferred from the White House.

LINDA AND MONICA

In June 1995, Lewinsky was a White House intern in Chief of Staff Leon Panetta's office. On November 26, 1995, she was moved to a paid position in the Office of Legislative Affairs and finally transferred on April 5, 1996, to work at the Pentagon. Linda Tripp met her shortly after she arrived at the Pentagon. With work obligations, Tripp did not have time to let the relationship between her and Lewinsky flourish until later that spring. As part of Tripp's public relations work, she had large photographic portraits of the president. Lewinsky noticed these photographs and a conversation with Tripp ensued; they discovered that they were the only two people working in the Department of Defense's public affairs office who had also worked at the White House. According to Tripp, the relationship quickly became intense. She characterized the relationship as both sisterly and, because of the age difference (Monica was twenty-four and Linda was forty-eight), like a mother and daughter.[9]

In the late fall of 1996, Tripp learned of Lewinsky's presidential liaison. Before confiding in Tripp, Lewinsky sought assurances that Tripp would keep the information confidential. Tripp told Lewinsky, "I have no intention of telling anyone."[10] Reportedly, Lewinsky confided in ten friends, and Tripp was the only one to reveal the confidence.[11] In her book *Monica's Story*, Lewinsky later wrote about her feeling toward Tripp after the betrayal: "I wanted to hurt her. I felt like an animal wanting to claw at her skin."[12]

After the initial disclosure, Lewinsky provided Tripp with a deluge of information. Lewinsky sought out Tripp five or more times a day at the Pentagon. At home, Lewinsky telephoned so frequently that Tripp resorted to a caller identification box to screen her calls. Tripp claimed that Lewinsky would often get frustrated with her because Tripp would often forget important details. Consequently, Tripp alleged that Lewinsky, at some point, urged her to take notes.

THE INFAMOUS TAPING

In September 1997, Lucianne Goldberg, a New York literary agent, urged Tripp to begin taping her conversations with Lewinsky: "You've got to really rat and you've got to tape."[13] According to Goldberg, Tripp did not agree to tape until she thought Paula Jones's lawyers might subpoena her to testify in the sexual harassment suit against President Clinton.[14] On October 3, 1997, Tripp began taping her conversations with Lewinsky. Then in December 1997, she informed Paula Jones's lawyers that she had taped her calls with Lewinsky, but she did not provide the tapes.[15] Sometime after the taping had commenced, Tripp learned that under Maryland law it was illegal to tape phone conversations without the consent of all parties.[16] In early January 1998, Jones's lawyers subpoenaed Tripp to testify at a deposition. On the evening of January 12, on the advice of her lawyer James Moody, Tripp called Starr's office.[17] In her ninety-minute phone conversation with Starr's deputy, Tripp revealed Lewinsky's sexual relationship with the president and said that it was corroborated by twenty hours of secret taping.[18]

Later that night, three Whitewater prosecutors and an FBI agent went to Tripp's Maryland home. In exchange for the tapes and an agreement to wear a body wire to record her meeting with Lewinsky scheduled for the next day, they granted Tripp immunity from prosecution. On January 13, she wore a wire when she met Lewinsky at the Ritz-Carlton Hotel. The device recorded Lewinsky telling Tripp that Vernon Jordan, a close friend and confidant of President Clinton, was busily investigating job opportunities for Lewinsky. Their conversation also confirmed other shared confidences previously recorded by Tripp. The Starr investigation ultimately reported that Lewinsky had tearfully asked Tripp to keep silent about the relationship she had revealed to her. Three days later, on January 16, Lewinsky and Tripp had lunch together. At this luncheon FBI agents and attorneys from Starr's office confronted Lewinsky, and for the first time, she learned of her friend's betrayal.[19]

A POLITICAL INFORMANT'S MOTIVATION

Next to her picture in her 1967 high school yearbook, Tripp listed as her pet peeve "a certain fair-weather friend."[20] Thirty-one years later, Tripp became an internationally known fair-weather friend. What motivated her to tape her friend Monica and then ultimately to turn the tapes over to special prosecutor Kenneth W. Starr? Tripp's comments, as well as other sources, reveal a multifaceted set of possible motivations, each of which likely played a part in her role as a political informant.

Tripp recalled that her initial conversations with Lewinsky were not documented in any way.[21] She simply provided a listening ear to her friend. Lucianne Goldberg, a literary agent, suggested taping the conversations.[22] After Tripp contacted Goldberg in September 1997, she decided to take Goldberg's advice and began taping the conversations so that she would be believed. Her credibility had earlier been questioned with regard to the Katherine Willey incident.[23] Willey allegedly told Tripp that during a meeting in the Oval Office Clinton had groped and kissed her. Stationed outside the Oval Office at the time, Tripp had reported to *Newsweek* that she had observed Willey "disheveled. Her face was red and her lipstick was off. She was flustered, happy and joyful."[24] When the *Newsweek* story ran in August 1997, Robert Bennett, the president's lawyer, dismissively responded to Tripp's account: Ms. Tripp "should not be believed."[25] Interestingly, Tripp's testimony before the grand jury several months later was more detailed than her initial disclosures. She said that she had been invited into the West Wing elevator by Willey and recounted the following about the occurrence:

[T]he elevator is tiny in the West Wing, it's very, very compact and she was all red in the face, all here, here, here, here, all red. And her lipstick was gone. Now she didn't look like she had been raped, she didn't look anything like that, but Kathleen is very put together, everything, in my opinion, is always perfect on Kathleen. Kathleen even has—everything perfect. On this day, she came out and she looked completely different than when she had gone in.[26]

Regarding a subsequent conversation that took place between Tripp and Willey outside in the parking lot, Tripp testified as follows:

Well, she said that "His tongue was down my throat," was the first thing. And I said, "Did you kiss him back?" And she said, "Well, I think I did." And she kept telling me the powerfulness of it and the forcefulness of it. And she kept saying, "He put my hand on his penis. It was [redacted material]." And I said, "What?" And she said, "I am not kidding. This is exactly what happened."[27]

Given the vividness of the description, it is not surprising that Tripp was upset when her credibility was questioned and characterized the questioning of her truthfulness as an unfair attack. Thus, Tripp's zeal to prove that she was telling the truth might have made her receptive to Goldberg's suggestion. In addition, Tripp was insulted by Bennett's remarks; she was worried that she would become enmeshed in Clinton's legal problems if Paula Jones's lawyer were to subpoena her. "I felt especially at risk if I told the truth in my deposition in the Jones case because the President, through his counsel Robert Bennett, was quoted in the national media last August saying 'she is not to be believed.'"[28] Consequently, she decided to substantiate her claims by taping her conversations with Lewinsky.[29]

Greed could also have played a part in Tripp's motivation. Did she betray her friend for financial gain as Judas Iscariot betrayed Jesus for thirty pieces of silver? In 1996, before she had found out about Lewinsky's involvement with the president, Tripp had contacted Goldberg. She was planning to write a book entitled *Behind Closed Doors: What I Saw at the Clinton White House*, under the pseudonym Joan Dean (after John Dean, the attorney whose testimony helped bring down the Nixon presidency during the Watergate scandal).[30] When Goldberg and Tripp discussed the book's monetary potential, Goldberg suggested that Tripp contact conservative columnist Maggie Gallagher, who would help her write a proposal for the book.[31] According to Tripp's testimony, Gallagher wrote a synopsis, but Tripp terminated the book idea both for monetary reasons and because the proposal was too sensational. Tripp commented after reviewing the twelve-chapter synopsis:

> I was horrified. I realized that this was way too dangerous and simultaneous to realizing it was way too dangerous and that I'd lose my job, . . . she hadn't made anything up, but when she put her own creativity to it, in the way the words flowed on the page, I was horrified. It was—it was sensational. It sounded sensational.[32]

With regard to compensation Tripp said,

> I also found out from Maggie that Lucy had promised her an entirely different figure than we had agreed on originally. . . . Not only that, you've insured by what you've promised to Maggie that now I'm down to only one year's salary essentially and I can't give up my retirement, my health benefits, my life insurance for my kids, everything that I've worked for, for that. It's not worth the risk. It's not worth the gamble.[33]

Tripp terminated the book deal by phone, and at the end of their conversation Goldberg slammed down the phone. Tripp recontacted Goldberg again in September 1997 with Lewinsky's story perhaps because she thought this new story might be substantially more marketable. It is interesting to note that if greed was indeed a factor, Tripp substantially undermined her own financial interest once she had gone public by agreeing to become an informant for Starr.

A third possible motivation might have been political considerations. There were a number of conservative figures associated with Tripp.

Former Bush staffer Tony Snow had introduced her to Goldberg. According to Tripp, Snow was "a dear friend and colleague of mine in the Bush White House. He was the head of speech writing for George Bush."[34] As she spoke to Snow about her experience in the Clinton White House, he encouraged her to write it down and promised that if she decided to write the book he could introduce her to Lucianne Goldberg, a well-known conservative literary agent. Goldberg, in turn, put her in contact with Maggie Gallagher.

In addition, Tripp met with with Paula Jones's lawyers in the fall of 1997. They apparently contacted her as a result of a lead provided by Goldberg.[35] Jim Moody, the lawyer who suggested that Tripp contact Kenneth Starr, once worked for the U.S. intelligence community. Tripp met Moody through some conservative lawyers with close ties to Paula Jones's lawyers.

Closely aligned with Tripp's political motivation is her so-called patriotic duty. In an interview on the *Today* show Tripp described her taping as patriotic duty: "I was honored to be at the White House. I came from a military—a 20-year military background. These are patriots who live their patriotism every day. To—to then take that and go to the White House, where I saw this potentially criminal activity on a daily basis, it was astounding to me."[36]

Still another motivation was the depth of Tripp's friendship with Lewinsky. Tripp described herself as Lewinsky's "only friend."[37] "I always saw Monica as a kid, I always saw her as a lost soul. . . . I believe she and the country will never understand that I believed this was in her best interest, and that makes me very sad."[38] In speaking about their friendship, Tripp claimed that she tried to extricate herself from the relationship as it intensified but could not do so because her closeness with Lewinsky. Tripp described herself as Lewinsky's surrogate mother, since Lewinsky's biological mother was across the country in California.[39] Tripp also claimed that Lewinsky repeatedly threatened to commit suicide. Tripp claimed she did what she did to prevent her friend, this young, distraught, and obsessed woman, from killing herself: "In fact, I still, to this day, believe it benefited Lewinsky as well. Embarrassing, yes. She's alive today. She has a future today. I would not have given you odds on that in December [1997]."[40]

One more possible motivation stems from Tripp's vehement reaction to Clinton's behavior. "What I wanted was the behavior to stop. . . . I wanted him to have to face that this is completely unacceptable behavior. . . . I was not vested in Paula Jones's case, but I found that horrifying."[41] As a teenager, Tripp had witnessed her father's marital infidelity.

"I had an extremely strict upbringing and suffered through my parents' painful divorce."[42] Moreover, she suffered through her own divorce. Could her reaction reflect sensitivity to marital problems?[43]

All of these motivations could have played a role in compelling Tripp to contact Starr. Once Starr had been contacted, she sought immunity on the advice of her counsel, Jim Moody. Moody said, "I asked for immunity and she got it. . . . I knew it was routine for whistle-blowers to be in fear of retaliation and so I made the request for the immunity."[44] Starr granted Tripp immunity from federal prosecution on the evidence she presented. This immunity deal did not involve Maryland authorities, however, so she was still subject to state prosecution for illegal wiretapping. Tripp's request for immunity suggests another more common possible motivation: the fear of criminal sanctions. She had hoped that immunity from Starr's office would eliminate any future criminal charges she might face as a result of her taping.

DID TRIPP'S TAPING VIOLATE THE FOURTH AMENDMENT?

Federal constitutional protections are only implicated when the government is somehow involved. Much of Tripp's taping was done as a private citizen. Even when she acted under the direction of Mr. Starr, a government official, she did not violate federal law. The Supreme Court, in *Hoffa v. United States*, interpreted the fourth amendment to not require the consent or knowledge of all parties with regard to conversations between individuals. 385 U.S. 293, 302–303 (1966). In these conversations, the court stated that no matter how much a defendant may trust an individual this trust is not protected by the fourth amendment if the individual later turns out to be a government informer. The court reaffirmed this holding in *Lewis v. United States*, finding that a defendant is not protected from government agents who pose as drug buyers and are then invited into the defendant's home, where they proceed to arrest the defendant. 385 U.S. 206, 211 (1966). Congress codified these cases in 18 U.S.C. secs. 2510–2520, which require only one-party consent to taping a private conversation.

A brief history of the fourth amendment may be useful before returning to Ms. Tripp's situation. In 1967, in *Katz v. United States* the Supreme Court revised the fourth amendment doctrine, which governs government searches and seizures. 389 U.S. 347 (1967). In *Katz*, the court moved from a notion of privacy that was closely tied to property concepts, such as common law trespass, to a more comprehensive theory of privacy. Federal agents in *Katz* had placed a listening device on the outside wall of a public phone booth. Since there was no actual penetration of the booth and therefore no trespass, the Ninth Circuit Court of Appeals ruled that the agents had not conducted a "search" within the meaning of the fourth amendment when they listened to Katz's conversation. *Katz v. United States*, 369 F.2d 130, 134 (9th Cir. 1966). The Supreme Court reversed, ruling that the fourth amendment "protects people, not places," and pointed out that it does not make sense to continue to rely on antiquated property law concepts. See 389 U.S. at 351.

From the *Katz* decision, an analysis evolved that made the fourth amendment applicable when an individual had an "expectation of privacy." Expectation of privacy, as defined by subsequent cases, has become an elusive concept. It is not enough that the individual has a subjective expectation that his activities will be private; the expectation must be one that society accepts as "objectively reasonable." What society is prepared to accept as reasonable becomes in fact what a majority of the Supreme Court regards as such. See *California v. Greenwood*, 486 U.S. 35, 39 (1988). This brings us back to Tripp's situation. Four years after *Katz*, in *United States v. White*, the court held that there is no reasonable expectation of privacy when a party divulges information to a third party. 401 U.S. 745 (1971). In *White*, the court faced a situation in which a government informant allowed agents to record his conversations with a suspected drug dealer. During eight encounters with the suspect, the informant carried a radio transmitter that relayed his conversations with the drug dealer to a nearby agent with a radio receiver. During four of the eight conversations, an additional agent eavesdropped from the informant's kitchen closet. The *White* court, relying on earlier decisions involving informers, limited the *Katz* expectation of privacy rationale by ruling that subjects of investigation bear the burden of risk that their compatriots might inform on them. Thus, an individual has no reasonable expectation of privacy when talking to other individuals. Under this rationale, Lewinsky had the burden of realizing that her "friend" Tripp could possibly be a government informer.

Justice Harlan, in his *White* dissent, expressed concern about the potential damage the majority's approach might wreak on a free society. He noted that electronic eavesdropping could make George Orwell's "Big Brother" a reality. See 401 U.S. at 770. He recognized

[t]he expectation of the ordinary citizen, who has never engaged in
illegal conduct in his life, that he may carry on his private discourse
freely, openly, and spontaneously without measuring his every word
against the connotations it might carry when instantaneously heard
by others unknown to him and unfamiliar with his situation or analyzed in a cold, formal record played days, months, or years after the
conversation. Interposition of a warrant requirement is designed not
to shield "wrongdoers," but to secure a measure of privacy and a
sense of personal security throughout our society. 401 U.S. at 790.

In reaching its decision, the *White* court cut the reach of *Katz* back
severely. Initially, *Katz* seemed to be a significant expansion of fourth
amendment protections, but this expansion did not occur. Post-*Katz* decisions have continued to recognize an "expectation of privacy," but that
expectation has proven fragile indeed, for it is easily eliminated as soon as
a compatriot becomes a government informer. There does not even need to
be a government informer in order for the expectation of privacy to be
found unreasonable. The expectation of privacy is also destroyed if information is conveyed to institutional third parties. For instance, in *United
States v. Miller* the court held that bank records could be subpoenaed without a warrant. 425 U.S. 435 (1976). In *Smith v. Maryland* the court found
no fourth amendment protection for phone numbers automatically
recorded for billing purposes by means of a pen register to the telephone
company. 442 U.S. 735 (1979). Finally, in *California v. Greenwood* the
court held that individuals do not have an expectation of privacy for their
garbage once it is placed on the curb for pick up by a third party. 486 U.S.
35 (1988). This line of cases stands for the proposition that the Supreme
Court will not recognize an objective expectation of privacy if the claimant
voluntarily conveys information or other evidence to a third party.

   Thus, although Lewinsky felt her privacy was violated by Tripp's disclosure and taping of their conversations, Lewinsky's fourth amendment
rights were not implicated by Tripp's activity.

INFORMANTS AND MARYLAND'S
WIRETAPPING LAW

Maryland is one of several states that have made it a criminal offense
to tape conversations without the consent of all parties to the communication. As previously mentioned, this is not the case in the federal system. In
response to U.S. Supreme Court decisions that have limited the protection

of individual rights, states such as Maryland have interpreted their own laws to provide greater protection.[45] Among the states that do require consent of all parties are California, Delaware, Florida, Massachusetts, New Hampshire, Pennsylvania, and Washington. Illinois' statute requires all parties to consent, but case law has interpreted this to mean one-party consent if the person doing the intercepting is a party to the communication. Montana requires "knowledge" of all parties.

Since Linda Tripp taped her conversation with Lewinsky from her home in Howard County, Maryland, Maryland law governed her conduct. The Maryland criminal statute, in pertinent part, is as follows:

(a) Except as otherwise specifically provided in this subtitle it is unlawful for any person to:
   (1) Wilfully intercept, endeavor to intercept, or procure any other person to intercept or endeavor to intercept, any wire, oral or electronic communication;
   (2) Wilfully disclose, or endeavor to disclose, to any other person the contents of any wire, oral, or electronic communication, knowing or having reason to know that the information was obtained through the interception of a wire, oral, or electronic communication in violation of this subtitle; or
   (3) Wilfully use, or endeavor to use, the contents of any wire, oral, or electronic communication, knowing or having reason to know that the information was obtained through the interception of a wire, oral, or electronic communication in violation of this subtitle.[46]

Intercept is defined in the preceding statute as:

the aural or other acquisition of the contents of any wire, electronic, or oral communication through the use of any electronic, mechanical, or other device.[47]

Pursuant to this statute, on July 30, 1999, a Maryland grand jury handed down two indictments against Tripp. The first count of the indictment dealt with illegally taping a telephone conversation with Lewinsky on December 22, 1997.[48] This tape was one of twenty-seven that Tripp made. The December 22 date was chosen probably because it was both before Tripp had received the grant of immunity from Starr's office and after she had been informed that surreptitious taping in Maryland was illegal, which is an essential element in making out a violation of the statute. In her grand jury testimony, Tripp indicated that although she knew it was illegal, she had made this tape to protect herself. However, this grand jury testimony could not be used in any way because of her grant of immunity. In the conversation, Lewinsky and Tripp discussed their upcoming testimony about Lewinsky's sexual relationship with Mr. Clinton in the sexual misconduct suit brought against Clinton by Paula Jones.[49]

Because Tripp used a tape recorder to record telephone conversations with Monica Lewinsky, her conduct constituted interception of "oral communication" as defined by the statute.[50] Furthermore, she did not fall under any of the exceptions, since the statute requires that in order for the interception to be lawful "a person [doing the intercepting] is a party to the communication and . . . *all of the parties* to the communication have given prior consent to the interception"[51] (emphasis added).

The second count of the indictment alleged that on January 17, 1998, Tripp instructed her attorney to disclose the contents of the conversation to *Newsweek* magazine while knowing that the contents had been obtained by the actions in the indictment's first count. This charge was consistent with subsection (2) of the statute. In interpreting its statute, Maryland case law has set a high standard for meeting the "willful" requirement. The key question is whether Ms. Tripp did "*wilfully* intercept" the communication (emphasis added). "Wilfully" is not defined explicitly in the statute and has been the subject of two reported Maryland appellate court decisions. In *Petric v. State*, 66 Md. App. 470, 504 A.2d 1168 (1986), a union official was prosecuted for secretly recording his conversations with management during a labor dispute. The court instructed the jury that to convict the jury would have to find that the defendant "knew or should have known that he was violating the [state] law." *Petric*, 504 A.2d at 1172. The defendant's testimony that he thought federal law preempted Maryland law, if the jury believed it, would be a defense. The court nevertheless upheld the conviction because there was ample evidence that the defendant in fact knew that he was violating state law. As is the case with any specific-intent crime, much of the evidence as to the intent was circumstantial. In *Hawes v. Carberry* Hawes, a Virginia attorney, traveled to Maryland to interview Carberry and secretly recorded the conversation. 103 Md. App. 214, 653 A.2d 479 (1995). Carberry sued. Under Maryland law, a plaintiff suing for damages for illegal interception must prove the same thing that a prosecutor would have to prove in a criminal case, that is, that the defendant intercepted the conversation willfully. See *Fearnow v. C. & P. Telephone Co., et al.*, 104 Md. App. 1, 655 A.2d 1 (1995) (duty to inquire into illegality is but a factor for the jury to consider in making a determination of willfulness). This means that the plaintiff who sues under sec. 10-402 must show that the defendant knew that it was illegal to tape the proceedings without the consent of all parties. *Earley v. Smoot*, 846 F. Supp. 451, 453 (D. Md. 1994). At trial, Hawes, the defendant, testified that at the time the only thing he knew about wiretapping or eavesdropping was what other lawyers had told him: that federal law permitted him to tape his own conversations. Plaintiffs offered evidence to the contrary and argued that "willfully" means "intentionally." Rejecting the plaintiff's argument, the appellate court held that the trial judge should have granted a directed verdict for Hawes because "willfully" means more than "intentionally"; it requires proof that the defendant knew he was violating the law. See *Hawes v. Carberry*, 103 Md. App. 214, 222, 653 A.2d 479, 483 (1995). Thus, to prove the case against Linda Tripp, her conduct would need to meet the willfulness requirement under the statute; that is, Maryland prosecutors would have to prove that she actually knew her conduct was illegal prior to taping the conversations.

Despite earlier assertions to the contrary by Maryland prosecutors,[52] Tripp was indicted. Not surprisingly, there is considerable speculation that the indictments were politically motivated. The case was originally handled by Attorney General Marna McLendon, a Republican. After state Democrats put pressure on McLendon, she turned the case over to Stephen Montanarelli, an appointed Democrat who had fifteen years of experience directing the Office of the State Attorney General that deals in white-collar and public corruption cases. Reportedly, more than forty Democratic state legislators sought the indictment.[53] Despite Tripp's spokesman's assertions that "[Tripp] is the victim of political persecution,"[54] McLendon defended the decision to indict by claiming that as a result of the case's notoriety the public now demanded accountability. She also indicated that the prosecutors had considered Tripp's possible defenses before concluding that they could still prove the charges beyond a reasonable doubt.

IMMUNITY AGREEMENT

With her wiretap indictments, Linda Tripp was the last player in the Lewinsky-Clinton scandal to face criminal prosecution.[55] Lewinsky was given a broad grant of immunity by Starr and has never been prosecuted. The Senate acquitted Clinton after his impeachment. Starr granted Tripp use immunity as well as derivative use immunity from federal prosecution for her testimony and for the evidence she had presented before the grand jury. This means that Maryland could not use Tripp's testimony or any evidence from this testimony. In order for Maryland to make a case against her, the prosecution would have to demonstrate that the evidence had come from a source completely independent of Tripp's grand jury testimony and other evidence (the tapes) that she provided. Stephen Montanarelli, the Maryland state prosecutor in charge of the Tripp investigation, had indicated from the start of this prosecution that "immunity will be a problem but we will face it in the future."[56] He felt that he could make a circumstantial case without using the actual tapes.[57] Such was not the case, however.

The immunity agreement raised potential legal ramifications involving the relationship between two sovereign entities—the United States government and the government of Maryland. There are, in general, two types of immunity: use and transactional. In the federal system a statutory grant of immunity provides for use immunity, which means that the prosecutor may not use the compelled testimony either directly or indirectly against the witness in a later prosecution. See 18 U.S.C. sec. 6002–6003. Transactional immunity is a broader form of protection; it provides that the government may not prosecute the witness at all for the crimes that were the subject of the immunized testimony. When Kenneth Starr granted Ms. Tripp use immunity from federal prosecution, what effect, if any, did this have on state prosecution?

The tenth amendment leaves the police power to the states.[58] The police power is the power to legislate for the people's health, safety, morals, and general welfare. Most criminal prosecutions in this country are conducted by the state under its police power. Prosecutors in each of the fifty separate states and the federal government have the power to grant immunity under specific statutory requirements. Mr. Starr's power to grant immunity emanated from the Independent Counsel Act, 28 U.S.C. sec. 594(a)(7)[59] and 18 U.S.C. sec. 6002. Starr gave Ms. Tripp use immunity, which pledged that the federal government would not prosecute her based on any evidence obtained directly or indirectly from her testimony about the tapes and conversations with Ms. Lewinsky.

The relationship between the federal government and the state of Maryland raises interesting federalism issues. Various aspects of interjurisdictional immunity deals often come down to comity between state and federal officials. For example, in the Tripp case, Maryland prosecutors decided to delay pursuing an indictment in deference to federal authorities, at least as long as the federal grand jury was still meeting. Moreover, Maryland prosecutors probably did not want to get in a long, drawn-out legal battle with Starr's Office of Independent Counsel, even though they were fully within their jurisdictional power to pursue independent sources of evidence and prosecute Ms. Tripp.[60] To ensure the viability of future immunity deals, federal prosecutors fought to keep Ms. Tripp from being prosecuted. The question of whether Maryland's indictments were valid after Ms. Tripp had testified before the federal grand jury is surrounded by two conflicting policy objectives which the Supreme Court has wrestled with for over a century. First, "[e]very good citizen is bound to aid in the enforcement of the law," and immunity deals are often necessary in order for investigators to find the culprits. *Brown v. Walker*, 161 U.S. 591, 600 (1896). Yet, at the same time, under the fifth amendment witnesses should not be forced to testify against themselves. See *Murphy v. Waterfront Comm'n of New York Harbor*, 378 U.S. 52, 55 (1964). Thus, in order for an immunity statute, state or federal, to be constitutional, it must provide at least the same protection as required by the fifth amendment. See *Brown v. Walker*, 161 U.S. at 600–610.

In 1896, in *Brown v. Walker* the court for the first time held a federal immunity statute to be constitutional because it also encompassed use or transactional immunity, which gave a witness complete protection from subsequent prosecution. This level of immunity was broad enough not to violate the constitutional privilege against self-incrimination provided by the fifth amendment. Five years prior, in *Counselman v. Hitchcock*, 142 U.S. 547, 584–585 (1892), the court held that use immunity alone was inadequate as a statutory substitute for the fifth amendment's protections. In *Brown v. Walker*, however, the court reasoned that since the fifth amendment privilege was intended to "secure the witness against a criminal prosecution," if prosecution were impossible under an immunity grant, the grant was necessarily not in conflict with the fifth amendment. See *Brown* at 595. Theoretically, the immunity statute's protections were equal to the protections provided if the witness had been allowed to remain silent. See *Murphy*, 378 U.S. at 79.

Also in *Brown*, the court held that a federal immunity statute coextensive with the fifth amendment was binding on state prosecutors. The court did not delve into the relationship between the state and the federal government, the so-called federalism issues, but instead brushed aside this possible infringement on state sovereignty with two arguments: First, the court argued that the immunity statute, as a federal law, overrides any and all conflicting state laws under the supremacy clause.[61] Second, the court found the danger of state prosecution to be too remote and hypothetical. This "two-sovereignty" rule reflects the nineteenth-century American Federalist system in which the federal government and the separate state governments were treated more like foreign entities than members of the same country. In fact, the court rested its argument on English cases that dealt with the issue of witnesses' refusal to testify because they feared prosecution in another country.

These arguments floundered in subsequent Supreme Court decisions because, as the *Brown* dissenters predicted, there was a growing overlap between federal and state criminal law. *Brown v. Walker* was a 5–4 decision. As a dissenting opinion by Justice Shiras noted,

> [A]s we have seen, it is entirely within the range of probable events that the very same act or transaction may constitute a crime or offence against both governments, state and Federal. . . . But, as already observed, not only may the same act be a common offence to both governments, but the disclosures compulsively made in one proceeding may give clues and hints which may be subsequently used against the witness in another, to the loss of his liberty and property. *Brown v. Walker*, 161 U.S. at 626–627 (Shiras, J., dissenting)

The federal government through the constitutional power provided by the commerce clause has continued to expand in their federal criminal jurisdiction.[62] Because of the substantial overlap between the federal and state systems, it is possible for an individual to face criminal prosecution for the same basic act in both systems without implicating the double jeopardy provisions of the fifth amendment. See *Bartkus v. Illinois*, 359 U.S. 121 (1959); *Heath v. Alabama*, 474 U.S. 82 (1985). With the greater possibility of a governing parallel state statute, the danger of state prosecution of federal witnesses based on their testimony in federal court became more likely. Consequently, the court moved toward a two-sovereignty rule, departing from *Brown*'s reasoning and holding that state and federal prosecutors were not bound by each other's immunity deals. *Knapp v. Schweitzer*, 357 U.S. 371 (1958); *Feldman v. United States*, 322 U.S. 487 (1944); *United States v. Murdock*, 284 U.S. 141 (1931). The two-sovereignty rule was possible because the court did not find the fifth amendment to be applicable to the states. See *Knapp v. Schweitzer*, 357 U.S. at 379–380. Thus it became possible for the states to use federal immunized testimony.

In 1964, however, in *Malloy v. Hogan*, the court incorporated the fifth amendment through the fourteenth amendment, making it applicable to the states. 378 U.S. 7 (1964). Prior to *Malloy*, state governments were allowed to compel self-incriminatory testimony. Once the fifth amendment had been applied to the states, a statutory immunity protection coextensive with the fifth should logically be applicable to the states. In a unanimous decision, the *Malloy* court abandoned the two-sovereignty rule and held that state prosecutors could not use evidence obtained directly or indirectly from federal grand jury testimony under a federal immunity agreement.

Developing this theory, the court, in *Murphy v. Waterfront Comm'n of New York Harbor*, recognized a new era of "'cooperative federalism,' in which the federal and state governments are waging a united front against many types of criminal activity." *Murphy*, 378 U.S. at 56. This decision paved the way for Congress to pass 18 U.S.C. §6002–6003, which limited federal immunity to use immunity, as opposed to transactional immunity. With this legislation, Congress sought to balance the competing goals of maximizing the volume of evidence available to grand juries while minimizing the affect of the testimony on subsequent criminal prosecutions.

Maryland state prosecutors were compelled to honor Starr's immunity deal which rendered all evidence obtained from Ms. Tripp's testimony inadmissible. See *Murphy*, 378 U.S. 53–79; *Reina v. United States*, 364 U.S. 507 (1960); *In Re Grand Jury Proceedings: United States v. Buckley*, 860 F.2d 11 (2nd Cir. 1988); *In Re Bianchi*, 542 F.2d 98 (1st Cir. 1976); *Carter v. United States*, 417 F.2d 384 (9th Cir. 1969); cert. denied, 399 U.S. 935, *reh'g denied*, 400 U.S. 855; *United States v. Rice*, 421 F.Supp. 871 (E.D. IL, 1976). However, under the Supreme Court's holding in *Kastigar v. United States*, which upheld the federal immunity statute, Maryland state prosecutors could utilize evidence obtained in a wholly independent manner to prosecute Ms. Tripp under Maryland's wiretapping statute. See *Kastigar v. United States*, 406 U.S. 441 (1972); *Rowe v. Griffin*, 497 F.Supp. 610 (M.D. Ala. 1980), aff'd, 676 F.2d 524.

Maryland law requires state prosecutors to show by a preponderance of evidence that the evidence sought to be admitted was derived from a wholly independent source, unconnected with the testimony given at the grand jury. Essentially, state prosecutors needed to prove they obtained evidence that existed before Ms. Tripp testified and was not influenced in any way by her grand jury testimony. An example of this would be the prosecutor's intention to use statements that Tripp made to friends prior to her grand jury testimony. The source of this information are members of Tripp's former bridge club. Tripp spoke to them about recording Lewinsky's conversations.[63] The most crucial testimony, however, was that of Monica Lewinsky's. Could the state prove that Lewinsky's testimony regarding the conversation on December 22, 1997 (the subject of the indictment) was derived from a legitimate, wholly independent source? The state's position was that Lewinsky's memory was based entirely on her own conversation with Tripp, not on her knowledge of Tripp's immunized statements to the grand jury. Lewinsky claimed that the date was "etched in my mind because it was a pretty frightening time for me."[64] The defense counsel argued at a

Kastigar hearing that Maryland was violating the immunity deal because Lewinsky's testimony was derived from Tripp's grand jury testimony. To support this contention, they pointed to the fact that Lewinsky failed to provide specific dates of conversations when questioned by Stephen Montanarelli's office in July 1998, making her recollection of the December 22 phone call at the hearing ten months later highly unlikely.[65] Judge Diane Leasure of Maryland's Howard County District Court in suppressing Lewinsky's testimony found that Lewinsky had "substantial exposure to Ms. Tripp's immunized testimony" and that Ms. Lewinsky's recollection of the events was derived from her review of the testimony of Tripp and was, therefore, not wholly independent.[66] As a result of this ruling, the prosecutor had to dismiss the charges against Linda Tripp.[67] Tripp commented, "Despite the federal grant of immunity, the state of Maryland pursued its selective prosecution of me for more than two years."[68] Her attorney, Joseph Murtha, said, "[S]he would do it all again, because she had no choice."[69]

It is important to note that this would have been a different inquiry if Mr. Starr had granted Linda Tripp transactional immunity. Transactional immunity would have made her immune from being prosecuted for anything that she testified to before the grand jury. For a transactional immunity deal to be binding on Maryland, most courts would likely rule that Starr would have to obtain Maryland's consent to the deal.

CONCLUSION

The story of the political informer, Linda Tripp, is a story of a low-level government employee's power to almost topple a presidential administration. Other examples of political scandal can often be traced back to a single, until-then-unknown individual. For example, in sixteenth-century England at the famous trial of St. Thomas More, if Richard Riche had not informed against More, the fourth and last count of the indictment would have been dismissed and More would have been set free. If White House aide Alexander P. Butterfield had not disclosed the elaborate Oval Office taping system, the Nixon presidency might have survived. Particularly in this media age, the threat of public exposure is easily wielded by government employees. The unseen and unknown Washington staffers and bureaucrats are sometimes the ones who see the most. Thus, political informants are a power to be reckoned with since they have the potential to change the course of history.

APPENDIX
CHRONOLOGY OF EVENTS:
LINDA TRIPP, POLITICAL INFORMANT IN
THE CLINTON-LEWINSKY SCANDAL

April 1991	Under the Bush administration, Tripp enters the White House secretarial pool as a "floater," a staffer who supported executive assistants as needed.
November 1992	William Jefferson Clinton is elected as the forty-second President of the United States.
April 1993	Tripp is assigned to work in White House Counsel Bernard Nussbaum's office.
July 1993	Tripp, while still on staff in Nussbaum's office, is one of the last persons to see then-Deputy White House Counsel Vince W. Foster Jr. alive before he allegedly kills himself.
November 1993	Tripp reportedly observes Kathleen E. Willey emerge from the Oval Office disheveled and anxious.
Spring 1994	Lloyd Cutler replaces Bernard Nussbaum as White House Counsel. Tripp is reassigned within the White House.
August 22, 1994	Tripp takes a position in the Pentagon's Office of Public Affairs for the Secretary of Defense.
June 1995	Lewinsky begins work as an unpaid intern in the Office of Chief of Staff Leon Panetta.
November 1995	Lewinsky has the first of ten sexual encounters with President Clinton.
November 26, 1995	Lewinsky is transferred to the Office of Legislative Affairs.
April 5, 1996	After White House aides notice she is spending too much time in the West Wing, Lewinsky is transferred to the Pentagon's Office of Public Affairs for the Secretary of Defense.

April 1996	Tripp and Lewinsky meet and talk about their White House days, both having transferred from the White House to the Pentagon.
September–October 1996	Lewinsky tells Tripp about her relationship with the president.
May 24, 1997	Clinton breaks off his affair with Lewinsky.
May 27, 1997	In a unanimous opinion, the Supreme Court rejects Clinton's argument that he should not be subject to Paula Jones's sexual harassment suit while in office.
August 1997	*Newsweek* quotes Tripp as a witness to the incident involving Clinton's alleged sexual advance toward Kathleen Willey in the Oval Office. Clinton's attorney, Robert Bennett, dismisses Tripp's account.
August–September 1997	Tripp fears she will be called to testify in the Jones sexual harassment suit against the president. Lucianne Goldberg, a literary agent, advises Tripp to tape her conversations to bolster her story in the face of detractors.
October 3, 1997	Tripp begins surreptitiously taping phone conversations with Lewinsky.
November 24, 1997	Tripp's attorney, Kirby Behre, states that secretly taping conversations is illegal under Maryland law.
December 12 and 22, 1997	Tripp continues to record her conversations with Lewinsky.
December 1997	Tripp tells Jones's lawyers about the taped conversations. She does not hand over the tapes, however.
January 7, 1998	Lewinsky signs an affidavit in the Jones sexual harassment suit, claiming she had no sexual relationship with President Clinton.
January 1998	Jones's lawyers subpoena Tripp to testify in a deposition for the sexual harassment suit.
January 12, 1998	On the advice of her attorney, James Moody, Tripp contacts Independent Counsel Kenneth Starr's office. Later

that night three Office of Independent Counsel (OIC) prosecutors and an FBI agent go to Tripp's home. OIC prosecutors grant Tripp immunity in exchange for the tapes and agreeing to wear a body wire.

January 13, 1998   Tripp wears a body wire to a lunch with Lewinsky. The device records Lewinsky talking about the affair.

January 15, 1998   Tripp tapes her final two conversations with Lewinsky under the supervision of Starr's office.

January 16, 1998   While Lewinsky and Tripp are having lunch, FBI agents confront Lewinsky and ask her questions for nine hours in a hotel room.

January 17, 1998   At Tripp's request, Moody plays recorded conversations with Lewinsky to a *Newsweek* reporter.

January 21, 1998   The Clinton-Lewinsky scandal is revealed in the press.

January 26, 1998   Howard County State's Attorney Marna McLendon, a Republican, says she will not open a criminal investigation against Tripp under Maryland's wiretapping law.

February 11, 1998   After pressure from Democratic state legislators, McLendon hands the case over to Maryland State Prosecutor Stephen Montanarelli, a Democrat.

July 7, 1998   Montanarelli begins a grand jury investigation of Tripp for possible violations of Maryland's wiretapping law.

July 28, 1998   Starr grants Lewinsky inmunity from prosecution in exchange for her testimony.

July 29, 1998   Tripp testifies under oath before a federal grand jury that she continued taping despite knowing it was illegal.

September 9, 1998   Starr submits a report to Congress, citing eleven possible grounds for impeachment.

December 19, 1998   The House of Representatives passes two articles of impeachment against the president.

February 12, 1999   The Senate acquits the president.

June 16, 1999   Montanarelli questions Lewinsky about Tripp's tapes. Transcripts of her answers are given to the Howard County grand jury.

July 30, 1999   Tripp is indicted on two counts of violating Maryland's wiretapping law: One count of illegal interception of phone conversations on December 22, 1997, and one count of illegal disclosure of the contents of that conversation to *Newsweek* on January 16–17, 1998. She faces up to twenty years in prison and $20,000 in fines.

May 5, 2000   Judge Diane Leasure of the Maryland Howard County District Court refuses to allow Lewinsky to testify because her recollection of the events were derived from the Tripp grand jury testimony.

May 31, 2000   Prosecutor Montanarelli, because of the judge's decision to bar Lewinsky's testimony, moves to dismiss the Tripp prosecution. Judge grants motion.

Chapter 3

The Nonexistent Informant

The Story of Officer Carlos Luna

INTRODUCTION

Through the Bill of Rights, the original ten amendments to the Constitution, our constitutional framers sought to limit the power of the government and protect the rights of the individual. One of the most notable rights is found in the fourth amendment, which establishes

> [t]he right of the people to be secure in their persons, houses, papers, and effects, against unreasonable searches and seizures, shall not be violated, and no Warrants shall issue, but upon probable cause, supported by Oath or affirmation, and particularly describing the place to be searched, and the persons or things to be seized.

This right protects individuals against unreasonable search and seizure from the police or government officials. Two provisions in this amendment effectuate the protection. First, the fourth amendment requires probable cause, or justification, before the police may conduct a search or an arrest. The Supreme Court, in *Illinois v. Gates*, established that the probable cause would be determined by a "totality of the circumstances" test. 462 U.S. 213, 238 (1983). The court recognized that the determination is based on "only the probability, and not a *prima facie* showing, of criminal activity" *Illinois v. Gates*, 462 U.S. 235 (quoting *Spinelli v. United States*, 393 U.S. 410, 419, [1969]). Second, the fourth amendment requires a warrant, which is a court order issued by a neutral judicial officer (either a judge or magistrate) to authorize a search or an arrest. A warrant is sometimes required in order to do a search outside a home and usually required for home searches. If the court finds a violation of the fourth amendment, the remedy is exclusion of the evidence that was found as a result of this violation. This remedy is referred to as the exclusionary rule. See *Weeks v. United States,* 232 U.S. 383, 392–393 (1914), made applicable to states by *Mapp v. Ohio*, 367 U.S. 643, 655 (1961).

The warrant-authorized search has become a very important law enforcement weapon in the war on drugs. In many instances, unnamed informants provide the information to establish the probable cause needed for a warrant to make a drug bust. Given the nature of the information they provide, these informants are typically addicts or otherwise involved in the drug enterprise.[1] Often, they inform in order to collect a reward or avoid criminal prosecution. Ironically, these incentives may enable them to continue their drug addiction.[2] These informants often live a transient existence, having no fixed address nor a place where they can be reached. In addition, because of the danger of retaliation associated with informing, the courts are very protective of the confidentiality of informants.

In the utilization of informants, courts tend to presume that police are truthful. This presumption exists to a large extent in our legal culture, but it is also supported by case law. See *Franks v. Delaware*, 438 U.S. 154, 171 (1978). Thus, with little or no oversight from the courts, some police officers have found it possible to fabricate drug informants without detection. This chapter details a case in which the lies were discovered despite the presumption that police do not lie and the protection afforded the confidentiality of the informant. It teaches us valuable lessons concerning the use and abuse of informants in the criminal justice system, especially in the war on drugs.

THE FACTS OF THE LUNA CASE

The Warrant Application

On February 17, 1988, Officer Carlos A. Luna of the Boston Police Department's Drug Control Unit applied for a search warrant to conduct a "no-knock" search of "apt. #3 on the third floor" of 102 Bellevue Street.[3] In his sworn affidavit, a copy of which is included in Appendix A, Luna stated that he had received information from a reliable informant, referred to as "IT":

"IT" has proven reliable in the past by providing your affiant with information that led to the arrest and now pending case in Suffolk Superior Court of one Miguel Sarracent for Trafficking in Cocaine, Possession of Class D with Intent to Distribute and unlawful Possession of a firearm, also for the conviction in Suffolk Superior Court of one June Samaniego for Possession of Class B with Intent to Distribute.

Officer Luna claimed "that for the last three weeks and more recently within the last two days 'IT' had been present at apartment #3, 102 Bellevue Street . . . which was the home of a H/M [Hispanic male] (med built, med skin, @ 5'06'', 30's) known to 'IT' as 'STEVIE.'" "IT" said he observed Stevie "engaged in the cutting, weighing, packaging and selling of paperfolds of white powder, believed to be cocaine." Officer Luna stated that he himself had seen people purchase drugs through a hole in the door of Apartment #3, 102 Bellevue Street. Finally, Officer Luna stated that on February 15 and 16 he had personally purchased cocaine from Apartment #3, 102 Bellevue Street. On the basis of this information, the judge granted Luna a warrant to conduct a no-knock search of Apartment #3, 102 Bellevue Street for drugs and drug paraphernalia. As is the usual procedure, the judge did not ask to meet with the informant or for any additional information about the informant.

The Execution of the Warrant

On February 17, 1988, at 8 P.M., Officer Luna, along with three other members of the Drug Control Unit, including Officer Paul Schroeder and Detectives Sherman C. Griffiths and Hugo Amate, attempted to execute the search warrant. The four-man team pounded on the heavy metal door with a sledgehammer. As Officer Griffiths took his turn wielding the heavy hammer against the door, shots from a handgun rang out from inside the apartment. A .45-caliber bullet ripped through the door and hit Officer Griffiths in the head, killing him. Luna, Schroeder, and Amate remained in the hallway until backup officers arrived at the scene.

The Protective Sweep

Once backup had arrived, the officers did what they call a "protective sweep" of the entire building, looking for the assailant or for more victims. The officers used this as justification to engage in an extensive warrantless search lasting until early morning. Several items were seized, including bullets, shell casings, fingerprints, and the heavy metal door on the apartment. At 3:30 A.M. on February 18, 1988, several officers left the scene to obtain a search warrant for the entire premises. This warrant was executed at 4:45 A.M.; however, most of the evidence had already been seized by this time. In *Commonwealth v. Lewin*, 407 Mass. 617 (1990), the Massachusetts Supreme Judicial Court suppressed most of this evidence, finding that the scope of the protective search exceeded its original justification because the officers had continued to search without a warrant after the exigency that justified the protective search had ceased.[4]

During the course of the protective sweep of the building, the officers found seven people, including Albert Lewin. The people at the apartment building implicated Lewin in the shooting. It is interesting to note that of the seven witnesses, three were related. Also, in exchange for their later testimony against Lewin, murder charges for their involvement in Officer Griffiths's death were dropped, as were serious drug charges. Although no direct grant of immunity from prosecution for the murder of Officer Griffiths was given, the implication was that they would not be charged if they truthfully cooperated with the prosecution. In fact they were never charged. In addition, police promised relocation and protection. *Commonwealth v. Lewin*, 405 Mass. 566, 569 & n.1 (1989).[5]

The Search for "IT"

On May 11, 1988, based largely on statements of the people found in the apartment building, a grand jury indicted Albert Lewin for numerous criminal offenses, including the murder of Officer Griffiths. On June 24, 1988, Lewin's counsel asked the court to order the state to disclose the identity of the informant "IT." Defense counsel believed that "IT" had material exculpatory information, which is evidence that could be helpful to the defense for this murder charge. The defense believed that this evidence showed that someone other than Lewin had operated the cocaine business at 102 Bellevue Street. In *Brady v. Maryland*, 373 U.S. 83 (1963), the Supreme Court held that suppression of evidence favorable to the accused, when the evidence is material to guilt, violated due process. Thus, the prosecution is obligated to provide exculpatory evidence to the defendant. 373 U.S. at 86–87. Mr. Lewin was a 6'2'' tall, dark-complected Jamaican man. Luna's affidavit citing information from "IT" indicated that a 5'6'' tall, medium-complected, Hispanic male named Stevie was conducting a drug business from the Bellevue location. Certainly this information is both material and exculpatory. In August, the court granted the defendant's motion to compel the disclosure of the informant, and for the next month Luna claimed he was attempting to locate "IT." Although Officer Luna and Sergeant Amate spent substantial time and expense allegedly searching for "IT," and filed several written reports documenting the search, they were unable to locate "IT." On October 20, 1988, the defense counsel moved to dismiss the indictment, arguing that "IT's" identity was essential to constructing his defense.

The Pretrial Motions

A Superior Court judge (trial court) conducted a hearing on the defendant's motion to dismiss the indictment to determine if the police had falsified the existence of "IT" and/or their attempt to find "IT." At the hearing, Luna described in detail "IT's" height, weight, hair, skin color, and approximate age. He also described several occasions on which he had allegedly met with "IT." Suspicious of the existence of "IT," defense counsel presented thirty-one search warrants issued between June 1987 and March 1988 that Luna had obtained by relying on information from "IT." Defense counsel noted that "IT" had never been interviewed by a judge. On February 22, 1989, the Superior Court judge granted the motion to dismiss the indictment because Luna could not locate "IT," whom the judge found to be a material exculpatory witness.

On February 22, 1989, the same day that the judge granted the motion to dismiss the indictment, the prosecutor made a motion for reconsideration of the dismissal, indicating in his brief that he had further factual information on "IT." The prosecutor's motion told an elaborate and perplexing story, inconsistent with Luna's original affidavit. A controlled purchase of cocaine had been made at Apartment #3, 102 Bellevue Street on February 17, 1988, the day Griffith had been shot, by an informant known as "X." According to "X," Luna had brought "X" to 102–104 Bellevue Street and told "X" to make a drug purchase from Apartment #3, 102 Bellevue Street, the third floor apartment on the right. When "X" got to the third floor, however, "X" apparently realized that drugs were actually being sold from the apartment on the left. Based on the fact that Luna had directed "X" to the wrong apartment, the prosecutor had begun to doubt that Luna had actually purchased drugs from Apartment #3, 102 Bellevue Street on February 15 and 16 as Luna had earlier alleged. Furthermore, the prosecutor had discovered a second informant, known as "Y," who claimed that he had been the one who made the February 15, 1988, drug purchase from Apartment #3, 102 Bellevue Street, not Luna. Based on this information, the judge ordered Luna, Amate, and Schroeder to provide affidavits as soon as possible to clarify the confusion. In the meantime, the prosecutor discovered a third informant, known as "Z," who claimed he had made the February 16, 1988, drug purchase from Apartment #3, 102 Bellevue Street. See *Commonwealth v. Lewin*, 405 Mass. 566, 573–576.

The Truth Revealed

Finally, on March 21, 1989, following the advice of his attorney, Luna submitted a very different story from the one told in his February 17, 1988, search warrant affidavit. He related a convoluted story culminating with his admission that he fabricated the informant. His new story was that Officer Schroeder had arrested "Y" on February 9, 1988, for possession of controlled substances. "Y" offered to provide the Boston Police Department with information on drug sales in the Dorchester area, presumably to avoid prosecution. Pursuant to this deal, "Y" led Sergeant Amate to 102–104 Bellevue Street and told Amate of a Hispanic man named Stevie who sold drugs out of a third floor apartment. On February 15, 1988, "Y" met Amate and Schroeder at 102–104 Bellevue Street, and "Y" made a controlled purchase of drugs from Apartment #3, 102 Belevue Street. The following day, Luna and Amate met informant "Z" at 102–104 Bellevue Street, and "Z" also made a controlled purchase of drugs from Apartment #3, 102 Bellevue Street. Finally, on February 17, 1988, Luna applied for and received a warrant to search Apartment #3, 102 Bellevue Street. Just prior to executing the warrant, however, Luna met "X" at 102–104 Bellevue Street, and "X" also made a controlled drug purchase at Apartment #3, 102 Bellevue Street. At this point, however, Luna was apparently under the assumption that the drugs were being purchased from the door on the right, which was actually Apartment #4, 102 Bellevue Street. In his March 21, 1989, affidavit, Luna admitted that he had made the application for the February 17, 1988, search warrant based on collective information from Officer Schroeder and Sergeant Amate and based on the February 15 and 16 controlled purchases made by informants "X" and "Y." Luna claimed that he had substituted his name for informants "X" and "Y" and made up "IT" in order to protect the confidentiality of "X" and "Y." However, it appears more likely that Luna was concerned about the reliability of "X" and "Y" and thus used "IT" in order to ensure a probable cause finding. Thus, not only did Officer Luna lie about "IT" in the initial affidavit, but he also went through the charade of looking for "IT," knowing full well that "IT" did not exist.

The Superior Court judge reconsidered his decision to dismiss the indictment in light of the evidence that "IT" had never existed. After reconsideration, the judge sustained his decision to dismiss the indictments due to the misconduct of the prosecutor and the egregious misconduct of the police officers. The judge noted that the prosecutor had provided information that questioned the existence of "IT," and led to the "inescapable conclusion" that the police officers had fabricated this informant. See *Commonwealth v. Lewin*, 405 Mass. 566, 576–577 (1989). The Superior Court judge also criticized the conduct of the prosecutor for having maintained his position in opposing the defendant's motion to dismiss, even after he had developed doubts as to the existence of "IT." See 405 Mass. at 577–778. Attributing the police officers' misconduct to the prosecutor, the judge found that the behavior of the prosecutor "fell below required constitutional and ethical standards" and, therefore, warranted a dismissal of the indictments. 405 Mass. at 580. The judge found that the conduct of the police and the prosecutor had been so egregious that it called into question the reliability and validity of the new evidence that was presented and made a fair and non-prejudicial trial unlikely. See *Id.*

Not surprisingly, this case made it to the Massachusetts Supreme Judicial Court, which reversed the dismissal, holding that the prosecutor's misconduct did not prejudice the defendant's right to a fair trial. See 405 Mass. at 584. The court further held that the police misconduct, while egregious and reprehensible, did not merit the dismissal of a charge as serious as murder. The Supreme Judicial Court noted that "Luna's knowingly false application for the search warrant completely discredits a fundamental safeguard on which constitutional protection against unreasonable searches and seizures is based." See 405 Mass. 585. However, the court concluded that "[a]lthough we condemn the police misconduct in this case in the strongest terms and would have required the suppression of any evidence of drug law violations seized during a search pursuant to the search warrant, the charges against the defendant need not be dismissed because of egregious police misconduct." 405 Mass. at 586. The court reasoned that deterrence of this sort of conduct would be achieved by the fact that the "officers' police careers are over, their reputations greatly damaged, and they face serious criminal charges." 405 Mass. at 587. Indeed Officer Luna was later convicted of perjury and expelled from the police force. He accused the prosecutor on the case, Francis O'Meara, of encouraging him to lie in his affidavit. O'Meara was exonerated by the Supreme Judicial Court and in 1992 left the District Attorney's Office to go into private practice.[6] This entire story illustrates the extent to which some police officers and prosecutors will go not only to lie initially, to make up nonexistent informants, but to continue to lie repeatedly to cover up their initial fabrication. It also shows the limits of the judicial system's willingness to take corrective action.

THE FOURTH AMENDMENT AND THE NONEXISTENT INFORMANT

The Fourth Amendment, Informants, and the Search Warrant Process

The fourth amendment to the Constitution requires that there be a justification, or in legal language "probable cause," to make an arrest or perform a search. In order to search, a warrant is generally required. Once a search warrant has been obtained, the results of a search are largely insulated from the thrust of the exclusionary rule even if the search is later found to have been illegal. This is a result of the case of *United States v. Leon*, 468 U.S. 897 (1984) in which the Supreme Court created the good-faith exception to the exclusionary rule. When a police officer has obtained a warrant, this is an indication of good faith and there is no point in excluding evidence even if the warrant later proves to be illegal, as there is no reason to believe that this exclusion will serve as a deterrent or affect future actions of the police officer. See 468 U.S. at 919–920. Although, as we will explore, there are some limitations to this doctrine, such as knowing falsity in the affidavit for the warrant, the obtaining of a warrant largely insulates even a constitutionally invalid search from the exclusionary rule.

To obtain a search warrant police need to show probable cause to a neutral judicial officer, usually by a sworn affidavit. This showing is generally made by a law enforcement officer before a judicial officer in an ex parte proceeding. In an ex parte proceeding, unlike a trial-type confrontation common to our adversary system, only one side is presented— the officer's side. In evaluating probable cause, the judicial officer considers facts rather than conclusions so that she has a basis to evaluate the information. In addition, the judicial officer evaluates the credibility of this information, especially when an informant is the source of the information. The law enforcement officer must demonstrate the credibility of the evidence by providing specific information. Conclusory language such as "the informant is credible" is not sufficient.

The Supreme Court, in the 1964 case *Aguilar v. State of Texas*, 378 U.S. 108 (1964), developed a so-called two-prong test for evaluating warrant applications based on confidential informants. The first prong focuses on the credibility of the informant. The judge should ask, "Why should I believe this information is reliable?" See 378 U.S. at 114. The second prong focuses on the basis of the informant's knowledge. The judge should ask, "How does the informant know what she says she knows?" See 378 U.S. at 114. The information supporting each prong must be detailed facts, not conclusory statements. While the Supreme Court initially held that a deficiency in either prong would undermine the finding of probable cause, a later Supreme Court case, *Illinois v. Gates*, 462 U.S. 213 (1983), relaxed this two-prong test by replacing it with a commonsense "totality-of-the-circumstances" approach. This approach states that substantial satisfaction of either prong might be sufficient to establish probable cause. Nevertheless, the language from the *Gates* case indicates that the *Aguilar* test still has some importance, as it delineates two factors to be weighed in evaluating an informant. In interpreting their own constitutions, some states have retained the two-prong test and rigidly evaluate each prong. Massachusetts is one of these states. See *Commonwealth v. Upton*, 394 Mass. 363, 373 (1985).

As mentioned, the *Gates* court sought to modify the old test, finding it too rigid and thus difficult for police officers to satisfy. The difficulty of satisfying the two-prong test helps to explain Officer Luna's action in fabricating an informant. He had a description of an informant,[7] which had withstood previous search warrant challenges, so he continued to use the same description rather than risk using another. The complexity of establishing both prongs, coupled with poor training, constitutes some of the underlying reasons for Luna's lying. In addition, common sentiment that society is better served by finding evidence of drug dealing as opposed to following arcane procedural technicalities contributes to this lying.[8]

The fact that the lies were discovered makes the story of Carlos Luna unusual, because courts rarely allow for challenges to search warrants based on information provided by informants. In *McCray v. Illinois*, 386 U.S. 300 (1967), the Supreme Court held that the Constitution did not require disclosure of the informant's identity for purposes of challenging the probable cause determination. In deciding not to require disclosure, the court recognized the importance of informants: "The informer is a vital part of society's defensive arsenal. The basic rule protecting his identity rests upon that belief." 386 U.S. at 307 (1967) (quoting *State v. Burnett*, 42 N.J. 377, 385–388 [1964]). The court stated that if an informant's identity were required to be disclosed, people would be discouraged from becoming informants. The court also noted that revealing the identity of those who are presently informants would end their usefulness as informants.

The Supreme Court has created two exceptions to the nondisclosure of informants principle. While these exceptions do exist, they are rarely put into practice, due to the heavy burden that the court has placed on the defendant in showing that disclosure is necessary. The first exception, created by the court in *McCray*, goes to the veracity of the officer's affidavit. Discretion is left to the judge who hears the motion to suppress.[9] See 386 U.S. at 307–308.

The procedure enunciated in *McCray* left little opportunity for a defendant to prove the nonexistence of an informant. While a very conscientious judge will alleviate her suspicions as to the police officer's veracity by requiring the production of an informant for an in camera hearing, this, is unusual and rare. In *McCray*, the arresting officers testified in open court in precise detail regarding what they were told by the informant and why they believed the informant's information was reliable and trustworthy. The court then made a point to state that the officers were under oath and subject to cross-examination. These two facts were enough for the court to conclude that the judge was "obviously satisfied" that each officer was testifying honestly, "and for that reason he exercised the discretion conferred upon him . . . to respect the informer's privilege." 386 U.S. at 313. Traditionally, judges have found it difficult to believe that a police officer sworn to uphold the law would break the law by committing perjury. Even if this were the case, the courts have relied heavily on cross-examination of the officer as an effective safeguard to the truth.

McCray discussed disclosure of an informant's identity at a suppression hearing to assess probable cause prior to trial. The second exception is found in *Roviaro v. United States*, 353 U.S. 53 (1957), which addressed the issue of informant identity disclosure at trial. In this case, the court held that the privilege of the government to withhold the identity of informants could be overcome at trial if the defense were to show that disclosure "is relevant and helpful to the defense of an accused, or is essential to a fair determination of a cause." 353 U.S. at 61. In *Roviaro*, the informant was the only person, other than the defendant, who had participated in the illegal transportation of narcotics for which the defendant was arrested. See 353 U.S. at 64. The informant, therefore, was the only witness who could either support or contradict the testimony of the defendant. Taking this into account, the court held that if the disclosure were necessary to determine the guilt or innocence of the accused, then disclosure would be required. The court recognized that this was a case-by-case determination that required balancing the public interest in protecting the flow of information (keeping an informant's identity secret) with the individual's right to prepare a defense. The court explained that this balance must take into consideration the crime the defendant is charged with, the possible defenses available, the possible significance of the informer's testimony, and any other relevant factors. See 353 U.S. at 62. The court noted that "the public interest in effective law enforcement" must at times give way to "fundamental requirements of fairness." 353 U.S. at 59–60. The differences between *Roviaro* and *McCray* were clarified in *United States v. Raddatz*. 447 U.S. 667 (1980). The court explicitly stated that "although the Due Process Clause has been held to require the government to disclose the identity of an informant at trial, provided the identity is shown to be relevant and helpful to the defense, *Rovario v. United States*, 353 U.S. 53, 60–61 (1957), it has never been held to require the disclosure of an informant's identity at a suppression hearing. *McCray v. Illinois*, 386 U.S. 300 (1967)." 447 U.S. at 679.

None of the cases mentioned thus far have dealt directly with a situation in which it is believed that the police officer actually lied about the existence of the informant. Although a test for veracity was addressed in *McCray*, there was no allegation in that case that the police were actually lying about the very existence of the informant. Further elaboration on the veracity issue occurred in the 1978 Supreme Court case of *Franks v. Delaware*. 438 U.S. 154 (1978). Defendant Franks sought, based on the fourth amendment, to suppress evidence (clothing and a knife) found by the police in a search of his apartment. He challenged the truthfulness of certain factual statements made by the police in the affidavit supporting the warrant to search his apartment, and he sought to call witnesses to testify on his behalf to prove that statements in the affidavit were false. See 438 U.S at 155. The court placed a very heavy burden on the defendant before he could inquire as to the veracity of the search warrant; he was required to show, by a preponderance of evidence, that there was a false statement included in the warrant affidavit.[10] The *Franks* case established the standard that the defendant must show that the statement in the affidavit was knowingly and intentionally false or made with reckless disregard for the truth, and that the statement was necessary for the finding of probable cause. "Allegations of negligence or innocent mistake are insufficient." 438 U.S at 171. Further, even an intentionally false statement will withstand scrutiny if it is found not to have been required for the determination of probable cause. It is important to note that the affidavit is presumed to be valid and the defendant must factually support his allegation of falsity. Implicit in the *Franks* opinion is the justices' belief that the information provided by the police contained in warrant affidavits is truthful. When the source of the information is an unnamed informant, it is extremely difficult for a defendant to make the required showing because he simply does not have access to the necessary information.

The Carlos Luna case is extraordinary because it demonstrates the lengths to which the defense counsel must go to show that an affidavit is false. Since there was no central registry for search warrant applications in Massachusetts, Lewin's counsel had to search clerk's offices of many local district courts. Upon arrival at each clerk's office, counsel had to look through all the search warrants to find the ones Carlos Luna applied for, and then compare them to the existing affidavit. Even the most conscientious defense counsel does not generally undertake this this time-consuming and expensive investigative work.

Even if the defense somehow jumps through all the legal hoops and establishes that the police officer is lying, the officer rarely will be prosecuted for the perjury. This is because of the need for a good working relationship between police and prosecutors, and because of sympathy for the police officer's goal of ridding society of a criminal.[11] In addition, it is difficult for the prosecutor to know with certainty whether a police officer is lying. This, coupled with the prosecutor's desire to win convictions, may result in the prosecutor not following up on her intuition that the officer is lying. Many involved in the criminal justice system do not equate lying at a suppression hearing to perjury.[12] Those questioned in the Luna case considered the perjury to be mere "fudging" rather than lying, as lying had to do more with lying about guilt or innocence than lying in a situation such as this.[13] Another factor contributing to the low rate at which police affidavits and testimony are questioned is the reluctance of judges to implicate other government officials, particularly if they regularly appear in the judge's courtroom.[14]

"Testilying"

Ultimately, a jury acquitted Albert Lewin of Officer Griffiths's murder in October 1990. Officer Carlos Luna was convicted of twenty-five counts of perjury and filing false reports as a result of his fabricating the informant. In June 1991, he was sentenced to five years probation. At his trial, Luna testified that he was encouraged, and indeed ordered, to lie. "Luna, who testified in his own defense, said after he joined the drug control unit in 1987, his squad leader had told him to copy a used affidavit[15] that had passed legal scrutiny when he wanted to obtain a warrant."[16] In a subsequent trial of Luna's supervisor, Kenneth Acerra, who, on an unrelated matter, pled guilty to conspiracy, civil rights violations, and tax fraud,[17] Boston Police Detective John Brazil testified that Acerra taught him to be "efficient" in the preparation of search warrants. This efficiency was based on fabricating informants and surveillance results.[18] Lies intended to put criminals in jail are so common that police have coined a phrase to describe it: "testilying."[19]

The problem of testilying is not a new phenomenon.[20] The 1961 Supreme Court decision, *Mapp v. Ohio*, 367 U.S. 643 (1961), provided an incentive to lie about searches. The decision made the exclusion of evidence obtained as a result of a violation of the fourth amendment applicable to state criminal prosecutions. Prior to *Mapp*, there were no consequences associated with a violation of the fourth amendment in state criminal proceedings. Once the Supreme Court extended the exclusionary rule to state criminal trials, the incentive to lie increased.[21]

Several studies have documented the frequency with which police officers lie. A study of the Chicago criminal court system examined 269 search warrants in which the warrant affidavit utilized a "reliable" informant. The affidavits were all found to be disturbingly similar.[22] Reminiscent of Officer Luna, the study found eight warrant affidavits submitted by Officer Blue (an alias) to be nearly identical.

> Each of Blue's warrant affidavits stated that he had known the informant for 12 months. Each stated that the informant had provided information to Blue on two prior occasions, that this information had twice lead [*sic*] to the seizure of narcotics and twice to an arrest, that the substance obtained had been twice tested and found to be narcotics, and that there were two cases pending based on the information provided by the informant. In all eight warrant affidavits, the informant bought drugs there. In every affidavit, Blue stated that the informant had been using drugs for thirty-six months. Finally, all the affidavits state the informant tried the drug and got a high feeling like he had before.[23]

In response to several arrests of New York police officers for drug offenses, in 1992 Mayor David Dinkins appointed a commission to investigate the police department. In their study of the New York Police Department, the Mollen Commission documented an increase in police lying and other illegal activity. After a two-year investigation, the commission concluded that "clusters of police" throughout the city were engaged in illegal activity.[24] They further found that perjured testimony by police officers is particularly common in drug prosecutions.[25] "A nine month investigation by the *National Law Journal* . . . found . . . abuses by informants and law enforcement threaten the rights and the safety of innocent people, as well as the integrity of the courts. The war on drugs is the engine driving this development."[26]

Take, for instance, a typical prosecution of an individual for drug possession. If the drugs seized from the defendant are suppressed because the police violated the fourth amendment in obtaining the drugs, the case is likely to be dismissed because there will be no evidence available on which to convict the defendant. On the other hand, if officers lie about their search and seizure methods and the judge believes the testimony, the officers have avoided exclusion of the evidence and the defendant will most likely be convicted.[27] To justify unlawfully entering an apartment where they believe they can find narcotics or cash, officers pretend to have information from an unidentified civilian informant or claim they saw the drugs in plain view after responding to the premises on a radio run.[28]

Although the central objective is to evade the costs of the exclusionary rule, there are other justifications for this lying. First, the moral justification is simple: putting a guilty person behind bars outweighs small acts of illegality, "little white lies." "As one dedicated officer put it, police officers often view falsification as, to use his word, 'doing God's work'—doing whatever it takes to get a suspected criminal off the streets."[29] Thus, it is not surprising that the Mollen Commission reported that lying during the warrant process, especially with regard to confidential informants, seemed to be a common phenomenon.[30]

Second, as indicated by Luna's testimony, lying is ignored and at times even encouraged by supervisory personnel. Police supervisors, who usually have gone through the ranks of the police force, have a great deal of empathy for the frontline officers. They are, therefore, protective and supportive of their fellow officers. Further, unlike most organizational models, a police department's lower echelon—cops on the beat or detectives investigating crime—have a great deal of discretion and are often called on to make important and instantaneous decisions. Furthermore, politicians and the public put pressure on the police to put criminals behind bars but do not necessarily consider how the incarceration was accomplished.

A third, less altruistic reason that the higher echelon of the police departments ignores and indeed encourages police lying, especially with regard to drug prosecutions, is money. In 1984, Congress passed a civil forfeiture statute that allows seized drug money, assets, and items used to facilitate a drug crime, to be funneled to the seizing police agency. Among the items that have been forfeited are houses, boats, cars, and restaurants. This provides a financial incentive for a police department to engage in illegal seizures for the purpose of increasing its income. As a result of this financial incentive, police departments have adjusted their priorities. Instead of putting the perpetrator in jail, police departments will sometimes concentrate resources on drug control in an effort to fill their coffers. Given the financial incentive associated with these operations, it is not surprising that lying is tolerated and ignored.[31]

A fourth factor that promotes lying is that a police officer who lies is rarely caught. There are several institutional reasons for this failure to expose dishonest officers. Most criminal cases, about 90 percent,[32] end in plea bargains. Thus, the necessity for testifying and exposing oneself to a perjury charge does not exist. Moreover, a prosecutor who is aware of the possibility of false testimony or other police illegality, might seek to sweeten the plea bargain to avoid the possibility of a trial and the resulting perjury.[33] Thus, the illegality will never see the light of day.

Also worth noting is the so-called blue wall of silence. Police officers often face dangerous situations, and they need to be able to rely on each other for their very safety. As a result, what has evolved is great loyalty and trust of one another—a brotherhood. Even when officers know that other officers are perjuring themselves, they will not come forward and rat out a fellow police officer. In some instances, officers will even lie for fellow force members.[34]

As previously mentioned, police perjury is rarely prosecuted. While prosecutors and judges believe that perjury is systematic and frequently apparent, they rarely take action against it.[35] The Mollen Commission documented findings of prosecutors acknowledging perjury and falsifications of documents as serious problems in law enforcement, and while not condoned, these problems are largely ignored.[36] One obvious reason for this is that perjury is difficult to prove. Often there is conflicting testimony of witnesses, some of whom may not be regarded as credible. Also, prosecutors tolerate police perjury because they need to maintain a working relationship with the police in order to prosecute their cases effectively. Additionally, prosecutors may agree with the police that society's interest in convicting criminals outweighs the dishonesty that police may use to get the desired result.

Judicial indifference to testilying is often explained away by the failure of prosecutors to come forward with cases against the police. It all comes back to the notion of preserving relationships. Judges know that police officers appear in court regularly, and that they play an integral part in the process of criminal adjudication.[37] Police officers know judges likely will not damage the prosecution's case as long as procedural safeguards at least appear to be obeyed. Thus, the courts passively allow police officers' testilying.

REFORM PROPOSALS

Police Guidelines

Carlos Luna was a victim of a poor infrastructure within the police department. The war on drugs and the resulting rapid expansion within the drug control unit (from twelve to sixty officers) resulted in poor training. During the late 1980s warrant falsifications were common, as indicated by an independent examination of hundreds of warrants by *The Boston Globe*.[38] Ironically, if we believe the subsequent information presented by the prosecution in the pursuit of Lewin, then it is likely that the information known to Luna would have resulted in probable cause. Nevertheless, he filed a false affidavit. He resorted to an affidavit that had been successful in the past. Perhaps this was a result of inadequate training, or perhaps it was laziness on his part. It may have been difficult to establish the reliability of the actual informants. Finally, as indicated, Luna had no idea that there would be consequences to lying in an affidavit. He never thought his lie would see the light of day. He was eager to make as many busts as possible; he was ambitious.

As indicated, there are few safeguards within the court system to ensure the veracity of the information allegedly obtained from unnamed informants. In response to the publicizing of informant abuses such as Luna's, many law enforcement agencies have developed guidelines to combat the structural incentives to lie. These guidelines face a number of institutional obstacles: putting a supervisor in a position to monitor informants is contrary to the general operation of police forces that places a great deal of discretion on lower-level officers. In addition, in order to develop relationships with informants, police often act in ways that in essence could be seen to license criminal activity. These relationships would cause embarrassment if they were formally acknowledged. Additionally, the idea of formally reporting an informant who wishes to keep his identity a secret might reduce the availability of informants. Nevertheless, where money is exchanged for information, as opposed to criminal activity being ignored, most police departments would prefer to have some formal internal checks on the use of informants to ensure that the money is actually used for the information and not for the personal gain of the police officer.[39]

To curtail police misconduct, certain fundamental control procedures must be employed. A well designed policy would control and account for payments and nonmonetary benefits conveyed to informants, require physical verification of the existence of informants, impose corroboration requirements between information provided by the informant and that provided by the officer, require separation of duties to every extent practicable, and employ a system of checks and balances. The Boston Police Department has incorporated several such control procedures into its informant policy, which was adopted on June 10, 1996, by special order number 96-31, a copy of which is included as Appendix B. An analysis of some of the important provisions follows:

1. To ensure the actual existence of an informant, several safeguards are in place. In the Informant Recruitment Procedures,[40] an officer must report any initial contact with a potential informant to the commanding officer in charge of criminal investigations. The officer's supervisor should meet the informant. Also, officers shall generally meet with informants with another officer present.

2. Once the informant is approved, extensive filing requirements, including the attachment of a recent photo of the informant, must be met. When approved, the officer's supervisor should conduct a complete initial debriefing with the assistance of the recruiting officer. A report of the debriefing is provided to the Investigative Unit Chief. This measure will serve to corroborate the officer's version of the information with that of the informant's. This cross-checking will afford the supervisor a very high degree of confidence with respect to the use of the informant and to the officer's integrity. These types of provisions should help prevent the fabrication of an informant, as discussed in this chapter.

3. With regard to incentives provided to the informant, there are many checks. All payments and nonmonetary benefits to the informants should be recorded in the informant files. Furthermore, receipts should be written for all monetary payments to the informant, using his/her alias. This signature should be witnessed and cosigned by two officers. The receipt should be placed in the informant file as well as forwarded to various supervisory personnel. This "dual control" will allow internal auditors to trace and verify informant transactions.

4. The Auditing and Review Division, a division independent of the Investigative Unit, should conduct a yearly internal audit of all accounting records. They should not only check the monetary payment, but also verify that the informant files have been properly maintained.

These formal internal guidelines are a step in the right direction, but are not a cure-all, especially when corruption permeates a police department. Should there be a greater obligation on the part of the prosecutor to check on the informants? Should more police officers be prosecuted for this lying? Should charges be dismissed?

CONCLUSION

The story of Officer Carlos Luna and his nonexistent informant serves to highlight the ease with which informants are used and abused. Many warrants rely on information from unnamed informants. The *National Law Journal*, looking at a particular geographic area, found that in 1980, 46 percent of warrant applications used unnamed informants; in 1993 this increased to 93 percent. As long as law enforcement remains a competitive enterprise in which police are encouraged to find the perpetrators, nonexistent informants will continue to plague the criminal justice system. Of all the abuses of informants, the problem of the nonexistent informer may be one of the most egregious, but it is an abuse that will likely respond well to reform. Police guidelines, better training, greater judicial vigilance, and prosecution of police who perjure themselves might not totally eliminate the case of the nonexistent informant but will contribute to quelling the breadth and depth of nonexistent informer abuses.

APPENDIX A

AFFIDAVIT
IN SUPPORT OF APPLICATION FOR SEARCH WARRANT.
TRIAL COURT OF MASSACHUSETTS

Your affiant officer Carlos A. Luna has received information from a reliable informant; hereafter referred to as "IT", who has proven reliable in the past by providing your affiant with information that led to the arrest and now pending case in the Suffolk Superior Court of one Miguel Sarracent for Trafficking in Cocaine, Possession of Class D with Intent to Distribute and unlawfull Possession of a firearm, also for the conviction in the Suffolk Superior Court of one June Samaniego for Possession of Class B with Intent to Distribute.

"IT" now tells me that for the last three weeks and more recently within the last two days, "IT" has been present at #102 Bellevue St., Dorchester Mass. apt. #3 on the third floor of a multi-unit wooden dwelling; that being the home of a H/M (med built, med skin, @ 5'06", 30's) known to "IT" as STEVIE; and while there "IT" observed this H/M (STEVIE) engaged in the cutting, weighing, packaging and selling of paperfolds of white powder, believed to be Cocaine......these packages of white powder, believed to be Cocaine are numbered according to the price.....e.i. #4 representing a value of $40.00, #1 representing a value of $100.00, etc.; "IT" further tells me that STEVIE packages his POWDER (street term, referring to COCAINE) in Mass. Lottery Receipts in order to keep himself away from what STEVIE refers to as "having possession of drug paraphernalia items" in the event of his house getting busted.

"IT" goes on to say that STEVIE has rebuilt the door to the apt. thus making it an extremely heavy door to break-down.......STEVIE deals his POWDER through a hole (8 1/4") in his door; never opening the door to anybody, STEVIE believes this to be a safe and secured system giving him an edge in case of a Police raid on his apt.

As a result of the information received; I responded to the location and at diverse times over several days did set-up a series of covert surveillance posts; and while doing so, I observed an unusual high amount of foot traffic leading up to the apt.; I further observed these various persons knocking on the door of apt. #3 and asking for "one fifty", "one", "an eight-ball", etc., while rolling their monies and pushing it through a small hole in the door; these persons would then receive a paperfold through the same hole......I also observed these persons examining the contents of the paperfolds and I observed the contents to be a white powder, believed to be COCAINE.

On 02/15/88 I went to the location and knocked on the door; an H/M asked me what I wanted, I then replied "a sixty"; I was then told to place the money through the hole and received one lottery slip paperfold containing white powder believed to be COCAINE......please refer to police report.

On 02/16/88, again I went to the location and again knocked on the door; the same H/M asked me what I wanted, and again I responded "a sixty"; I was again told to place the money through the hole and again I received a lottery slip paperfold of white powder, believed to be COCAINE.....please refer to police report..........On both occasions I used official BPD drug funds; marked monies.

As a result of the information received, the observations and investigations concerning this location (including the two separate drug buys at this location and further based on your affiant's experience in the illegal drug field; your affiant does believe that large amounts of COCAINE, a Class B Controlled Subst. are being secreted and sold from this location; I further believe this to be an "on-going" illegal enterprise and that the drug laws of Massachusetts are being violated at this location; and due to the type of drugs involved and their Easy destruction as well as to maintain a safety factor for the officers involved a no knock warrant is hereby requested.

Your affiant has been a police officer for nine years; has served in various Special Enforcements Teams, has worked undercover, has made undercover drug buys and personally responsible for hundreds of drug related arrests, finally your affiant is currently a member of the Drug Control Unit.

PRINTED NAME OF AFFIANT	SIGNED UNDER THE PENALTIES OF PERJURY
X_____ Carlos A. Luna	X_____ /s/ Carlos A. Luna

Appendix B
Boston Police Guidelines Regarding Use of Informants

Boston Police
SPECIAL ORDER NUMBER 96-31

ALL BUREAUS, DISTRICTS
AREAS, DIVISIONS, OFFICES,
SECTIONS AND UNITS

COPIES TO: ALL SUPERINTENDENTS
DEPUTY SUPERINTENDENTS
AND DIRECTORS

_____ June 10, 1996 _____

SUBJECT: CONFIDENTIAL INFORMANT PROCEDURES

The provisions of this Special Order are effective immediately. Special Order 95-4, issued on January 18, 1995, and all previously issued Rules, Orders, Memorandums and Directives on this subject are hereby rescinded and replaced by its provisions.

PURPOSE

To detail procedures relative to the recruitment and record keeping requirements connected with the use of confidential informants.

GENERAL CONSIDERATIONS

One of the most important responsibilities of any police officer is the recruitment and development of informants to the point where they regularly contribute information concerning criminal enterprises and become a valuable resource to the Department.

Although individual officers are responsible for recruiting informants, informants do not "belong" to the officer, but represent a resource for the Department as a whole.

The specific procedures and requirements of this special order do not apply to persons providing information as anonymous participants in the "Crime Stoppers" program.

All reports and data relating to confidential informants and the information they supply, required to be forwarded or transported to a particular unit or person in accordance with this order, shall be hand-delivered in sealed envelopes and not placed in Department or U.S. Mail.

All references to information/documents being provided to a District/Division Commander by a Detective Supervisor are to be via the Detective Supervisor's chain of command.

In cases where there is disagreement between a District or Unit Commander and the Chief, Bureau of Investigative Services as to the appropriateness of any action or procedure being contemplated or performed in accordance with this Special Order, the Chief, Bureau of Investigative Services shall be the final arbiter of such disagreement and shall have complete authority to direct what actions or procedures shall be done or not done.

DEFINITIONS

1. **Source of Information** a person or organization, not under the direction of a specific officer, who provides information without becoming a party to the investigation itself (e.g., a business firm furnishing information from its records; an employee of an organization who, through the routine course of his activities, obtains information of value to the Department; or a concerned citizen who witnesses an event of interest to the Department).

   A **source of information** who seeks financial compensation shall be re-classified as a **paid confidential informant**. A **source of information** who becomes an active participant in the investigative process shall be re-classified as an **other informant**.

2. **Paid Confidential Informant**—a person who provides a police officer with information regarding a crime or criminal activity for monetary consideration and is compensated in any manner.

3. **Defendant Informant**—a person who provides a police officer with information regarding a crime or criminal activity for consideration in a pending criminal matter. Officers are not to enter into any agreement or promise with such a person without first notifying and receiving the approval of an Assistant District Attorney, Assistant U.S. Attorney or Assistant Attorney General. Upon receiving such approval, the officer shall complete a report which documents the date and time of such notification, what promises or considerations were made and who granted the approval. The original of such report shall be placed in the informant's District Unit confidential informant file with a copy being forwarded to the Chief, Bureau of Investigative Services, or his designee.

4. **Other Informant**—a person who has a criminal background, or who associates with a criminal element or with a person with a criminal background, who may or may not have a criminal case pending and who

wishes to act as an informant. Possible motivations for such informants include, but are not limited to, the following:

a. personal gratification, which may include collecting rewards;
b. revenge;
c. rivalry;
d. avoiding criminal prosecution.

5. **Significant Contact**—any contact or communication with an informant, planned or unplanned, in which the informant provides information of any intelligence value to any law enforcement agency regarding criminal activity or which is used as the basis of a search or arrest warrant.

6. **Code Number**—The Code Number is a combination of numbers and letters which will consist of the last two numbers of the calendar year that the informant is entered, followed by the numerical number of the District/Unit, followed by the first and last initials of the recruiting officer's name, followed by a sequential number. Thus, an informant entered in 1995 by the Drug Control Unit, Sgt. John Doe, would be coded 95-28-JD-01. Any reference to the confidential informant will be by the code number or alias. Informants identified as being used by multiple officers shall have a code number assigned by the Chief, Bureau of Investigative Services or his designee.

INFORMANT RESTRICTIONS

In addition to the definitions and categories described above, individuals fitting the criteria established below shall be subject to the additional requirements indicated:

1. **Persons less than 18 years of age**—may only be utilized with the written consent of their parent or legal guardian.

2. **Persons on probation or parole**—all persons on parole shall be informed that the Department will seek permission to have them released from any conditions of their parole that prohibit them from acting as an informant. The following procedures will be utilized:

   a. **Federal Probation or Parole**—the Department shall seek authorization and approval from the United States Regional Parole Commissioner, in accordance with the provisions of the U.S. Parole Commission requirements governing the Use of Parolees and Mandatory Releases as Informants/Confidential Sources, §2.40 (05). If granted, a copy of the agreement between the Department and the U.S. Parole Commission shall be placed in the informant's file at the District or Unit and in the confidential informant central file;

b. **State Parole**—the Department shall seek authorization and approval from the informant's parole officer. If granted, a copy of the Commonwealth of Massachusetts Parole Board Confidential Waiver Agreement shall be kept in the informant's file at the District or Unit and in the confidential informant central file (see Commonwealth of Massachusetts Parole Board Manual of Policies and Procedures, Chapter 500 §505.17);

c. **State Probation**—all persons on state probation shall be instructed that their use as an informant may create a conflict with their probation and that they should seek the advice of their Probation Officer.

3. **Persons who have previously been disqualified as an informant**—may only be utilized on a case by case basis with the concurrence of the District/Unit Commander and the written approval of the Chief, Bureau of Investigative Services, subject to such additional restrictions as he may require.

INFORMANT RECRUITMENT PROCEDURES

Recruiting/Control Officer's Responsibilities
Officers who identify and recruit individuals that are willing to provide information to the Department must comply with the following procedures for all individuals except those defined as a "**source of information**":

a. Report any initial contact with a potential informant to the officer's Detective Supervisor;

b. Conduct a criminal history check (BOP check; NCIC check; NLETS check);

c. Set up an appointment with the officer's Detective Supervisor to meet the potential informant to determine his/her potential use, to evaluate their credibility and to ensure that they provide satisfactory documentation to positively verify their true identity;

d. Fill out two Confidential Informant Cards, BPD Form 2468, and make one photocopy of the card once it is completely filled out. Attach a recent photograph (i.e., recent ID photo or a Polaroid) to each of the original Confidential Informant Cards and to the photocopy;

e. Read and explain the provisions of the Informant Working Agreement, BPD Form 2645, to the potential informant. If the potential informant agrees to abide by its conditions, have two originals of the agreement signed by the potential informant, the recruiting officer and the officer's Detective Supervisor and make one photocopy of it;

f. Give the Detective Supervisor all documents gathered that help to identify the informant or establish his reliability, including criminal history checks and both the originals and photocopies of the Confidential Informant Card, with the photographs attached, and the Informant Working Agreement;

g. If use of the informant is approved, assist the Detective Supervisor in conducting a complete initial debriefing of the informant;

h. All planned meetings or significant contacts with the informant shall be documented by recording all records of payment, if any, **and** the filing of debriefing reports. Debriefing reports shall not identify an informant by true name, but shall include the date of the meeting, the code number of the informant, the names of the officers who met with the informant, a summary of the information the informant supplied and what payment, if any, was made to the informant.

The original of all debriefing reports, including debriefing, and all payment-records and/or receipts shall be placed in the District/Unit Detective Commander's confidential informant's file. A copy of all debriefing reports, including the initial debriefing, shall be kept in the Detective Supervisor's confidential informant file and second copy sent to the Chief; Bureau of Investigative Services, or his designee.

Officers shall only hold planned meetings with an informant, or potential informant, with another officer present both for corroboration and for backup. Any exception must be authorized, in advance and in writing, by the officer's Detective Supervisor.

i. With the exception of the Confidential Informant Card and the Informant Working Agreement, all Department reports and/or forms shall refer to the informant only by their code number.

j. Officers are not to have any business, personal or planned meetings with an informant, other than a **source of information**, unless it is directly related to the informant providing information.

k. Officers shall immediately notify their Detective Supervisor, in writing, whenever they have reason to believe an informant has done any of the following:

1. Failed to follow the instructions of a control officer;

2. Knowingly violated any provision of the Informant Working Agreement;
3. Knowingly provided false information;
4. Engaged in any criminal conduct or enterprise that is not authorized by a control officer for the purpose of obtaining evidence.

The photograph and signature requirements of paragraphs (d) and (e) of this section may be waived by the District/Unit Detective Commander with the concurrence of the Chief, Bureau of Investigative Services, or his designee, if such requirements would tend to hinder effective law enforcement due to the sensitive nature of the informant's position or source of information. All such waivers shall be in writing with the original of the waiver placed in the District/Unit Detective Commander's confidential informant file and a copy placed in the confidential informant central file. In all such cases, the recruiting officer and the officer's Detective Supervisor shall ensure that the required two Confidential Informant Cards are filled out and document that the informant understands and has verbally agreed to abide by the conditions of the Informant Working Agreement.

Detective Supervisor's Responsibilities
a. Subject to any additional requirements listed under "Informant Restrictions", the Detective Supervisor is responsible for recommending the use of individuals as confidential informants after evaluating their suitability, potential usefulness, personal history and criminal record, if any. Detective Supervisors are responsible for ensuring that Board of Probation checks are performed on all active informants during each Tri-Annual Fitness reporting period and for forwarding the results of such checks to the central informant file. Detective Supervisors shall also be responsible for ensuring that satisfactory documentation has been provided that positively verifies an informant's true identity. All such recommendations and all documents gathered that help to establish the informant's identity and/or reliability shall be forwarded to the District/Unit Detective Commander for concurrence and approval. These documents shall include criminal history checks and both the originals and the photocopy of the Confidential Informant Card and the Informant Working Agreement.

b. Detective Supervisors are authorized, but not required, to maintain a "working" file on informants utilized by officers under their command. References to documents being kept in the "Detective Supervisor's file" are made with the understanding that the keeping of such a file is optional. Whether individual Detective Supervisors choose to maintain a "working" file or not, they are responsible for ensuring that the District/Unit Detective Commander's confidential informant file is kept accurate and current.

c. Once an individual is approved for use as a confidential informant, the Detective Supervisor is responsible for conducting a complete initial debriefing with the assistance of the recruiting officer. The original of the initial debriefing report shall be placed in the informant's file at the District or Unit with one copy being kept in the Detective Supervisor's file and one copy being forwarded to the Chief Bureau of Investigative Services, or his designee.

d. The Detective Supervisor is responsible for ensuring that all necessary entries are made on the Confidential Informant Card (BPD Form 2468) and that officers submit debriefing reports for all planned meetings or significant contacts that adequately summarize the intelligence or information gained from an informant. In addition, the Detective Supervisor is responsible for ensuring that copies of all debriefing reports are forwarded to the Chief, Bureau of Investigative Services, or his designee, as soon as practicable, but no more than seventy-two (72) hours after they are submitted.

e. The Detective Supervisor is responsible for approving or rejecting all payments to an informant up to and including payments of $250.00. Payments in excess of $250.00 must be approved by the Chief, Bureau of Investigative Services.

    All payments in excess of $25.00 must be approved in advance. Payments of $25.00 or less that were not approved in advance shall be reimbursed only with the Detective Supervisor's approval. The Detective Supervisor shall keep track of the amount of money paid to each informant, note same on his copy of the Confidential Informant Card and provide that information to the District/Unit Detective Commander in a timely manner.

    Personal funds are not to be utilized by officers for the procurement of evidence, to make controlled and/or undercover buys or for the purpose of paying informants.

    The Detective Supervisor shall ensure that all payments to an informant, whether approved or not, are properly entered on the Confidential Informant Card (BPD Form 2468) and receipted for by the informant, who shall sign his alias or code name, on a Department receipt form (BPD Form 8) that is witnessed and co-signed by two officers. The copies of the receipt form and a Request for Funds Form (BPD Form 2494) shall be placed in the District/Unit Detective Commander's Confidential Informant File with the **originals** being forwarded to the Bureau of Investigative Services Finance Officer.

District/Unit Detective Commander's Responsibilities

a. The District/Unit Detective Commander, or a Detective Supervisor so designated by the District/Division Commander, shall be responsible for approving or disapproving the recruitment of individuals as confidential informants that have been recommended for approval by Detective Supervisors under his command after determining that satisfactory documentation has been provided that verifies the informant's true identity.

b. The District Unit Detective Commander shall be responsible for ensuring that all Detective Supervisors under his command maintain the Confidential Informant Cards appropriately and forward all required materials.

c. Immediately upon approving a potential confidential informant for use, the District/Unit Detective Commander shall forward an original of the Confidential Informant Card, with the photograph attached, an original of the Informant Working Agreement and a copy of any criminal history checks to the Chief.

   Bureau of Investigative Services, or his designee. The other set of originals of such documents and all other documents relating to such confidential informant shall be kept in the District/Unit Detective Commander's confidential informant file.

d. The District/Unit Detective Commander shall be responsible for maintaining custody of the District/Unit confidential informant files and shall ensure that all such files are kept in a secure, central location.

District/Division Commander's Responsibilities

a. The District/Division Commander shall, in conjunction with the Tri-Annual Fitness Report, audit the District/Unit Detective Commander's confidential informant files to ensure that the files are being properly maintained and that they appear to contain all necessary documentation.

b. The District/Division Commander shall ensure that all Detective Supervisors in his command are in full compliance with the requirements of this special order.

Chief, Bureau of Investigative Services

a. The Chief, Bureau of Investigative Services, or his designee, shall be responsible for maintaining the confidential informant central file. This file shall contain individual files on each informant that include an original of the Confidential Informant Card (BPD Form 2468), with a photograph attached, and an original of the Informant Working Agreement (BPD Form 2645) and copies of any other reports or documentation forwarded by the District/Unit Detective Commander.

In addition, the file shall contain copies of all debriefing reports submitted, as well as copies of any reports that seek or grant approval from persons or outside agencies regarding the use of the informant, place restrictions on the use of the informant or change the informant's status.

b. The Chief, Bureau of Investigative Services, or his designee, shall ensure that incoming confidential informant debriefing reports are analyzed and that any patterns, trends or criminal intelligence information that is discovered during such analysis is reported to those Bureaus, Districts or Units that could benefit from such knowledge.

c. The Chief, Bureau of Investigative Services, or his designee, shall be responsible for deciding whether or not a carded informant will be permitted to be carded and/or used by a second officer or unit. Informants used by multiple officers shall have a code number assigned by the Chief, Bureau of Investigative Services, or his designee.

d. The Chief, Bureau of Investigative Services, or his designee, shall be responsible for immediately notifying all persons known to use a particular informant whenever that informant is disqualified for such use.

e. Only the Chief, Bureau of Investigative Services, may authorize a payment to a confidential informant that exceeds $250.00.

INFORMANT STATUS/DISQUALIFICATION PROCEDURES

Informants shall be classified as follows:
a. Active—informants currently providing information or who have done so within the last six months.

b. Inactive—any informant who has not provided information within the last six-month period shall be classified as inactive.

c. Disqualified—any informant who has been determined to be unsuitable for any reason, including, but not limited to:

1. Fails to follow the instructions of a control officer;
2. Knowingly violates any provision of the Informant Working Agreement;

3. Knowingly provides false information;
4. Engages in any criminal conduct or enterprise other than that specifically authorized by a supervisor for the purpose of obtaining evidence in a specific investigation.

Status Change Procedures

a. **Active to Inactive**—a Detective Supervisor who becomes aware that an informant has not provided information within the last six month period shall re-classify such informant as "inactive" and shall forward a report of such re-classification to the District/Unit Detective Commander and to the Chief, Bureau of Investigative Services, or his designee.

b. **Inactive to Active**—An officer may request that his Detective Supervisor reactivate an informant who has had their status changed from active to inactive after first conducting a new criminal history check. The officer shall assist his Detective Supervisor in evaluating the informant's suitability, potential usefulness; personal history, criminal record and past history as an informant.

The Detective Supervisor shall make a recommendation concerning such reactivation to the District/Unit Detective Commander for his concurrence and approval. If the District/Unit Detective Commander approves the reactivation, the supervisor shall complete a report documenting such reactivation for inclusion into the District/Unit Detective Commander's confidential informant's file and forward a copy of such report to the Chief, Bureau of Investigative Services, or his designee.

Once the decision is made to reactivate an informant, the officer and the Detective Supervisor shall conduct a complete debriefing, place the original of the debriefing report in the District/Unit Detective Commander's informant file, keep one copy for the Detective Supervisor's file and forward a copy of the report to the Chief, Bureau of Investigative Services, or his designee.

c. **Active to Disqualified**—an officer who has reason to believe that an informant may no longer be suitable for use as an informant shall make an immediate report of his recommendation, and the reasons therefore, to his Detective Supervisor.

A Detective Supervisor who receives a report recommending that an informant be disqualified for use as an informant, or who decides on his own authority that such recommendation is warranted, shall immediately notify the District/Unit Detective Commander of such recommendation in writing.

The District/Unit Detective Commander, after reviewing all reports and recommendations, shall approve or disapprove the request to disqualify an informant. Copies of all reports and recommendations concerning a request for disqualification shall immediately be forwarded to the Chief, Bureau of Investigative Services, or his designee, for inclusion in the confidential informant central file.

d. **Disqualified to Active with Restrictions**—Individuals who have been disqualified may only be utilized with the endorsement of the Chief, Bureau of Investigative Services.

Requests for such utilization shall include a report from **both** the officer and his Detective Supervisor that evaluates the informant's suitability, potential usefulness, personal history, criminal record and past history as an informant. In addition, the report shall specifically address the issues that resulted in the informant's being disqualified and must state why such past misconduct should no longer preclude the individual's use as an informant. Before being forwarded to the Chief, Bureau of Investigative Services, all such requests must be approved by the District/Unit Detective Commander

If approved, the Chief, Bureau of Investigative Services shall permit such informants to be utilized only on a case by case basis, subject to such additional restrictions as he may require. The original of each such request, whether approved or disapproved, shall be placed in the District/Unit Detective Commander's informant file and a copy forwarded to the Chief, Bureau of Investigative Services, or his designee, and placed in the confidential informant central file.

Once the decision is made to utilize such an informant, the officer and the Detective Supervisor shall conduct a complete debriefing of the informant. original debriefing report shall be placed in the District/Unit Detective Commander's informant file with one copy being kept by the Detective Supervisor and an additional copy being forwarded to the Chief, Bureau of Investigative Services, or his designee

AUDIT

The Auditing and Review Division shall conduct an annual audit of confidential informant files, both those kept at the District/Unit and the confidential informant central file. Such audit shall ensure that:

a. Confidential informant files are properly maintained and include all necessary documentation, i.e., payment receipts, debriefing reports, confidential informant cards, photographs, informant working agreements, criminal history checks (BOP), et cetera.

b. Documents required to be forwarded to the confidential informant central file and/or to the Chief, Bureau of Investigative Services, or his designee, are being delivered in a timely and prescribed manner.

FEDERAL OR STATE MULTI-AGENCY TASK FORCES

The provisions of this special order shall not apply to officers assigned to federal or state multi-agency task forces which have other written rules or procedures that govern the use of confidential informants by members of such task forces.

DISCLOSURE OF CONFIDENTIAL INFORMANT INFORMATION

All Department employees are reminded that, by definition, information concerning confidential informants is of a highly sensitive nature. Accordingly, Department employees shall be held strictly liable for the disclosure of any information in their possession, no matter how trivial, to any person or organization which may tend to confirm the existence of a particular confidential informant or otherwise tend to identify a particular confidential informant unless:

a. as necessary, in the body of an affidavit filed in support of a search warrant;
b. ordered to do so in a judicial proceeding or by court order;
c. requested to do so, in writing, by a member of a law enforcement agency with a demonstrated need to know that particular informant and with approval of a Detective Supervisor;
d. as otherwise provided in this order.

In the event of uncertainty as to whether a member of any law enforcement agency, including a member of this Department, has adequately demonstrated a need to know informant information, the Chief, Bureau of Investigative Services, shall be the final arbiter as to whether the requisite need to know has been demonstrated.

Paul F. Evans
Police Commissioner

Chapter 4

Jailhouse Informants

The Stories of
Leslie Vernon White and
Anthony Michael Sarivola

Don't go to the pen—send a friend.
Why spend time—just drop a dime.

INTRODUCTION

Like other informants, the jailhouse informant gathers information for the government. However, unique to this type of informant is the fact that this information gathering goes on by one who is incarcerated. In this chapter, we will explore two types of incarcerated informants: those operating in a jail that holds prisoners awaiting trial and those who operates within the prison system, where inmates have been convicted and sentenced. In both situations the quest for freedom, whether through the promise of a early release, dropped charges, sentencing recommendations, or early parole, makes informants highly motivated to inform and provides strong incentive to lie.[1] When an informant has no information to trade on, they frequently fabricate the needed information in order to "buy" leniency from the government. As the Fifth Circuit observed, "It is difficult to imagine a greater motivation to lie than the inducement of a reduced sentence." *United States v. Cervantes-Pacheco*, 826 F.2d 310, 315 (5th Cir. 1987).

The most common incarcerated informant is an individual in jail awaiting trial for pending charges. By informing on his cellmates or others who are facing pending charges, he seeks to strengthen his ability to plea bargain with prosecutors. This informant will testify against a fellow inmate in return for a reduction or dismissal of charges, a sentencing recommendation, payment upon release, or in-custody benefits such as more food, greater telephone privileges, pocket cash, and access to television. The jailhouse informant raises both due process issues as well as sixth amendment right-to-counsel issues for a defendant who is the target of the informant's information.

The second type of jailhouse informant is one in prison as opposed to jail. This informant has already been convicted of a crime and sentenced. He informs on his fellow inmates with regard to unsolved crimes or possible security matters internal to a prison. In addition to monetary compensation, an informant will often be recommended for early release either through the parole system or through a petition to a trial judge for reconsideration of the original sentence. In addition, prison informants receive prison-related benefits, including greater privileges or transfer to a more desirable setting. In obtaining a fellow inmate's confession, this informant's methods raise issues related to the fifth amendment's protection against self-incrimination.

THE ROGUE INFORMANT: THE STORY OF LESLIE VERNON WHITE

Born in 1958, Leslie Vernon White was a typical jailhouse informant: he would gather and/or fabricate information about an individual who was facing pending charges. He would then offer this information to the government in return for benefits from them. White reached the pinnacle of his career when he mastered the art of "booking"[2] his fellow inmates. His exploits were documented in a 1989 segment of *60 Minutes* and resulted in a Los Angeles County grand jury investigation on the use of jailhouse informants.[3]

White has led a long life of crime. In and out of jail since the age of eight, his rap sheet includes convictions for purse snatching, drugs, kidnapping, robbery, and perjury.[4] White used cocaine and amphetamines heavily. As a juvenile he was committed to a state facility as an incorrigible, where his information helped authorities find three murdered bodies. He once testified against the leader of an Aryan brotherhood prison gang in a prison murder case. He has provided information both while awaiting trial and while serving time but is most noted for the information he has provided while in jail awaiting trial.

In his appearance on *60 Minutes*, White admitted to consistently fabricating confessions of fellow inmates and offering perjured testimony to courts. White described an elaborate scheme in which he would ask his cellmate about his charges, and when the cellmate typically would respond protesting his innocence, White would obtain the prosecution version and utilize it to fabricate a cellmate's confession. He would trick police by impersonating a prosecutor or police officer and use their shorthand jargon to learn information that had not been otherwise publicly released. He would often do this from a jailhouse telephone. White used this inside information to make the fabricated confession more believable. Although he waited until 1988 to divulge his informing exploits, he began his nefarious enterprise in 1977.

A couple of examples are illustrative.[5] White claims that while riding in the backseat of a squad car with a burglary suspect, the suspect confessed to the burglary. This evidence was particularly damning as the only other evidence the police had was a receipt for the stolen goods. There was no evidence of breaking and entering at the burglarized location. In another instance, White even made up a confession when a suspect could not effectively speak English.

In 1990, largely as a result of a series of fifteen articles in *The Los Angeles Times* from October 29, 1988, to December 17, 1988, the Los Angeles County district attorney convened a grand jury to investigate White's allegations. This investigation was the most extensive investigation of jailhouse informants ever conducted. One hundred and twenty witnesses testified before the grand jury and 147 exhibits were introduced into evidence. In addition, there were hundreds of interviews not presented to the grand jury and thousands of documents that were obtained. The investigation encompassed all of the players within the system, including corrections personnel, prosecutors, defense attorneys, and informants.[6]

This grand jury found that, although it was possible that altruistic reasons had motivated some informants, the overwhelming majority of informants received benefits for their testimony.[7] The grand jury found that these informants had little difficulty lying.[8] When a strong motivation to receive benefits is coupled with the realization that lying informants are rarely, if ever, prosecuted, informants realize they have little to lose by testifying falsely.[9]

In-custody informers are almost invariably motivated by self-interest. They often have little or no respect for the truth of their testimonial oath or affirmation. Accordingly, they may lie or tell the truth, depending only upon where their perceived self-interest lies.

In-custody confessions are often easy to allege and difficult, if not impossible, to disprove.[10]

To enhance the credibility of his testimony, an informant often testified that there have been no promises of benefits made to them in return for their testimony. Even though nothing may be explicitly stated, both the prosecutor and the informant knew that there will be some compensation for the testimony.[11] "The practice (of promising rewards) was done by a wink and a nod and it was never necessary to have any kind of formal understanding."[12]

Probably the most disturbing aspect of the grand jury investigation was the findings concerning the involvement of those sworn to uphold the law. The grand jury found that detectives seeking to strengthen their case commonly sought aid in the informant tank, a section of the jail that housed informants.[13] The detective arranged with the jailer for their suspect to be placed in a section of the jail reserved for informants. Allegations of this practice, as well as further allegations of law enforcement officials deliberately providing information to informants, were not investigated and were ignored by the authorities.[14]

For his willingness to expose the horrors of the informant system, White received an excessive six-year sentence for purse snatching.[15] He became a more direct victim of the scandal that he created when on May 19, 1992, he was sentenced to three years in prison for perjury.[16] This perjury was discovered during his truthful testimony before the grand jury about how he had lied as an informant. White was the only person prosecuted as a result of the grand jury investigation, which he had a major role in initiating. This is somewhat ironic, considering the grand jury had found that there was not a single case in which an informant was prosecuted for perjury or for providing false information, despite the fact that numerous instances in which this had occurred were discovered.[17] At the time of his sentencing for perjury, White observed, "I was involved with law enforcement in a conspiracy to commit perjury. Unfortunately my co-conspirators will not be going to prison with me."[18]

LEGAL QUESTIONS: DUE PROCESS CONCERNS AND THE PROSECUTOR'S DUTY

I knew that informants, especially those [of] the jailhouse variety, were liable to say anything that would get them any advantage, and so I never even got to the point. . . . I just pretty well assumed [they] were all untrustworthy and that anything that they ever gave me or I ever used would have to be in some manner very thoroughly corroborated. I guess, in short, I never believed anything any of them said.[19]

What obligation does the prosecutor have to share these sentiments?

The system of determining guilt or innocence in our country is often referred to as the adversary system. In this system, each side is presumed to be equal and to vigorously advocate for their position. Through the advocacy of opposite positions, the truth supposedly emerges. However, in a criminal trial the state, as represented by the prosecutor, generally has considerably more resources than an individual defendant. These resources include the investigative services of various law enforcement agencies as well as financial resources to hire experts. Thus, the truth would rarely emerge if the adversary system were left untouched. Accordingly, the prosecutor has the heavy burden of proving guilt beyond a reasonable doubt. Further, the Constitution provides certain benefits to a defendant including the right to a jury trial, the right to confront witnesses, and the right not to be compelled to be a witness against himself. Finally, ethically, a prosecutor should not only advocate zealously for his client—the state—but also should ensure that wrongful convictions do not occur. "A prosecutor has the responsibility of a minister of justice and not simply that of an advocate. This responsibility carries with it specific obligations to see that the defendant is accorded procedural justice and that guilt is decided upon the basis of sufficient evidence."[20]

The Supreme Court has recognized the obligations of a prosecutor to act in a fair manner according to the Due Process Requirements of the fifth and fourteenth amendments. With regard to the testimony of witnesses, the court in 1935 readily found a violation of due process in *Mooney v. Holohan*, in which the prosecutor procured perjured testimony. 294 U.S. 103, 112–113 (1935). In 1957 the court found a due process violation when perjured testimony was not affirmatively sought but offered even though known to be false. *Alcorta v. Texas*, 355 U.S. 28, 31 (1957) (per curiam). In a particularly relevant situation, a witness-informant falsely testified that no promises had been made in exchange for his testimony. *Napue v. Illinois*, 360 U.S. 264 (1959). The court held that the prosecutor was required to correct this testimony, even though it was not related to the facts of the case, because it influenced the fact finder's assessment of the witness' credibility. This obligation extended even if the leniency agreement had been made by another prosecutor and the trial prosecutor was unaware of the arrangement. *Giglio v. United States*, 405 U.S. 150, 154 (1972).

As previously discussed, many agreements are not formalized before the informant testifies. Nevertheless, there is an implicit understanding that favorable benefits will be provided for the informant's testimony. The prosecutor is under no apparent obligation to bring this arrangement to the attention of the defendant. Should the defendant wish to bring information about this arrangement to the jury, he might present expert testimony regarding the traditional informant arrangement and cross-examine the informant about his expectations. The trial judge has discretion about how much of this issue the defendant can bring to the jury's attention.

The prosecutor's obligation to provide exculpatory information was expanded beyond the perjury scenario in *Brady v. Maryland*, 373 U.S. 83, 87 (1963). In this case, after Brady had been convicted of murder and sentenced to death, he learned that the prosecution had failed to disclose an extrajudicial confession of an accomplice who had admitted to the homicide. This confession may have been important in the jury's determination of sentencing, as they could have opted for life imprisonment. The court held that withholding evidence favorable to the accused violates due process when the evidence is material to either guilt or sentencing. It did not matter whether the state had acted in good faith or bad faith. In highlighting the obligations of the prosecutor the court said,

> Society wins not only when the guilty are convicted but when criminal trials are fair; our system of the administration of justice suffers when any accused is treated unfairly. An inscription on the walls of the Department of Justice states the proposition candidly for the federal domain. "The United States wins its point whenever justice is done its citizens in the court." 373 U.S. at 87

Much of the debate in the court since *Brady* has been around the issue of what constitutes materiality. *United States v. Agurs*, 427 U.S. 97, 104 (1976). In *United States v. Bagley*, the court faced a situation in which the defendant, in a discovery motion, asked if there were any inducements provided to the government witnesses in exchange for their testimony. 473 U.S. 667, 669–670 (1985). In response to this motion, the government produced an affidavit signed by the witnesses indicating that no inducements had been provided. This affidavit proved to be false, as the government had agreed to pay money to the informants in exchange for their testimony. The defendant argued that the government's action in response to his motion violated his due process rights, as he lost the opportunity to use the information to impeach the witnesses. The issue before the court was the materiality of this evidence. The court looked at the exculpatory information and asked whether there was a "reasonable probability" that, had the evidence been disclosed to the defense, the result of the proceeding would have been different. In this case, five of the justices did not find a *Brady* violation. This decision is somewhat troubling because even if the government deliberately suppressed evidence of inducement to witnesses, if there was sufficient other evidence of guilt, the suppression would not affect the outcome of the case, and, consequently, the government suppression would not be a due process violation. In *Kyles v. Whitley*, the court seemed to moderate its position somewhat by indicating that it would not be difficult for a defendant to demonstrate a reasonable probability that the favorable suppressed evidence could affect the outcome. 514 U.S. 419, 434 (1995). The defendant would not be required to show this by a preponderance of the evidence, but would merely need to show that the evidentiary suppression "undermines confidence in the outcome of the trial." 514 U.S. at 434 (quoting *Bagley*, 473 U.S. 667, 678 [1985]).

The *Kyles* case took the opportunity to reiterate the proposition first mentioned in *Giglio* that any information in the possession of the government is the responsibility of the primary prosecutor, even if the prosecutor has not been informed of the existence of this information. In *Kyles*, the information not communicated was in the possession of the police investigator. The court dismissed the logistical problems associated with this issue by stating that "procedures and regulations can be established to carry [the prosecutor's] burden and to insure communication of all relevant information on each case to every lawyer who deals with it." 514 U.S. at 438 (quoting *Giglio*, 405 U.S. 150, 154 [1972]). This presents a troubling issue with regard to informants. Often an informant develops a relationship with a police officer rather than a prosecutor. The police and prosecutor are two separate entities, and although in an ideal world they would work together, this is not always the case. Thus, although the prosecutor is obligated to disclose exculpatory evidence, he may never even learn of it.[21]

Sixth Amendment: Right to Counsel

The sixth amendment protects individuals against jailhouse informants such as Leslie White by providing that "in all criminal prosecutions, the accused shall enjoy the right . . . to have the Assistance of Counsel in his defense." This right is particularly pertinent when dealing with statements sought to be introduced against the accused. The first question we must ask in our analysis is, when does this right attach or become relevant? Initially it was thought that this right attaches whenever counsel would be useful. In *Escobedo v. Illinois* the Supreme Court searched for a solution to the problem of police coerced confessions. 378 U.S. 478, 479 (1964). The standard prior to 1964, the date of *Escobedo*, was the so-called voluntary standard. This approach analyzed the particulars of the individual case. The court considered the suspect's characteristics, such as age, mental competence, and experience with the criminal justice system. The court also looked at the conduct of the police during the interrogation, including duration of the interrogation, methods used, and promises made. All these fact were put into a blender called the "totality of the circumstances" to determine whether the suspect's will was overborne and the confession was, therefore, involuntary and not admissible. This approach, as can well be imagined, was rather subjective and fact-specific. In *Escobedo*, the court turned to the sixth amendment in their attempt to find a more standardized approach. Because of the tremendous impact a confession could have on the trial process, the court reasoned that counsel was necessaary at the time of the confession. "[The] right to use counsel at the formal trial [would be] a very hollow thing [if], for all practical purposes, the conviction is already assured by pretrial examination." 378 U.S. at 487 (quoting *In re Groban*, 352 U.S. 330, 344 [1957] [Black, J. dissenting]). Despite the court's rationale, *Escobedo* was limited to its specific facts and did not provide the standardized approach that the court was seeking. As a matter of fact, the later case of *Kirby v. Illinois*, 406 U.S. 682, 689 (1972), regarded *Escobedo* not as a sixth amendment case, but as a fifth amendment case seeking to guarantee the privilege against self-incrimination.

In *Kirby* the court did not adopt the rationale that counsel should be available whenever they might be needed. Instead, the court interpreted the sixth amendment language:

> [i]n *all criminal prosecutions*, the accused shall enjoy the right to a speedy and public trial, by an impartial jury of the State and district wherein the crime shall have been committed, which district shall have been previously ascertained by law, and to be informed of the nature and cause of the accusation; to be confronted with the witnesses against him; to have compulsory process for obtaining witnesses in his favor, and *to have the Assistance of Counsel for his defense* (emphasis added)

to mean the time when the government had actually committed themselves to prosecute, which is usually evidenced by some sort of court proceeding. The rationale for this limitation was that at this point in time the accused faced the forces of the state and needed counsel to aid in traversing through those forces. This point at which the sixth amendments attaches has been called the critical stage.

> Whatever else it may mean, the right to counsel granted by the Sixth and Fourteenth Amendment[s] means at least that a person is entitled to the help of a lawyer at or after the time that judicial proceedings have been initiated against him—"whether by way of formal charge, preliminary hearing, indictment, information, or arraignment." *Brewer v. Williams*, 430 U.S. 387, 398 (1977) (quoting *Kirby*, 406 U.S. at 689)

Since an accused, after he is taken into custody, is entitled to be brought before a court as soon as the court is open for business, the right to counsel quickly attaches. *Gerstein v. Pugh*, 420 U.S. 103, 122–123 (1975). Thus, in most instances an accused who is awaiting trial in a jail setting has had his right to counsel attach. An individual who is arrested pursuant to a warrant or a grand jury indictment is generally regarded as having had his right to counsel attach as well. One limitation on this right to counsel can be found in the case of *Moulton v. Maine*, which limited the right to counsel to the charges that had been brought before the court. 474 U.S. 159, 179–180 (1985). In this case the defendant, Moulton, expressed an interest in killing a state witness. To gain evidence of this threat, the police equipped a codefendant with a listening device. The court suppressed the evidence relating to pending charges, holding that it did not matter that there was an independent investigation (threat on a state witness). The police could use the information with regard to the threat on a state witness, an offense in which the sixth amendment had not yet attached. Thus, a statement about a crime to which no judicial proceedings have commenced does not implicate the sixth amendment.

Assuming the critical stage has occurred, what governmental action will constitute a violation of the sixth amendment? For an answer to this question we turn to the case of *Massiah v. United States*, 377 U.S. 201 (1964), which was decided shortly after the seminal case of *Gideon v. Wainwright*, 372 U.S. 335, 342 (1963), which made the sixth amendment applicable to the states through the fourteenth amendment. In *Massiah*, after the critical stage had attached, the government solicited the aid of a codefendant who initiated and recorded a conversation with the defendant Massiah. The court ultimately suppressed this conversation, holding that once the sixth amendment had attached the government may not "deliberately elicit" a statement from the accused in the absence of his attorney. Such solicitation would constitute a violation of the sixth amendment. Since the confession in *Massiah* was obtained while the suspect was not incarcerated, it was thought by some that *Massiah* had been displaced when *Miranda* was decided two years later, involving a police interrogation prior to the actual incarceration of a suspect. This, however, was not the case, as the court cited *Massiah* as precedent in the later case of *Brewer v. Williams*. 430 U.S. 387 (1977). In *Brewer*, the police questioned the defendant Williams during a car ride that took place after he had been arraigned and charged with murder. Williams's attorney had advised him not to speak with the police until he was present, and the police were aware of this arrangement. Nevertheless, Williams was questioned during the car ride, and the confession that Williams gave was used at trial. The court held that the police questioning violated Williams's constitutional right to counsel, upholding *Massiah*.

With this background in mind, we turn to the situation presented by Mr. White, the jailhouse informant. The *Massiah* doctrine of deliberate elicitation has been applied to jailhouse informants in two subsequent Supreme Court cases. In *United States v. Henry*, Henry had been indicted for armed robbery and was in jail awaiting trial. 447 U.S. 264 (1980). The FBI contacted Nichols, an individual who had previously served as a paid informant, and arranged to have him placed in Henry's cell. Nichols was told not to question Henry about the crime, but to keep his ears open and report to the FBI any incriminating statements Henry might make. Nichols would receive monetary compensation for such reports. Not surprisingly, at some point Henry made incriminating statements that Nichols dutifully reported to the FBI. The court suppressed these statements, finding that the government had deliberately solicited this information in violation of the sixth amendment. In their analysis, the court indicated that there were two separate inquiries to be addressed. The first consideration was what the government did to create this situation. The second consideration was the specific activities of the informant. In this case, the court felt that by creating a situation in which the government placed an informant who was working on a contingency-fee basis in the same cell as the defendant, they created a situation that was likely to make Nichols more than just a passive listener. In fact, Nichols did engage in conversation with Henry.

> [Even if we accept the FBI agent's statement that] he did not intend that [the informant] would take affirmative steps to secure incriminating information, he must have known that such propinquity

likely would lead to that result. [By] intentionally creating a situation likely to induce Henry to make incriminating statements without the assistance of counsel [after Henry's right to counsel had attached], the government violated [his] Sixth Amendment right to counsel. 447 U.S. at 270.

Although this broad language might indicate that any government plant, even if a completely passive one, would violate the sixth amendment, the court in *Henry* left open the situation of a completely passive listener who did not engage the suspect in conversation. Further, Justice Lewis Powell, in his concurrence, explicitly said that he would not join the majority opinion if it held that "mere presence or incidental conversation of an informant in a jail cell would violate [the sixth amendment]." 447 U.S. at 277.

In *Kuhlman v. Wilson* the court had more of an opportunity to distinguish between active and passive listeners. 477 U.S. 436, 459 (1986). Wilson was a suspect in a robbery and murder. After he was brought to court and the sixth amendment attached, he was placed in a cell with Benny Lee, who had agreed to act as a police informant. Lee was instructed not to ask any questions, but merely to keep his ears open. Wilson told Lee the same story he had told the police. Lee, in hearing the story, indicated to Wilson that the story "didn't sound too good" and that "things didn't look too good for him." 477 U.S. at 439–440. Several days later, after Wilson had a visit from his brother, he admitted his involvement in the crime to Lee. Lee informed the authorities. Wilson sought to suppress the statement, arguing that the government informant "deliberately used his position to secure incriminating information from [the defendant] when counsel was not present." 477 U.S. at 458 (quoting 447 U.S. at 270). The court, in a decision by Justice Powell, held that this was not enough to establish a violation of the sixth amendment; the defendant needed to demonstrate that the informant took some action beyond merely listening. Justice William Brennan's dissent took issue with the court's narrow interpretation of deliberate elicitation, indicating that there were more subtle forms of stimulating incriminating statements than overt questioning. These subtle forms included placing a perpetrator in a cell overlooking the crime scene, as well as having an informant who also happened to be the cellmate stimulate conversation by saying that the story did not sound too good. Brennan's dissent, referring to language in *Henry*, found that the government had "intentionally created a situation in which it was foreseeable that [the accused] would make incriminating statements." 477 U.S. at 476. Justice Brennan also pointed out the similarities to the *Henry* decision. Like Nichols, Lee was a paid informant who had received compensation in over 150 other cases. Also, Lee's information was obtained while the defendant was incarcerated in a hostile environment.

The difficulties in distinguishing between passive and active informants is rather apparent. This difficulty, coupled with an informant's propensity to mold his or her testimony to suit the government needs, makes it rather difficult for a defendant to claim a sixth amendment violation. Further, as previously mentioned, often there is no formal arrangement between the government and the informant (the informant assumes that they will derive benefit from their testimony), making the deliberate elicitation element of the sixth amendment difficult to establish.

CONFESSION FOR PROTECTION: THE STORY OF ANTHONY MICHAEL SARIVOLA

Anthony Michael Sarivola is representative of the type of informant who operates within the prison system where inmates have been convicted and sentenced.[22] Sarivola was born in Brooklyn, New York, in March 1955. His father was a truck driver and his mother was a housewife. The neighborhood where he grew up was inundated with organized crime figures. Sarivola proudly recalled that the home of the mother of the legendary Gallo brothers was down the block from his house on East Fourth Street. As a juvenile, Sarivola was arrested on more than one occasion for auto theft. On his seventeenth birthday, Sarivola joined the army for a six-year hitch. In October 1973, after completing basic and advanced training, Sarivola was discharged from the army for going AWOL. In 1979 his status was upgraded to an honorable discharge.

After his discharge in 1973, Sarivola returned to Brooklyn, where he worked an assortment of jobs including auto mechanic, police officer, armed car guard, and manager of a limousine company. While working at the limousine company, Sarivola became involved with members of the Columbo crime family. Sarivola did a variety of jobs for them, including collecting delinquent loans and hijacking trucks. In his sworn testimony he readily admitted that although he was not a made guy, he worked for a captain in the Columbo crime family and did so while he was a police officer for the Seagate Police Department, a cooperative on the southwestern edge of Brooklyn.[23] Although Sarivola had been arrested on a number of occasions, his first criminal conviction was in 1983 for extortion in a credit transaction, otherwise known as loan-sharking.[24] In April

1983, despite the fact that he was facing a twenty-year sentence, a judge sentenced Sarivola to only six months in prison. His accomplice, on the other hand, received a five-year sentence. Around the start of his prison term in September 1983, at Ray Brook Federal Correctional Institute in upstate New York, Sarivola became a "top-echelon" informant for the FBI.[25] FBI Agent Walter Ticano, the handler for Sarivola, related that Sarivola supplied information on high-ranking members of four of the five major New York crime families.[26] While at Ray Brook, however, his most valuable information was not mob-related.

Sarivola became friends with Oreste Fulminante, a career criminal in prison on a federal gun charge. Fulminante was a suspect in the September 1982 Arizona murder of his eleven-year-old stepdaughter in Arizona. Sarivola heard about this. In an October 20, 1983, meeting with Agent Ticano, Sarivola was encouraged to obtain stronger information about Fulminante. Later that day, Sarivola called Ticano and told him that he had obtained a confession from Fulminante. It seems as Sarivola and Fulminante were having a conversation while walking around the prison track, "Sarivola said he knew Fulminante was 'starting to get rough treatment and whatnot' from other inmates because of the rumor." *Arizona v. Fulminante*, 499 U.S. 279, 283 (1991). Sarivola, who masqueraded as an organized crime figure, offered to protect Fulminante, who was slightly built, from the other inmates in exchange for the truth about the girl's death. At this point, Fulminante allegedly confessed to Sarivola. 499 U.S. at 283. Fulminante admitted to Sarivola that he drove the child out to the desert on a motorcycle "where he choked her, sexually assaulted her, and made her beg for her life, before shooting her twice in the head." 499 U.S. at 283.

Sarivola was released in November 1983 after having served only seventy-two days for his extortion sentence. Upon his release from prison, he left his wife and five-year-old son, and eventually married Donna Simone, his wife's best friend. Anthony continued to work as a paid FBI informant and entered the Witness Protection Program with Donna. Donna became entangled in the Fulminante saga in May 1984, when Anthony and Donna picked Fulminante up from a bus terminal upon his release from prison. In the ensuing car ride to Pennsylvania, Fulminante confessed again, this time in the presence of Donna.

Sarivola had never testified against an organized crime figure, but in December 1985, he and Donna were called to testify at Fulminante's Arizona trial for the murder of his stepdaughter. Anthony testified to Fulminante's alleged jailhouse confession, and both he and Donna testified about the second admission that allegedly occurred while they drove with Fulminante following his release from Ray Brook. Fulminante was convicted on December 19, 1985, and subsequently was sentenced to death in the gas chamber. He immediately appealed.

Sarivola's testimony at the Fulminante trial was the only time Sarivola testified for the government at a trial. Sarivola was quoted as saying that he did not consider his testimony as evidence that he cooperated with law enforcement officials. "The guy Fulminante, nobody even counts that because that's a piece of shit who killed his stepdaughter and left her out in the desert. . . . If I couldn't have done that as a human being, I would've probably tried to kill the guy." After the Fulminante trial, the Sarivolas were involved in a number of schemes and swindles involving millions of dollars throughout the country. Sarivola received several convictions for his fraudulent activities and served substantial jail time.

According to Sarivola, he was motivated to become an informant for a number of reasons: "I arranged a meeting with a Special Agent Walter Ticano . . . and told him that I did not want to participate in the life I was participating in any more and that I would assist him in making cases against members of organized crime." Despite his claimed altruism, Ticano said that Sarivola was paid for verified information. As of the end of 1984, he had received a total of $22,400 from the FBI. Anthony was not always forthright with the FBI. In January 1984 when he was being pressured for specific information, he made a phony tape by playing both parties to a conversation.[27] In addition to receiving cash from the government, Sarivola participated in the Federal Witness Protection Program out of fear for his safety.

THE LAW OF CONFESSIONS OF PRISON INMATES

For the Constitution to protect a defendant, there must be government action. In this case, government action came through the person of Anthony Sarivola. In examining the Fulminante confession, we first may eliminate the sixth amendment protections previously discussed. Although it is evident that Sarivola deliberately elicited the confession of Fulminante, Fulminate had not yet been charged with the murder of the little girl. Thus, the "critical stage" as required by the sixth amendment had not yet occurred. Had Fulminante been indicted for the murder of his stepdaughter, his right to counsel would have attached and Sarivola's conduct would have amounted to deliberate elicitation, thus implicating the sixth amendment.

The famous case *Miranda v. Arizona*, 384 U.S. 436, 437 (1966), familiarized on popular dramas, requires that a suspect be warned of certain rights prior to any custodial interrogation. These warnings are: You have the right to remain silent; anything you say can and will be used against you; you have the right of counsel; and if you can't afford an attorney, one will be appointed at the state's expense. 384 U.S. at 444–445. *Miranda* sought to address the problems associated with incommunicado police interrogation. It defined custodial interrogation as "questioning initiated by law enforcement officers after a person has been taken into custody or otherwise deprived of his freedom of action in any significant way." 384 U.S. at 444. Here, Sarivola, although a government agent, was not a questioner as envisioned by *Miranda*. *Miranda* was concerned about techniques used by police investigators that would likely force the suspect to speak. See *Illinois v. Perkins*, 496 U.S. 292, 296 (1990). Further, the custody associated with the prison setting is not the type of police-dominated atmosphere envisioned by *Miranda*. In *Illinois v. Perkins*, the police placed an undercover agent in the cell with a suspect. 496 U.S. at 297. The Perkins court rejected the argument that *Miranda* warnings were required whenever a suspect is in custody in a technical sense and speaks with a government agent, as this was not the coercive situation that *Miranda* had in mind.

Does the action of Sarivola somehow implicate the privacy protections afforded by the fourth amendment? This question brings to mind an earlier case involving the former head of the teamsters: Jimmy Hoffa, which we mentioned in Chapter 2. In that case Hoffa, during a criminal trial in Nashville, Tennessee, for a Taft-Hartley violation—extorting funds from the Teamsters—schemed to bribe jurors. Edward Partin, a local union official from Baton Rouge, Louisiana, who faced both state and federal charges, decided to become a government informant. He gained access to Hoffa's hotel suite and reported conversations about the scheme to tamper with the jury. The court, in refusing to apply the fourth amendment to this situation, said that a wrongdoer, in this case Hoffa, does not enjoy fourth amendment protection for a "misplaced belief that a person to whom he voluntarily confides his wrongdoings will not reveal it." *Hoffa v. United States*, 385 U.S. 293, 302 (1966). Chief Justice Earl Warren dissented, arguing that the method used by the government was unfair and that the Supreme Court, in the exercise of its control over lower courts (supervisory powers), should not sanction this governmental strategy. It is interesting to note Chief Justice Warren's attitude about informants.

> Here, Edward Partin, a jailbird languishing in a Louisiana jail under indictments for such state and federal crimes as embezzlement, kidnapping, and manslaughter (and soon to be charged with perjury and assault), contacted federal authorities and told them he was willing to become, and would be useful as, an informer against Hoffa who was then about to be tried in the Test Fleet case. A motive for his doing this is immediately apparent—namely, his strong desire to work his way out of jail and out of his various legal entanglements with the State and Federal Governments. And it is interesting to note that, if this was his motive, he has been uniquely successful in satisfying it. In the four years since he first volunteered to be an informer against Hoffa, he has not been prosecuted on any of the serious federal charges for which he was at that time jailed, and the state charges have apparently vanished into thin air. . . . This type of informer and the uses to which he was put in this case evidence a serious potential for undermining the integrity of the truth-finding process in the federal courts. Given the incentives and background of Partin, no conviction should be allowed to stand when based heavily on his testimony. And that is exactly the quicksand upon which these convictions rest, because without Partin, who was the principal government witness, there would probably have been no convictions here. 385 U.S. at 317–318.

Let us return to the Oreste Fulminante story and explore its impact on the law of informants. After his conviction, Fulminante appealed. The Arizona Supreme Court suppressed the confession obtained by Anthony Sarivola and ordered that Fulminante be retried, this time without the use of the testimony of Sarivola. *State v. Fulminante*, 161 Ariz. 237, 245–246 (1988). On March 26, 1991, the Supreme Court affirmed the decision of the Arizona Supreme Court and overturned Fulminante's conviction. *Arizona v. Fulminante*, 499 U.S. 279, 282 (1991).

The court turned to the so-called voluntary standard. This approach was the primary approach to deal with incommunicado police interrogation up until the *Miranda* decision. Where there is no custodial interrogation pursuant to *Miranda* and the sixth amendment is not applicable, the voluntary standard still exists. Utilizing the voluntary standard, the court analyzes the particulars of the individual case, examining the suspect's characteristics, such as age, mental competence, and experience with the criminal justice system. The court then considers the conduct of the government during the interrogation, including the duration of the interrogation, methods used, and promises made. All these facts would be considered in applying the totality of the circumstances to determine whether the suspect's will was overborne and the confession was, therefore, involuntary and not admissible. In *Fulminante*, the Supreme Court accepted the finding of the Arizona Supreme Court. They found that because of the rumors of Fulminante being a child murderer, he was in danger of being harmed by his prison mates. Sarivola's offer to protect him in return for a confession was found to be a credible threat of physical violence. The court went on to point out that it was not necessary for there to be actual physical violence, as coercion can be mental as well as physical. The court concluded in a 5–4 decision "that Fulminante's will was overborne in such a way as to render his confession the product of coercion." 499 U.S. at 288.

The court then went on to determine the effect of their ruling. Four justices—Byron White, Thurgood Marshall, Harry Blackmun, and John Stevens—thought that admission of a coerced confession should result in an automatic reversal of a conviction, even if there was ample other evidence to support the conviction. In arguing for this approach, they felt that a coerced confession is different than other trial errors because it represents the most probative and damaging evidence and there is really no way to measure its impact on the jury. A majority of five justices—William Rehnquist, Antonin Scalia, Anthony Kennedy, David Souter, and Sandra Day O'Connor—disagreed and applied the harmless-error rule to coerced confessions. This rule comes from *Chapman v. California*, 386 U.S. 18 (1967), which held that coerced confessions should not be subject to the harmless-error analysis. The majority in *Fulminante* distinguished coerced confessions from trial structural defects such as deprivation of right to counsel or lack of an impartial judge. They pointed out that because these defects would effect the entire trial from beginning to end, they would not lend themselves to a harmless-error analysis. The harmless-error rule looks at the confession along with the other evidence presented and asks whether its introduction was harmless. The state then must demonstrate beyond a reasonable doubt that there was sufficient other lawful evidence introduced so that the introduction of the confession was harmless, or in other words, had no real effect on the jury's decision given the other evidence. Finally, once having decided to apply the harmless-error rule, another majority of five justices—White, Marshall, Blackmun, Stevens, and Kennedy—found that the introduction of the coerced confession was not harmless and referred the case back to the trial court for a new trial. This majority believed that the introduction of Sarivola's testimony made Donna's testimony regarding the second confession more credible.

As a result of the suppression of the coerced confession, Anthony was no longer able to testify at the retrial of Fulminante. But what about Donna's testimony? This question relates to the so-called fruits of the poisonous tree doctrine, a term that originated in the case of *Wong Sun v. United States*, 371 U.S. 471, 488 (1963). Did the illegality of Fulminante's first confession to Anthony result in the second confession to Donna? If this was the case, Donna's testimony would be suppressed. The state can avoid the fruits doctrine by demonstrating that the second confession was very attenuated from the first confession, thus dissipating the taint. In their argument that the taint has been dissipated, the state might show the time lapse between the two confessions, as well as Fulminante's free will, intervened in his decision to talk to Donna. See *United States v. Ceccolini*, 435 U.S. 268, 276 (1978). A decision on this matter was never reached because Donna failed to appear at three scheduled pretrial conferences that would have determined this issue.[28] The trial judge ruled that because of these three absences within a five-week period, the prosecution would not be allowed to use Donna Sarivola as a witness against Fulminante.[29]

At the second trial of Oreste Fulminante on June 21, 1994, this time without the testimony of either Anthony or Donna Sarivola, he was again found guilty of first-degree premeditated murder and sentenced to death.[30] This sentence was overturned on March 2, 1999, by the Supreme Court of Arizona, which found that evidence that the victim expected to be killed by Fulminante was wrongly admitted because it was inadmissible hearsay. *Arizona v. Fulminante*, 975 P.2d 75, 90 (Ariz. 1999). Fulminante, who suffers from a severe heart condition, pled guilty to second-degree murder and a kidnapping charge in late summer 1999. He received a sentence of twenty-five years, getting credit for the time he has served since his first trial. According to a conversation with James Belanger, attorney for Fulminante, on June 5, 2000, Fulminante should be released sometime in 2004.

Sarivola continued his life of crime while he was in the Witness Protection Program. He would often brag that he never testified against the mob: "I'd walk in any prison in the world and hold my face up because I didn't testify. I never ratted."[31]

Chapter 5

High-Level Informants

The Story of
James "Whitey" Bulger and
Stephen "The Rifleman" Flemmi

INTRODUCTION

This chapter examines the use of informants who provide the Federal Bureau of Investigation (FBI) with direct evidence of high-level organized crime activity.[1] According to FBI guidelines, they are referred to as organized crime (OC) or top-echelon (TE) informants. This chapter will specifically look at two informants (Bulger and Flemmi) whose major incentive for serving as informants was to promote their own criminal enterprises through the elimination of their competition. In addition to their personal benefits, these informants received monetary compensation[2] as well as sentencing concessions from the government. *Roy v. United States*, 38 Fed. Cl. 184, 186 (1997). In the situation that follows, the FBI befriended and nurtured two leaders of a rival criminal entity to acquire information that was used to break up their competition. When the government sought ultimately to prosecute these two leaders, the informants' relationship with the FBI was exposed and used as a defense to the indictment. In this chapter, largely as a result of extensive hearings held at the Federal District Court level,[3] as well as indictment from a federal grand jury, we have a unique opportunity to learn a great deal about what had previously been a very clandestine operation.

In return for information on the Italian Mafia, the FBI sanctioned criminal activity including loan-sharking and gambling by James "Whitey" Bulger and Stephen "The Rifleman" Flemmi, members of the rival Irish organized crime group. The vexing questions faced in this chapter are whether Bulger and Flemmi violated the deal they had with the FBI and committed more serious crimes, such as murder. How much did the FBI know of this activity? And, finally, how much of a role did the FBI play in this activity?

FACTS

James J. "Whitey" Bulger and Stephen "The Rifleman" Flemmi were reputed heads of the so-called Winter Hill Gang, a criminal organization sometimes referred to as the "Irish Mob." The Winter Hill Gang, named after the working-class Somerville, Massachusetts, neighborhood where the gang was headquartered, was a predominantly Irish-American organized crime group.[4]

Howie Winter emerged from the gang wars of the 1960s to head the Winter Hill Gang.[5] He succeeded James "Buddy" McLean, who was killed in a feud with a gang led by the McLaughlin brothers. Winter brought leadership and stability to the Irish gang. During the 1970s, he became the most powerful gangster in Massachusetts, next to Gennaro (Jerry) Angiulo—an underboss of the powerful Providence, Rhode Island, based Patriarca Mafia family. In 1979, Winter's leadership of the Winter Hill Gang ended when he was convicted of a scheme to fix horse races. Bulger and his second in command, Flemmi, replaced Winter. It is interesting to note that the U.S. Attorney had considered indicting Flemmi and Bulger for the race-fixing case, but decided not to at the request of the FBI.

This chapter focuses initially on James "Whitey" Bulger, who turned seventy-two in September 2001. In the legal analysis section, the focus shifts to Flemmi, because he has been caught, whereas Bulger is still a fugitive. In 2000, the FBI posted a $1 million reward for information leading to Bulger's capture, earning him membership in the elite club of million dollar fugitives.[6] A copy of the wanted poster is included in Appendix B.

Whitey Bulger grew up in a South Boston housing project. South Boston, or Southie, is a close-knit Irish neighborhood. Bulger began his criminal career as a youngster committing petty thefts. Petty thievery led to bank robbery, for which Bulger spent nine years in various federal prisons, including a stint at Alcatraz.[7] Although Bulger received a twenty-year sentence for his bank robbery conviction, he was released eleven years early after agreeing to participate in LSD experiments.[8]

In the 1970s, Bulger forged an association with Stephen Flemmi, six years his junior, through their mutual association with the Winter

Hill Gang. A few years earlier, Flemmi had rejected an offer to join the Mafia because of his dislike for local Mafia leaders Larry Zannino and Gerry Angiulo.[9]

During the 1980s, Bulger and Flemmi carved out such an extensive illegal enterprise that *The Boston Globe*, on September 20, 1988, reported, "With the Mafia in disarray, some now consider Bulger the most powerful mobster in Boston."[10] Despite Bulger's prosperity, he lived a relatively low-key lifestyle and never outwardly displayed his wealth.[11]

HOW DID THE BOSTON MAFIA GET INTO SUCH DISARRAY?

Bulger and Flemmi assisted the federal government in their attempt to prosecute the Italian Mafia, known as La Cosa Nostra (LCN), which in Italian means "our thing" and is synonymous with Mafia. Apparently, the LCN members never used the term "Mafia," preferring to use the more innocuous "Cosa Nostra." To avoid embarrassing J. Edgar Hoover, who for many years denied the existence of the Mafia, the FBI adopted this term, turned it into a proper name, La Cosa Nostra, and shortened it to LCN.[12]

For nearly two decades ending in December 1990, Bulger and Flemmi[13] gave the FBI information about rival mobsters, helping the federal government while promoting their own interests in getting rid of their competition.[14] Assistant U.S. Attorney Fred Wyshak acknowledged this arrangement, stating that Flemmi and Bulger worked as informants "to put their competition out of business."[15] Most members of the law enforcement community recognized Bulger and Flemmi's authority and power.[16] They were so protected by the federal government that *The Boston Globe* characterized Bulger and Flemmi as the only leaders left standing after federal prosecutors wiped out the New England Mafia in the 1980s.[17] "Jimmy Bulger and his partner in crime, Stevie Flemmi, ended up using the FBI to take down the New England Mafia so that they could have a monopoly in the crime business. He was sort of way ahead of his time. He was the Bill Gates of the criminal world. He had a monopoly in criminal enterprises in New England."[18]

One indictment characterized Bulger's criminal enterprise as the Bulger Group, with income in excess of $12.5 million. Similar to any business, their objective was to eliminate the competition. However, for Bulger, crushing the competition took on a new meaning.[19]

Why did the Boston FBI favor one criminal enterprise over another? The FBI receives its directives from Washington, D.C. The Boston branch of the FBI followed a national policy to destroy LCN, "the most powerful organized crime group in the United States."[20] "Our mission was to bring down a Mafia Family. We were told to be imaginative, to use our intuition, to use our resources. That's what we did."[21] As one agent put it, "priority one was the LCN."[22] Policy makers at FBI headquarters in Washington probably did not consider the unique situation existing in Boston, where the Irish criminal element also exerts a powerful influence.[23] Further, the LCN had nationwide influence, whereas Bulger and his associates were initially thought to have influence only in the Boston area.

Some argue that there may have been ethnic reasons for the FBI targeting LCN members. For example, John Mitchell, an attorney for an alleged LCN member, argued, "There was a coming together of people of Irish descent to target people of Italian descent."[24] Many commentators attempt to refute this claim by pointing out that Flemmi and Sonny Mercurio (a Mafia member and informant) are both Italian. Nonetheless, a better question is not why a particular individual was targeted, but rather why the Italian Mafia was targeted, and not the Irish Winter Hill Gang. Whatever the reason, Mitchell did not appear to have any hard evidence to support his claim. Neither the media nor Judge Mark Wolf, who held numerous months of hearings on the issue, seem to have given it much credence. As one unnamed federal source stated, "The Mafia was targeted because it was full of murderers and extortionists, not because it was full of Italians."[25] More recently, Nicholas Gianturco, a former FBI agent, testified that the Mafia was targeted "strictly because they're the most powerful organized crime group in the United States."[26] The recent indictment of James "Whitey" Bulger for the murder of eighteen people puts this assessment into question, at least in Boston. The indictment described a bloodthirsty organization that clawed its way to the top and stayed there, leaving a heap of bodies in its wake.

U.S. Attorney Donald K. Stern concurs with this assessment. "They were at least as bad and at least as violent as the Mafia. . . . Certainly based on what we now know, it was a horrible mistake for these guys to be used as informants."[27]

BULGER BECOMES AN FBI INFORMANT

John Connolly, a member of the FBI organized crime squad, grew up in South Boston. As a young FBI agent he was assigned to New York City. There he got got a lucky break when he recognized "Cadillac

Frank" Salemme, a wanted criminal and friend of Flemmi's, in a crowd in December 1972. Connolly arrested Salemme, earning him praise as well as a return ticket to Boston (with just four years of service in the FBI).[28] It was somewhat unusual to get a transfer home after such a short time in the employ of the FBI.

Starting in 1971, FBI attempts to develop an informant relationship with Bulger were largely unsuccessful. Although Agent Dennis Condon was able to get some information about an Irish gang war from Bulger in May 1971, the information dried up in September 1971.[29] When Connolly returned to Boston, the stage was set for another attempt. In 1975 Connolly met Bulger in a secluded parking lot facing Wollaston Beach in Quincy, Massachusetts. Young agent Connolly realized that bringing Whitey into the fold would be a real feather in his cap. In fact, Connolly's success in developing informants earned him accolades from FBI agents.[30] He began his sales pitch by pointing out that the local head of the Mafia, Gennaro Anguilo, had the ability to use dishonest cops to get someone arrested by planting evidence, and that Bulger might be a target of this. At this meeting, Connolly also discussed a vending machine dispute, which could result in a gang war between the local Mafia and the Winter Hill Gang. Two weeks after this initial contact, the deal was finalized. In return for his cooperation, Bulger would be protected from criminal investigation. Bulger, who studied military strategy in prison, commented, "You can't survive without friends in law enforcement."[31] In this way, the relationship that would span two decades was forged. *United States v. Salemme*, 91 F.Supp. 2d at 185–188. In fact, at a meeting in 1975, Connolly made it clear to Flemmi that he and Bulger would be "protected" for the criminal activity they engaged in while furnishing information. *Id.* Although Connolly was the prime FBI handler, over time many members of the FBI came to participate in protecting Bulger and Flemmi.

To fully appreciate the relationship between John Connolly and James "Whitey" Bulger, one must have some knowledge of their early roots. South Boston is an insular, both geographically and culturally, tight-knit Irish Catholic community where loyalty and an unquestioned chauvinism predominate. Whitey Bulger was the reputed king of Southie. One resident said, "No one made us feel better about where we lived than Whitey Bulger."[32] Despite the fact that his brother, Senator William Bulger, was reputed to be the most powerful state legislator in Massachusetts, Whitey was regarded as the most powerful within Southie. He was the protector of Southie pride, a benevolent gangster who could fix any problem as long as you played by the rules. One of those rules was "Thou shalt not rat." In his book, William Bulger said, "We loathed informers . . . our folklore bled with the names of informers who had sold out their brethren to hangmen and worse in the lands of our ancestors."[33] It is interesting to note that throughout his time as an informant, neither Connolly nor Whitey ever used the term "informant," preferring to use such words as "source," "liaison," and "strategist."[34] It is ironic that Whitey Bulger, the once-legendary South Boston figure, is now referred to as "King Rat." It is further ironic that his most trusted associate, Kevin Weeks, has provided much of the information implicating Bulger.

John Connolly grew up with the Bulger brothers in the Old Harbor Project. Although the academically oriented Billy Bulger more likely influenced him, he regarded Whitey, eleven years his senior, as a folk hero. "Like meeting Ted Williams" is how he described a chance meeting with Whitey as a young boy in 1948.[35] Whitey reportedly saved an eight-year-old Connolly from a vicious thrashing by an older boy.[36] In Connolly's words, "I was getting a good shellacking and then the next thing I heard is [words of Bulger] 'A—a—a—that's enough. That's enough.'"[37] Thus, this peripheral relationship between two children, with its deep Southie roots, continued years later between a law enforcement leader and a lawless leader. Bulger, in describing why he became an informant, said "a close feeling towards Special Agent John Connolly because [we] both grew up in the same neighborhood in Boston and had mutual childhood problems, as well as a deep hatred for La Cosa Nostra." 91 F.Supp. 2d 141, 186 (D.Mass. 1999).

This close relationship continues today in the form of an indictment. Agent Connolly has been indicted for providing information to Bulger resulting in the slaying of two FBI informants. Commenting on the indictment, U.S. Attorney Donald Stern said, "Today's indictment fills out a dark picture of corruption and obstruction of justice by a former FBI agent. . . . The handler of criminals became one himself."[38]

RELATIONSHIP WITH THE FBI, OR HOW THE FBI CONTRIBUTED TO THE CRIMINALITY OF BULGER AND FLEMMI

The relationship between Bulger, Flemmi, and the FBI was more than just an exchange of information for turning a blind eye to criminal activity, it was a social relationship. In 1985, at a dinner at which Connolly and his supervisor, John Morris, were present, Morris told Bulger and Flemmi, "You can do anything you want as long as you don't 'clip' anyone." 91 F.Supp. 2d at 242. They enjoyed each others' company. They ate dinners together, shared beers, and exchanged

Christmas gifts throughout this two-decade-long relationship. Flemmi and Bulger periodically dined not only with Connolly but also with a number of his colleagues from the Boston Organized Crime Squad, including John Morris, who was Connolly's supervisor, and fellow agent Nicholas Gianturco. These dinners, which took place at agents' homes or at Flemmi's mother's house, were often scheduled to commemorate successful milestones in the informant relationship. "Isn't he a great guy?"[39] said one FBI agent of Bulger. At one dinner, Agent Morris got so drunk that Bulger drove him home. When James Ring replaced Morris as the supervisor of the Organized Crime Squad in 1983, he began to question this close bond. Ring feared that Connolly was treating Bulger and Flemmi more like friends and consultants than as informants. He felt that meeting at Flemmi's mother's home was inappropriate. Probably the most unseemly aspect of the relationship was the payment of money to John Morris. Morris received a loan of $5,000, which he never paid back, as well as money for an airline ticket for his mistress.

FBI handlers carefully protected Bulger and Flemmi. Other law enforcement agencies attempted to investigate the activities of Flemmi and Bulger numerous times. When the investigations came to their attention, Connolly or their other FBI handlers tipped off Bulger and Flemmi, thus thwarting the investigation. For example, in 1980 the FBI frustrated an attempt by the state police to bug a garage where known criminal activity existed. The bug was extremely productive for the first two weeks, but by the sudden way in which the information dried up, it was evident that Flemmi and Bulger had been tipped off. Indeed, it appears that virtually every law enforcement agency with a Boston office had targeted Bulger and Flemmi, including the U.S. Attorney's Office; the Suffolk County District Attorney; the Massachusetts State Police; the Drug Enforcement Administration (DEA); the Boston Police Department; the Internal Revenue Service (IRS); the Department of Alcohol, Tobacco, and Firearms (ATF); and even U.S. Customs.[40] Some sources argue that although some of these investigations simply did not pan out, many were compromised intentionally by FBI agents.[41]

Former FBI Agent Roderick Kennedy recently testified that although he became aware that a Charlestown drug dealer was paying $60,000–$90,000 "rent" money to Bulger and Flemmi, he did not pass on the information about the drug dealer to the DEA. Moreover, Kennedy also stated that over the years DEA agents asked him repeatedly whether Bulger and Flemmi were informants. Kennedy would tell them that he did not know.[42]

The story of the South Boston Liquor Mart captures the essence of the leeway afforded Bulger and Flemmi. Julie Rakes and her husband Stephen bought a liquor store in Southie. Bulger and Flemmi, thinking that it would be a good headquarters for their activities, visited the Rakes' home and told the couple that they wanted to buy the store. When the Rakeses refused, Flemmi pulled out a gun, commented on how lovely the Rakes' young child was, and then reiterated his desire to buy the store. Rakes informed Boston Police Detective Joseph Lundbohm of this extortion. Thinking that the FBI was the appropriate agency to handle this matter, Lundbohm gave the information to Connolly. Connolly, who never informed his supervisor of this information, told Bulger. Subsequently, Bulger and Flemmi purchased the store. No investigation of the extortion occurred until many years later. (A grand jury has handed down an indictment for this issue.) Other examples of this FBI protection include the warning of a wire being used to investigate Flemmi for loan-sharking, the dissuading of officials of a vending machine company from pursuing their claims that Bulger and Flemmi used threats to promote their own vending machine company, the failure to investigate claims that Bulger and Flemmi were shaking down independent bookmakers, and the failure to investigate illegal gambling and trafficking in cocaine.

The most serious example of complicity between the FBI and Bulger and Flemmi involves the murders of informants who were informing on Bulger and Flemmi. On May 28, 1981, Roger Wheeler, the owner of World Jai Alai, was murdered in Tulsa, Oklahoma. Brian Halloran, a Winter Hill Gang soldier facing an unrelated murder charge, decided to provide information to the FBI about the crime. He indicated that Flemmi and Bulger solicited him to murder Wheeler, who had attempted to eviscerate a Winter Hill Gang skimming operation.[43] At the request of Morris, Connolly informed Flemmi and Bulger of Halloran's cooperation. Two weeks later Halloran was killed. Morris apparently believed that Flemmi and Bulger were responsible for this death but did not disclose this to investigating FBI agents.

The lack of trust within the FBI itself is evident in the actions of Agent Robert Fitzpatrick. He was so suspicious that John Connolly was rifling through the case file, probing the murder of Roger Wheeler, and forwarding the information to Bulger, that Fitzpatrick locked the case file away.[44] Recently, Kevin Weeks, a close associate of Bulger's and Flemmi's and known as Bulger's "surrogate son," indicated, as part of a plea arrangement with the government, that he acted as a lookout in the murder of Halloran while Bulger and Flemmi killed him.[45] Bulger has been indicted for the murder of Halloran, and both Bulger and Flemmi have been indicted for the murder of Roger Wheeler.

Further indication of complicity in murder comes from the story of John McIntyre, an informant who allegedly implicated Bulger and Flemmi in a gun-smuggling operation for the Irish Republican Army. Connolly reportedly warned Bulger and Flemmi of McIntyre's cooperation when McIntyre was brought in for questioning by the Quincy, Massachusetts, Police Department with regard to a break-in at his estranged wife's residence.[46] McIntyre related stories of a botched gun-smuggling operation to the Irish Republican Army and of a drug operation. These stories implicated the crew from the South Boston Liquor Mart. The Quincy detective contacted FBI agent Roderick Kennedy. Although it is not clear that Kennedy contacted Connolly with regard to the McIntyre allegation, in the past he had "often exchanged information" with Connolly. McIntyre left his parents' home one day indicating that he was going to meet with Patrick Nee, a close associate of Bulger. It was the last time McIntyre was seen alive. Kevin Weeks has admitted to abducting McIntyre and to assisting in moving his body to a makeshift grave where it was later found.[47] Bulger and Flemmi have been indicted for the murder of John McIntyre.

Along with McIntyre's body, police discovered two other bodies in the grave with close ties to Bulger and Flemmi. The bodies are those of Deborah Hussey, the daughter of a longtime girlfriend of Flemmi, and Arthur "Bucky" Barrett, a suspected bank robber who was believed to be cooperating with the government. Both Flemmi and Bulger have been indicted for these murders. All of these murders occurred in the first half of the 1980s, during the time that Bulger and Flemmi were FBI informants.[48] Weeks, who was indicted for federal racketeering charges in November 1999, has entered into a plea arrangement with the government and will be an important witness in connecting Bulger and Flemmi to these unsolved murders, as well as to the FBI corruption probe.[49]

Anthony Cardinale, a Boston lawyer, who represents organized crime figures, regarded the Bulger-Flemmi relationship with the FBI as a partnership. In a March 13, 2000, interview on *Fox the Edge with Paula Zahn*, he said, "They killed the individuals they believed were threats to them . . . [u]sing FBI information."

Robert Fitzpatrick, the second in command in the Boston office of the FBI from 1980 to 1986, characterized agent Connolly as the informant who let Bulger into the FBI. "When everybody was asleep, this guy (Connolly) went down and grabbed all this stuff and gave it out, anything that Bulger needed, the information about criminal competitors, information about others ratting him out, information about other law enforcement agencies."[50] During their tenure as FBI informants, Flemmi and Bulger were involved with gambling, loan-sharking, extortion, and, as recent indictments would indicate, murder.[51] Fitzpatrick further indicated that the corruption in the Boston office was systemic, resulting in TE informants empowered to murder without fearing prosecution.[52] Fitzpatrick said:

> [Agent] Connolly became the informant for Bulger, and, in effect, Bulger is now inside the kingdom, if you will. He now has the keys to the FBI vault, to the FBI kingdom. Bulger can get any information he wants through Connolly and, as we now know, did. That, to me, is shocking. And—and I might add, I'm angry over the fact that people were killed or murdered. I'm angry over the fact that it went on for so long.[53]

WHAT FLEMMI AND BULGER DID TO HELP THE FBI

Bulger and Flemmi provided much valuable information to the FBI. The U.S. Court of Appeals found that the information provided by Flemmi and Bulger greatly aided the FBI in their investigation of LCN leaders. *United States v. Flemmi*, 225 F.3d 78, 80 (1st Cir. 2000). Probably their most important contribution was their role, albeit indirect, in the taping of a Mafia induction ceremony in 1989. The crucial information that resulted in the taping of the induction ceremony came from Angelo "Sonny" Mercurio, a made member of the LCN, as well as a TE informant. Bulger and Flemmi were largely responsible for Sonny's recruitment.

The story of this recruitment captures Bulger and Flemmi's importance to the FBI. Evidently, after the Angiulo brothers were sent to prison in 1983, there was a period of three years during which the Winter Hill Gang dominated Boston's organized crime scene. In 1986, upon his release from prison, Sonny Mercurio sought to reestablish his control over the Boston Mafia. A new group of Mafioso, which included Vinnie Ferrara, Joe Russo, and Bobby Carrozza, among others, was also vying to take the reigns from Bulger and Flemmi. Mercurio, hoping to assert his position in the Mafia, sought to ensure that two bookies continued to make payments to the Mafia. Bulger and Flemmi had approached these bookies, but Mercurio warned Bulger and Flemmi to keep away from them, that the Mafia would be collecting from these bookies from now on. Mercurio explained to Bulger and Flemmi that the bookies were going to be told of the new regime at Vanessa's Italian food shop. Flemmi and Bulger gave this information to the FBI, who then got a bug for Vanessa's.

The bug at Vanessa's provided much incriminating evidence against Mercurio and his Mafia associates. Connolly used the information he received from the bugging operation as well as Mercurio's responsibility for the obtaining of the warrant for the bug as leverage to convince Mercurio to become an informant. In addition, while Mercurio was in prison the Mafia ignored him, whereas Bulger and Flemmi sent weekly payments to his girlfriend during this period. Thus, Mecurio was ripe to "flip." Mercurio was working as an informant for the FBI when they sought to obtain court permission to tape the LCN induction ceremony.[54]

The taping of the mafia induction ceremony in 1989 was the first time that the FBI had ever captured an induction ceremony on tape. Jim Ahearn, special agent in charge of Boston, characterized the ceremony in the following way: "[T]he Bureau for the first time ever, . . . overhear[d] and record[ed] an LCN induction ceremony, which would be invaluable for years to come at other LCN trials and Congressional hearings." The June 17, 1997, edition of *The Boston Globe* describes this tape of the ceremony as "something right out of 'The Godfather,'" and as one of the FBI's greatest coups.

In January 1981, Bulger and Flemmi reportedly provided the information that led to the government's successful bugging of the LCN's Boston headquarters in the North End section of Boston. The FBI used this information against Gennaro Angiulo and Ilario Zannino.[55] Other exploits of Bulger and Flemmi included saving the lives of two FBI agents.[56] In the late 1970s, Bulger informed the FBI that two agents, Billy Butchka and Nicholas Gianturco, were in danger because the mob suspected their status as undercover agents in Boston. Supposedly, Bulger intervened with the hitmen on Butchka's behalf. In addition, according to FBI documents, in the 1960s Flemmi tipped the FBI that local Mafia members were plotting the murder of then Suffolk County District Attorney Garret Byrne and "possibly a judge," as well as plotting to murder U.S. Attorney Paul Markham.

Bulger is also said to have supplied information that led to the arrest of participants in the Depositors Trust heist in Medford, Massachusetts, which occurred over Memorial Day weekend 1980,[57] and to have fingered Joseph Russo in connection with the murder of mobster Joseph Barboza Baron in 1976.[58]

In 1980, then FBI Boston Office Chief Lawrence Sarhatt stated that he considered dropping Bulger as an informant, but Connolly, Morris, and

U.S. Attorney Jeremiah O'Sullivan, head of the New England Organized Crime Task Force, convinced Sarhatt that Bulger was too valuable to cut loose.[59] In a memo, Sarhatt wrote that O'Sullivan told him that there was no improper conduct on the part of the FBI by continuing the Bulger relationship. Quoting O'Sullivan in his memo, Sarhatt wrote that "Mr. O'Sullivan . . . stated that there was sufficient justification for continuing him regardless of his current activities to be able to eventually prosecute LCN members." 91 F.Supp. 2d at 204.

Bulger's activities were not limited to providing information involving the LCN. Rather, in the words of criminal defense attorney Ed McDonald, "[H]e was providing information on people to the sides of him."[60] It has recently come to light, according to former FBI Special Agent Nicholas Gianturco, that Bulger and Flemmi informed both on the Mafia and on other members of the Winter Hill Gang.[61] Bulger and Flemmi received high praise for their work; internal FBI documents praised Bulger and Flemmi as "excellent" and "of the highest caliber."[62]

THE DILEMMA: HOW MUCH TO TURN A BLIND EYE, OR WHO WILL MONITOR LAW ENFORCEMENT?

In 1924, when Attorney General and future Chief Justice of the Supreme Court Harlan Fiske Stone created the modern FBI, he commented, "There is always the possibility that a secret police may become a menace to free government and free institutions because it carries with it the possibility of abuses of power which are not always quickly apprehended or understood; it is important . . . that its agents themselves be not above the law or beyond its reach." 91 F.Supp 2d. at 189. This warning by Justice Stone was largely ignored until 1976, when Attorney General Edward Levi sought to limit the power of the FBI by issuing a memorandum to the director of the FBI regarding standards for the use of informants. This memo was the forerunner to later FBI guidelines. Levi, in attempting to deal with this issue, recognized the importance and sensitivity of the informant issue and allowed for much of the responsibility to remain with the investigatory agent. In the case of Bulger and Flemmi, agents ignored these suggested guidelines, as the agents in charge thought they had no applicability to TE informants who dealt with organized crime matters. As the court found, Morris and Ring ignored provisions of the attorney general's guidelines that required authorization of criminal activity and reporting of unauthorized crimes committed by informants." 91 F.Supp. at 196.

> The FBI and attorney general informant guidelines, together with FBI administrative controls, are intended to provide the necessary checks and balances and to ensure that often difficult decisions are made at the appropriate level, based on complete and accurate information. . . . While admittedly no system is foolproof, clearly those objective[s] were not met here, at least in certain critical respects. 91 F.Supp. at 197.[63]

Many other law enforcement agencies today criticize the FBI for keeping Bulger on as an informant for so long. One DEA agent stated, "Everybody in this business knows that you have to make deals with bad guys. . . . But at some point, you have to cut them off when they're bigger than the people they're giving you."[64] Some argue that the FBI was justified in keeping Bulger and Flemmi active as informants up until 1983, the time of the downfall of Angiulo, Zanino, and other high-ranking members of the Providence, Rhode Island, based Patriarca crime family. However, subsequently, Bulger and Flemmi assisted in getting Angelo Mercurio to flip.[65]

Given what has come to light regarding the heinous crimes committed and investigations stifled, as well as the closeness of the relationship between the FBI and Flemmi and Bulger, it appears that Bulger and Flemmi flourished with the help of their FBI friends. In retrospect, the warning of Chief Justice Stone is certainly poignant.

U.S. Attorney for Massachusetts Donald Stern characterizes the activity as follows:

> Layer upon layer of myth, fear and protection have been stripped away—leaving a chilling and profoundly disturbing core of shakedowns, drug dealing, corruption and murder.[66]

THE INDICTMENTS

On January 10, 1995, Bulger and Flemmi were indicted on multiple charges, including racketeering, extortion, and murder. Connolly, who had retired from the FBI in 1990, maintained a close relationship with his former colleagues at the Organized Crime Squad of the FBI. He allegedly learned of the indictments and informed Bulger of their pendency. As a result of this information Bulger disappeared and became a fugitive. Flemmi, not expecting to be subject to arrest before January 10, was arrested on January 5, 1995. He is presently incarcerated, awaiting trial. Bulger remains a fugitive and is currently on the FBI's "Ten Most Wanted" list. In a somewhat ironic twist, despite his considerable legal efforts, which we will discuss in the next section, on May 16, 2001, Flemmi entered into a plea bargain with regard to this 1995 indictment and a 1999 indictment to be discussed. Flemmi, in exchange for the release of some of his property, dropping of some charges (namely, the murder charges), and a sentencing recommendation, pleaded guilty to extortion, money laundering, and obstruction of justice. He still faces federal indictments issued in September 2000 for the murder of ten people as well as murder charges in the states of Oklahoma and Florida.[67]

On December 22, 1999, additional racketeering indictments were issued against Flemmi and Bulger. These include indictments against FBI agent John Connolly for participating in a racketeering conspiracy with Bulger and Flemmi. In addition, Connolly was indicted for obstruction of justice. The indictments charge Connolly with taking part in bribing Morris and ignoring the takeover of the South Boston liquor store, described previously. Connolly was also charged with warning Flemmi of the January 1995 indictments.[68] Connolly's former supervisor, John Morris, was given immunity, and has admitted to taking $7,000 from Bulger and Flemmi.[69] Connolly's defense is simply that he was playing by the rules. He claims that his activity with regard to these informants was sanctioned, and indeed encouraged, by his superiors.[70]

On September 28, 2000, Bulger was indicted for eighteen murders over a period of twelve years. Flemmi was indicted for teaming up with Bulger on ten of these murders. Ironically, the victims included individuals who were brought to Bulger's attention by the FBI because they were informing on Bulger's activity. It is interesting to note that eleven of these murders occurred after 1975 while Bulger was working as an FBI informant. On October 11, 2000, additional indictments were issued against former FBI agent John J. Connolly Jr. for being part of the criminal enterprise headed by James "Whitey" Bulger. These indictments further accuse Connolly of leaking confidential information to Bulger and Flemmi resulting in the murder of informants Richard Castucci in 1976 and Brian Halloran in 1982, as well as John Callahan who was a witness in the Wheeler murder in 1982.[71]

LEGAL ISSUES

The preceding scenario raises a number of legal issues. It should be pointed out that these issues were raised in extensive pretrial hearings and then appealed by Flemmi who has since entered into a plea bargain, thus for the time being mooting these issues from further litigation. The primary issue is whether the FBI authorized the criminal activity engaged in by Bulger and Flemmi. If it was indeed authorized, what is the appropriate remedy? Should they be prosecuted for what was apparently authorized? Can the government use any information provided by the informants in prosecuting them? Was the government conduct so outrageous that charges should be dismissed? The final issue relates to the wiretapping and whether the government must disclose informant relationships in seeking wiretap warrants.

IMMUNITY FROM PROSECUTION

The primary legal issue before the court is whether, given the status of Bulger and Flemmi as TE informants, they were authorized to engage in the criminal activity, which is the subject of the indictments. Would this authorization make them immune from prosecution? The issue of immunity from prosecution was first addressed in the Linda Tripp chapter. Tripp was granted immunity from prosecution for past acts (her illegal wiretapping) in exchange for her testimony before the grand jury. In the Bulger case, the immunity in question is for continuing acts while the informants were associated with the government. This type of immunity is more like an authorization to commit illegal acts.

The Supreme Court case of *Santobello v. New York* provides useful guidelines for this issue. 404 U.S. 257 (1971). In this case, the government agreed as part of a plea bargain arrangement not to make a sentencing recommendation. A prosecutor who was unaware of this original agreement later made a sentencing recommendation. The court held that the government had to honor the original agreement, otherwise it would be unfair and a violation of due process. This case has been extended beyond the plea bargain stage to include other grants of immunity, even if those grants are informal. *United States v. Harvey*, 869 F.2d 1439, 1442 (11th Cir. 1989). In a situation out of the Court of Appeals for the Boston area, the Securities and Exchange Commission obtained substantial information from a defendant in return for a promise to recommend to the U.S. Attorney not to prosecute. When the government failed to honor their agreement, the court dismissed the case because of the unfairness to the defendant. See *United States v. Rodman*, 519 F.2d 1058 (1st Cir. 1975) (per curiam).

Some courts have looked at the agreement to determine whether the government official had the authority to make such an agreement. If the official was without authority, then the defendant cannot rely on it. See *United States v. Baptista-Rodriguez*, 17 F.3d 1354, 1367 n. 18 (11th Cir. 1994). The First Circuit has refused to adopt this approach, instead determining whether a promise was actually made as opposed to whether there was authority to make it. See *Bemis v. United States*, 30 F.3d 220, 222 (1st Cir. 1994).

The FBI's informant guidelines include provisions detailing when it is appropriate to authorize criminal activity by informants. But under no circumstances are informants permitted to participate in violence. In any event, only a high-ranking official—at least the second in command of a regional office—may authorize criminal activity. Moreover, any such decision is to be reviewed every ninety days by the head of the regional office.[72] However, according to Assistant U.S. Attorney Fred Wyshak, only federal prosecutors, not FBI agents, have the authority to grant immunity.[73]

In his finding of facts, Judge Wolf avoided the immunity agreement issue in his determination of the parameters of the agreement Flemmi and Bulger had with the government.[74] 91 F.Supp.2d at 321–325. He found that the term immunity was never used. The government never agreed that Bulger and Flemmi would not be prosecuted or investigated. The government did, however, agree to overlook some of their criminal activity and to warn and provide information about ongoing investigations. To support his findings, the judge pointed out that Flemmi never complained about ongoing investigations. Further, when Flemmi escaped indictment for race fixing, he expressed gratitude rather than an entitlement to not having been indicted. The judge concluded that based on the facts "that [the] protection permitted Flemmi and Bulger to survive repeated efforts by various law enforcement agencies to investigate them and allowed them to profit from their contribution to the FBI . . . [they] did not have either an express agreement or an agreement implied in fact that [they] would not be prosecuted." 91 F.Supp. 2d. at 324–325. Since there was no promise of immunity from prosecution, the court denied Flemmi's motion to dismiss.

USE IMMUNITY

A subsidiary issue is whether information provided by the informant can be used against him, called "use immunity." This is similar to the problem faced by the Maryland prosecutor in the Tripp case. Morris, as well as Supervisory Special Agent James Darcy, indicated that the maintenance of the confidentiality of the relationship was sacred and the FBI position was that no information furnished by an informant could be used to prosecute that informant. In this case, the central issue was whether any of the information provided by Bulger or Flemmi was used to secure the indictment against them. This brings to mind the *Kastigar* case, which was discussed in Chapter 2. *Kastigar v. United States*, 406 U.S. 441 (1972). In this case the U.S. Supreme Court held that any information the government secured with an express indication that they would not use it against the source cannot be used to secure the indictments of the informants, or to prove the case against them at trial. If there is an indication that similar information was used, the government must show that their source of the information was separate and distinct from the informant, or that the information was not really necessary for securing the indictment. *United States v. Schmidgall*, 25 F.3d 1533, 1536–1537 (11th Cir. 1994). In order to preserve the confidentiality of the informant, information provided may be used as long as it does not compromise the informant relationship or the identity of the informant. In his findings, Judge Wolf found an express agreement with regard to the wiretaps at both the Mafia headquarters and Vanessa's restaurant. Thus, Judge Wolf ruled that direct evidence or evidence derived from those tapings could not be used against Flemmi or Bulger either during the grand jury proceeding or the trial. See 25 F.3d at 1533; *United States v. North*, 920 F.2d 940 (D.C. Cir. 1990) (per curiam).

The Court of Appeals reversed the Wolf decision. *United States v. Flemmi*, 225 F.3d 78 (1st Cir. 2000). The court indicated that an FBI agent did not have the authority to grant use immunity. Although an agent could promise confidentiality, he did not have the authority to grant use immunity because use immunity was a separate and distinct assurance. In the Court of Appeals, Flemmi argued that even if the FBI lacked authority to grant use immunity, their promise resulted in his involuntary statements. Consequently, the result of these statements—the surveillance—should be suppressed. To analyze this, the court considered the totality of the circumstances, taking into account the suspects' particular characteristics as well as the actions by the government. See generally

Arizona v. Fulminante, 499 U.S. 279 (1991). This issue was discussed in Chapter 4. The Court of Appeals did not find Flemmi's statements involuntary. They pointed out that mere promises were not sufficient to make a statement involuntary. There needed to be some coercive activity by the government, an element that did not exist in this case. As a matter of fact, recall that Flemmi enjoyed a social relationship with Morris and Connolly in addition to his informant relationship. *United States v. Flemmi*, 225 F.3d. 78 (1st Cir. 2000).

OUTRAGEOUS GOVERNMENT ACTIVITY

Was the government activity so outrageous that the court should dismiss the charges? The preceding scenario demonstrates a pattern of government activity that is at a minimum offensive. The allegations and indictments indicate that the FBI assisted Bulger and Flemmi in avoiding prosecution for at least one murder as well as provided information that resulted in other murders.

The case of *United States v. Payner* illustrates the lenient way in which the Supreme Court has dealt with police misconduct. 447 U.S. 727 (1980). In this case, the IRS, while investigating tax evasion in the Bahamas, employed a nongovernmental investigator named Payner to break into a banker's briefcase and obtain documents. The IRS used the documents against Payner. Payner could not suppress the documents pursuant to the fourth amendment because he lacked standing to complain about the willful illegality. In order to have standing in a fourth amendment argument, there must be an expectation of privacy in the place searched. In this case, there was no expectation of privacy in the banker's briefcase. Because he lacked standing for fourth amendment arguments, Payner instead argued that the court should utilize their supervisory powers to suppress the documents. Using these powers allows the court to address and monitor bad conduct by government officials beyond the scope of the Constitution or statutes. In *Payner*, however, the Supreme Court refused to exercise their supervisory powers, feeling that the use of the probative evidence outweighed the importance of addressing the police misconduct.[75]

Given the court's refusal to suppress evidence in *Payner*, it is not surprising that the court rarely will consider dismissing charges because of the outrageous nature of government conduct. The outrageous conduct must be grossly shocking or shock one's conscience. *Rochin v. California*, 342 U.S. 165 (1952); and *United States v. McCown*, 711 F.2d

1441 (9th Cir. 1983). The court grants dismissal pursuant either to the due process clause, other constitutional authority, or under the court's supervisory powers. In addition to outrageous conduct, the prejudice to the defendant must be so severe that no remedy (e.g., suppression of the evidence) short of outright dismissal would be adequate. For example, in *United States v. Morrison*, the court held that even where there was a showing of a deliberate sixth amendment violation, dismissal was inappropriate without a demonstration of actual prejudice. 449 U.S. 361 (1981). A case from the Eighth Circuit is a good example of how much the defendant must demonstrate to show actual prejudice. *United States v. Crow Dog*, 532 F.2d 1182 (8th Cir. 1976). In this case, an informant had infiltrated the sacred attorney-client relationship. The informant was present at a meeting between the defendant and his attorney and had access to the legal files of various defense attorneys. Since there was no evidence that the informant passed on any of this information to the FBI, no prejudice was shown and dismissal was not granted, despite the extreme conduct by the government.

The cases in which prejudice has been demonstrated are usually cases in which the government gained access to defense strategies, which would affect the actual trial process. The Third Circuit Court granted a dismissal in a case in which a DEA informant not only sat in on meetings between a defendant and his attorney, but subsequently disclosed information to the prosecution. *United States v. Levy*, 577 F.2d 200 (3d Cir. 1978); see also *United States v. Valencia*, 541 F.2d 618 (6th Cir. 1976). The court held that it was virtually impossible to accurately measure the prejudice to the defendant. The court also noted that it would be impractical to attempt to correct the violations through a retrial with different prosecutors, and found dismissal the only viable remedy. Although the Bulger case raises substantial issues of prejudice, precedent does not support a dismissal, as the governmental conduct arguably did not affect the ultimate fairness of the trial process.

THE WIRETAP APPLICATION ISSUE

In drafting the wiretap provisions of Title III, Congress had to be cognizant of the provision of the fourth amendment that requires that any warrant "particularly describe the place to be searched, and the persons and things to be seized." This is known as the particularity clause of the fourth amendment. Our founding ancestors inserted this language to avoid general warrants, which gave colonial officials a license to search "whenever, wherever and whomever they chose."[76] The language of the fourth amendment seeks to limit the scope of such searches to the confines of the warrant so that nothing is left to the discretion of the executing officer. *Marron v. United States*, 275 U.S. 192 (1927). Congress, cognizant of the extensive privacy implications that a wiretap can have, especially since most conversations will not be incriminating, enacted Title III. Title III contains many specific requirements, which are more rigorous than a normal search warrant. The congressional purpose was to limit the thrust and scope of an authorized wiretap as well as to conform to the fourth amendment. See generally 91 F. Supp.2d 351–381. These requirements include full and complete statements about what less intrusive alternatives were tried and why they were not successful. In addition, the warrant must describe the location of the tap, but also the type of communication sought to be intercepted.

In 1984 and 1985, the DEA and the FBI wiretapped the cars and phones of Bulger, Flemmi, and their associate George Kaufman, who operated a garage that served as a front for the Winter Hill Gang, and later for Bulger and Flemmi. As mentioned previously, in order to obtain the necessary court orders for electronic surveillance, there needs to be complete disclosure to the judge issuing the court order. The legal standard pursuant to 18 U.S.C. sec. 2518 (1)(c) is that a "full and complete statement" explaining why conventional techniques (a.k.a., the use of informants) "are unavailable or unlikely to succeed" must be provided (see Appendix A). The FBI, wanting to continue to protect the confidentiality of their prized informants, did not divulge their relationship to Bulger and Flemmi in the affidavit for these wiretaps.[77]

This failure to divulge raises two issues. First, the defendant can argue that the government provided misinformation. This argument, which we previously discussed in Chapter 3, involves the case of *Franks v. Delaware*. 438 U.S. 154 (1978). In order to be successful in a *Franks* motion, the defendant must show that the government provided information that they knew was false, or provided it with reckless disregard for the truth, and that the information was necessary to establish probable cause. In analyzing whether the specific affiants meet this standard, a government agent, in this case a DEA agent, must obtain and is held responsible for all the information within the control of the government. See *United States v. Mastroianni*, 749 F.2d 900 (1st Cir. 1984). In the Bulger case, the DEA did not consult with the FBI. If they had consulted, it is not clear that they would have received the pertinent information. Nevertheless, by law they are responsible for this information.

The second issue is whether government conduct violated 18 U.S.C. sec. 2518 *et seq*. Pursuant to *United States v. Giordano*, the remedy for a violation of full disclosure is exclusion of the evidence found as a result of the electronic surveillance. 416 U.S. 505 (1974). In his decision, Judge Wolf indicated that either the *Franks* approach or the *Giordano* approach would work to exclude the evidence, but when there has been a violation of sec. 2518 the statutory approach is preferred. 91 F.Supp.2d at 170. Accordingly, Judge Wolf found the Flemmi motion to suppress on this issue meritorious and suppressed the wiretapped conversations.

The bugging of the Mafia induction ceremony raises a number of other issues. In its wiretap application, the FBI requested a "roving bug," which is considered more intrusive than the traditional bug since the roving bug targets a given individual in any number of locations, not just a given conversation in a fixed location. As a criminal becomes aware of the government's ability to intercept conversations, he or she moves around to stifle the government's efforts. Thus, in 1986, Congress amended Title III to include a "roving intercept" and "roving wiretap." According to 18 U.S.C. sec. 2518, a judge can dispense with the usual particularity requirements and allow a roving wiretap provided that the government provides "a full and complete statement as to why such specification is not practical" as well as a demonstration that the person targeted has "[t]hwart[ed] interception from a specified facility." In applying for the roving bug in this case, the government presumed that they had some discretion in what they reported to the court. They sought to rely on 18 U.S.C. sec. 2518 (1)(b) in describing the probable cause requirement for electronic surveillance. This section states that "a full and complete statement of the facts and circumstances relied upon by the applicant to justify his belief that an order should be issued" be given. The government used the language "relied upon by the applicant" to justify their failure to fully disclose the informants who provided information. The judge ruled that the language in the roving bug section of sec. 2518 (11) requiring a full and complete statement is not qualified by discretionary language.

Thus with regard to establishing probable cause, the government generally has legitimate discretion not to rely on singular information that could lead to the identification of a source and, therefore, to omit such information from the section of its application for a warrant that seeks to establish probable cause. With regard to an application for a roving bug, however, if such singular information also relates to whether it is impractical to specify the location to be bugged, the government does not have the discretion to withhold it from the court. 91 F.Supp.2d at 278.

Evidently, Mercurio was referred to as "Confidential Informant I" in the October 1989 bugging application for the Medford induction ceremony. However, it appears that the government never informed the judge who authorized the wiretap that Mercurio would take part in the conversations that were to be bugged, or that it was an induction ceremony that would be bugged.[78] Had the government sought to maintain the confidentiality of the informant, there were methods of submitting sealed information to advise the court of specific information that could not be revealed. The FBI seemed to argue that it needed the roving bug, among other reasons, to protect its informants.[79]

In seeking these warrants it appears that there were violations of Title III and the fourth amendment. The remedy for such violations is the suppression of the evidence, otherwise known as the exclusionary rule. One of the major limits of this remedy is the doctrine of standing. In order to have standing it is not enough that the government seeks to introduce evidence against you, but you must also demonstrate that you have been the victim of a privacy invasion. *Alderman v. United States,* 394 U.S. 165 (1969). This can be achieved by showing an expectation of privacy in the place searched. *Rakas v. Illinois*, 439 U.S. 128 (1978). The case law developed the factors that go into establishing an expectation of privacy. These factors include having a possessory interest in the item seized, and the person being legitimately on the premises. For example, an overnight guest who was invited onto another's property and is seized while there has an expectation of privacy, but a business guest on another's property for a few hours, who has no prior relationship with the occupant of the premises, would not have an expectation of privacy if seized. *Minnesota v. Carter,* 525 U.S. 83 (1998); and *Minnesota v. Olson*, 495 U.S. 91 (1990).

In addition to raising fourth amendment standing issues, this situation also raises Title III standing issues. Flemmi argues that Title III grants a broader standing than that allowed under the fourth amendment. He sought to suppress evidence derived from the taping of Vanessa's restaurant. Title III gives standing to any "aggrieved person," which means a person who was a party to any intercepted wire communication or a person against whom the interception was directed. Because Flemmi was the person against whom the interception was directed, he argued that he had standing. In analyzing the language of the statute, Judge Wolf turned to the legislative history of sec. 2510 (11). "It states, in pertinent part, that the statutory definition of 'aggrieved person' 'is intended to reflect existing law.'" 91 F.Supp.2d at 383 (citing Sen. Rep. No. 90-1097 at 2169 (1968), reprinted in 1968 U.S.C.C.A.N. 2112, 2180). Existing law does not confer standing on a named target to a bug who was not actually intercepted. *Id.* at 384 (citing *United States v. Ruggiero*, 928 F.2d 1289, 1303 [2d Cir. 1991]). Thus Flemmi might not necessarily have standing to complain about the illegal wiretap.

CONCLUSION

The story of James "Whitey" Bulger and his trusted associate Stephen "The Rifleman" Flemmi raises serious questions about just how far the government should go in sanctioning criminal activity. To infiltrate high-level criminal enterprises such as the Mafia, the FBI must deal with informants who have been and continue to be involved in serious criminal activity. With regard to the continuing criminal activity, is it appropriate for the government to allow it as long as you don't clip anyone? What if the continuing activity involves murder, and more sadly, what if the government actually, albeit arguably inadvertently, contributed to that activity? Or to put this question another way, is it ever proper for the government to sanction murder in exchange for valuable information? There have been instances in which underworld enforcers have admitted their crimes and implicated others in exchange for reduced charges. For example, John Martorano pleaded guilty to ten murders and implicated himself in twenty murders. U.S. Attorney Donald Stern indicated that without his cooperation the murders would have remained unsolved and nobody would ever be punished for them.[80] This situation is starkly different in that much of Bulger's and Flemmi's activities were ongoing while their friends in the FBI were protecting them. This is also the story of a close relationship that developed between the enforcers of the law and the lawbreakers. This association was allowed to flourish without oversight. It is not enough for FBI Director Louis Freeh to acknowledge that "significant mistakes were made,"[81] or for John Connolly to be indicted.

Finally, as U.S. Attorney General Janet Reno was leaving office she issued *Department of Justice Guidelines Regarding the Use of Confidential Informants* (see Appendix D). In analyzing them you can see that the Justice Department dealt with some of the specific problems I have addressed in this chapter. The primary safeguard found in the guidelines is greater involvement by prosecuting attorneys in the informant enterprise.

The guidelines are applicable to the following Department of Justice law enforcement agencies: the Drug Enforcement Administration, the Federal Bureau of Investigation, the Immigration and Naturalization Service, the U.S. Marshall Service, and the Department of Justice Office of the Inspector General (IB). To deal directly with the problems discussed in this chapter, law enforcement officials cannot make promises or commitments with regard to prosecution for criminal activities or limit the use of any evidence uncovered unless there is prior written approval from the Federal Prosecuting Office (which includes the U.S. Attorney's Office and various divisions in the Department of Justice) who has primary jurisdiction to prosecute such criminal activities (IC).

To prevent the information sharing that became a concern in the Bulger situation, the guidelines require that law inforcement agents, "take the utmost care to avoid conveying any confidential investigative information" to a confidential informant (IF). The information mentioned includes the existence of a search warrant and identities of other informants.

Other issues addressed by the guidelines include compliance and training (II), suitability determination (IIA1) with continuing review of suitability yearly (IIA2), more extensive review after six years (IIA3), and monetary payments with a prohibition against contingent payments (IIIB).

High-level informants are defined as those who are in a senior leadership position in enterprises important to the Justice Department and who are involved in serious crimes (IB9). These informants must be approved in writing by the Confidential Informant Review Committee, which includes a law enforcement official at or about the level of Deputy Assistant Director and two representatives designated by the Assistant Attorney General for the Criminal Division of the Department of Justice, including a Deputy Assistant Attorney General for the Criminal Division or an Assistant U.S. Attorney (IID1).

It is interesting to note that concerns about the type of relationship that has evolved between the law enforcement handler and the informant are addressed (IIIA1 and IIIA2). First, the law enforcement agent should not interfere with any impending investigation or arrest of the informant or the existence of any investigation unless authorized by the Chief Federal Prosecutor. In addition, the agent shall not socialize, exchange gifts, or engage in any business or financial transaction with the informant.

Finally, the guidelines seek to perform a cost-benefit analysis when illegal activity is part of the equation. To authorize any illegal activity, agents must document in the informant file that the activity was necessary to obtain essential evidence otherwise not obtainable for an investigation or that the information was necessary to prevent death, serious bodily injury, or significant damage to property. These benefits to be obtained must outweigh the cost of the illegal activity (IIIC). In no event should the illegal activity result in violence or obstruction of justice (perjury, witness tampering, and/or intimidation, entrapment, or the fabrication, alteration, or destruction of evidence). The guidelines also provide for notification of the prosecutor's office whenever the informant is being prosecuted or is a target of an investigation. In addition, law enforcement must notify the prosecutor when the informant has engaged in unauthorized activities (IV).

Appendix A
The Cast of Characters

James "Whitey" Bulger: FBI informant dating back to about 1970. He spent time in several of the nation's toughest prisons, including Alcatraz. Whitey grew up in South Boston, where he remained and went on to become the principal organized crime figure in the Irish mob. Throughout his time as an informant he forged close relationships with several FBI agents, exchanging gifts and having social meetings with them on a regular basis. He informed on his rivals in the Italian Mafia as well as members of his own organization, and is now referred to as "King Rat."[82] Whitey has been on the lam since 1995.

Stephen "The Rifleman" Flemmi: Bulger's longtime friend and second in command of the Winter Hill Gang. Flemmi's status as an informer was much more inconsistent than Bulger's. After a six-year period in the 1960s during which time he provided information to FBI agents Dennis Condon and Paul Rico, Flemmi was terminated as an informant in 1968. He did not begin working for the FBI again until 1980. According to Assistant U.S. Attorney Fred M. Wyshak Jr., he was terminated as an informant two years later following an FBI review.[83] Flemmi is reported to be "Confidential Informant 2" in the government's application to bug the 1989 Medford Mafia induction ceremony.

Angelo "Sonny" Mercurio: LCN soldier and FBI informant. Sonny was in charge of Vanessa's restaurant, which the FBI bugged based on information provided by Bulger and Flemmi. He became an informant himself and provided the bulk of the information used to show probable cause in the warrant application for the induction ceremony wiretapping.

Francis P. "Cadillac Frank" Salemme: Mafia boss who rose to power in the 1980s. He was the target of an attempted assassination in 1989 outside a Saugus, Massachusetts, pancake house. He was apprehended in Florida and is a codefendant with Martorano, Flemmi, and Bulger. Evidently, the FBI tried to recruit Salemme as an informant in 1969.[84]

Robert DeLuca: Reputed Mafia soldier from Lincoln, Rhode Island, and a codefendant with Salemme and the others. DeLuca is said to have been present at the Medford induction ceremony. He was indicted along with Salemme and Flemmi.

James Martorano: Winter Hill Gang member and codefendant with Salemme, Bulger, and Flemmi.

JOHN MARTORANO: Reportedly a high-ranking member and hitman of the Winter Hill Gang. He agreed to cooperate with the prosecutors in their case against Bulger and Flemmi, and pleaded guilty to murdering ten people for the mob. He will be tried separately from Flemmi, Salemme, and DeLuca.

GENNARO "JERRY" ANGIULO: Not really a player in the current litigation, but a key Mafia boss who was convicted partially on the strength of the 1981 wiretap of Angiulo's Prince Street headquarters and the infamous 1989 Mafia induction ceremony recorded in Medford.

RAYMOND "JUNIOR" PATRIARCA: Patriarca crime family boss and participant in the taped Mafia induction ceremony. He pleaded guilty in 1991 after Judge Wolf ruled that the Medford induction ceremony wiretap was legally obtained.

JUDGE MARK WOLF: Federal judge at the heart of the proceedings. Interestingly, Judge Wolf, upon graduating from Harvard Law School, became a deputy to U.S. Attorney General Edward Levi. Levi and Wolf proceeded to rewrite the Justice Department guidelines for the handling of informants for federal law enforcement agents.[85]

JOHN CONNOLLY: FBI handler who "inherited" Bulger and Flemmi from Rico.[86] Connolly grew up in South Boston and revered Whitey Bulger as a child. He formed a relationship with Bulger and Flemmi while they were informants, which grew to become a social relationship as well, including the exchanging of gifts. Connolly passed information along to Bulger and Flemmi, allowing them to evade investigation and arrest for two decades. He has been charged with racketeering, racketeering conspiracy, conspiracy to obstruct justice, and obstruction of justice along with Flemmi and Bulger. He pleaded innocent to these charges.[87]

JOHN MORRIS: One of Connolly's former supervisors in the FBI's Organized Crime Squad. Supposedly, Flemmi and Bulger loaned Morris $5,000, which has not been paid back.[88] He also received two cash gifts of $1,000 each. Recently, Morris has been offered immunity from prosecution in exchange for testimony.[89] He has moved to Florida.

H. PAUL RICO: FBI agent who forged the FBI's bond with Bulger, Flemmi, and many other mob figures.[90] Supposedly, Rico tipped Flemmi that he was about to be indicted for the attempted murder of Boston attorney John Fitzgerald.[91] It is unclear whether Rico actually signed on Bulger as an informant. He denies it, but a 1980 FBI memo states the story this way: "When Bulger was incarcerated on Alcatraz for bank robbery, Rico was helpful to Bulger's family, which impressed Bulger and caused him to turn away from his deep hatred for all law enforcement."[92] Judge Wolf identified Rico as one of the major characters in the FBI mishandling of Flemmi and Bulger. *Salemme*, F.Supp.2d at 149–150.

DENNIS CONDON: Rico's partner and an original handler of Bulger and Flemmi. He passed along information to Connolly as to Salemme's whereabouts, which led to Salemme's arrest and Connolly's transfer back to Boston. In 1971, Condon closed Bulger as an informant after deciding that he was not productive enough. When Condon took the stand as a witness he claimed not to remember much of the relationship between the FBI and Bulger and Flemmi.[93]

NICHOLAS GIANTURCO: Undercover agent in Boston, he first met Bulger and Flemmi in 1979 when Connolly was their handler.[94] He either succeeded Connolly as one of Bulger's and/or Flemmi's handlers, or simply served as an "alternate handler" from 1980 to 1983.[95] He admits to accepting gifts from Bulger and Flemmi in the 1980s.[96]

JEREMIAH O'SULLIVAN: U.S. Attorney and former Chief of the New England Organized Crime Strike Force. O'Sullivan is expected to testify at the hearings, although he is recovering from a heart attack.[97] He is expected to deny that Bulger or Flemmi were ever given FBI permission to commit crimes.

HOWIE WINTER: Leader of the Winter Hill Gang, and owner of Marshall Motors, the auto shop that served as a business front and gathering place for the Winter Hill Gang. In 1979, he was indicted and jailed as part of the race-fixing indictment that Bulger and Flemmi avoided. In 1992 when he chose to plead guilty to drug charges rather than inform on Bulger, he was sentenced to another ten years in prison.

FRED WYSHAK: U.S. Attorney who was able to convict Howie Winter on drug charges, and who is currently prosecuting Flemmi and Salemme.

JOHN MITCHELL: An attorney from New York City. He previously represented an alleged LCN member and is currently working with Anthony Cardinale to represent Frank Salemme.

WILLIAM BULGER: Whitey's brother. He served in the Massachusetts Senate as president and had a private law practice in Boston. He is now president of the University of Massachusetts.

RODERICK KENNEDY: FBI agent, served for a short time as liaison to the DEA. He was included in Judge Wolf's list of agents who were connected to the mishandling of Flemmi and Bulger.

JULIE AND STEPHEN RAKES: South Boston Liquor Mart's original owners. Flemmi and Bulger threatened them and their family in order to gain ownership of the liquor store. Although they went to the police, the intimidation was not investigated until years later.

JOSEPH LUNDBOHM: Police officer to whom Julie and Stephen Rakes told their story of extortion. He went to the FBI with the information; the incident was not investigated.

JAMES F. AHEARN: Supervisor in the Boston office of the FBI and a friend of Connolly's. He supported keeping Bulger on as an informant and publicly denied any special treatment toward Bulger by the FBI.[98] He is also included in Judge Wolf's list of agents who were involved in the mishandling of Bulger and Flemmi.

ROGER WHEELER: Oklahoma businessman and owner of World Jai Alai, a company from which Bulger and Flemmi had been taking money. He was murdered in Oklahoma, and his death has been linked to Bulger and Flemmi (140–145).

BRIAN HALLORAN: Associate of Bulger and Flemmi, he knew about the plan to kill Roger Wheeler. He was killed himself when it was suspected that he had informed on Bulger and Flemmi to the FBI (146–150).

KEVIN WEEKS: Associate of Bulger and Flemmi, he was known as Bulger's surrogate son (159). He took over the South Boston Liquor Mart when it came under Bulger's control. After being arrested and facing charges for racketeering, extortion, murder, drug trafficking, and loan-sharking, he told police where to find the bodies of three people Bulger had killed (322–323).

ROBERT FITZPATRICK: FBI agent in the Boston office, assistant special agent in charge and Connolly's supervisor. He went to the prosecutor, Jeremiah O'Sullivan, to warn of possible danger to Brian Halloran after Halloran informed on Bulger, and then to O'Sullivan's supervisor when O'Sullivan did not act on his concerns. However, despite his concerns about Connolly's mishandling of Bulger and Flemmi, he did not act and was included in Judge Wolf's decision as an agent involved in the mishandling (315).

JOHN MCINTYRE: Told police about Bulger's gun-smuggling operation to the Irish Republican Army. He was one of the bodies found in the mass grave in South Boston and is believed to have been murdered by Bulger and Flemmi (323).

PATRICK NEE: Involved in the arms smuggling to the Irish Republican Army and acted as liaison between Bulger and drug smugglers. He was convicted for his involvement in the gun shipment (343).

DEBORAH HUSSEY: Daughter of Flemmi's girlfriend, she was involved with Flemmi as well. Her body was found in the mass grave in South Boston (83, 323).

ARTHUR "BUCKEY" BARRETT: Involved in a bank robbery in 1980, he was forced to give Bulger a large amount of the money he had stolen. He was also found in the grave in South Boston (151–152).

ANTHONY CARDINALE: Boston attorney representing Salemme. He asked the court to disclose the names of FBI informants, claiming that there had been FBI misconduct in the investigation of his client (282).

BILLY BUTCHKA: FBI agent working undercover. Bulger told the FBI of a plan to kill him, and Butchka was warned in time for him to escape danger (338).

PAUL MARKHAM: U.S. Attorney. Flemmi told FBI of a plan to murder him.

LAWRENCE SARHATT: Special agent in charge of the Boston FBI office. At first he questioned Bulger's usefulness as an informant, but later accepted it and turned a blind eye.

JAMES RING: Supervisor of the Organized Crime Squad, took over from John Morris. He participated in the social gatherings Morris, Connolly, Bulger, and Flemmi attended. Ring was included in Judge Wolf's list of agents connected to the mishandling of Bulger and Flemmi.

APPENDIX B

FBI TEN MOST WANTED FUGITIVE

RACKETEERING INFLUENCED AND CORRUPT ORGANIZATIONS (RICO) - MURDER (18 COUNTS), CONSPIRACY TO COMMIT MURDER, CONSPIRACY TO COMMIT EXTORTION, NARCOTICS DISTRIBUTION, CONSPIRACY TO COMMIT MONEY LAUNDERING; EXTORTION; MONEY LAUNDERING

JAMES J. BULGER

Photograph taken in 1994　　　Photograph taken in 1994　　　Photograph altered in 2000

Aliases: Thomas F. Baxter, Mark Shapeton, Jimmy Bulger, James Joseph Bulger, James J. Bulger, Jr., James Joseph Bulger, Jr., Tom Harris, Tom Marshall, "Whitey"

DESCRIPTION

Date of Birth:	September 3, 1929	**Hair:**	White/Silver
Place of Birth:	Boston, Massachusetts	**Eyes:**	Blue
Height:	5′7″ to 5′9″	**Complexion:**	Light
Weight:	150 to 150 pounds	**Sex:**	Male
Build:	Medium	**Race:**	White
Occupation:	Unknown	**Nationality:**	American
Scars and Marks:	None known		

Remarks: Bulger is an avid reader with an interest in history. He is known to frequent libraries and historic sites. Bulger is currently on the heart medication Atenolol (50 mg) and maintains his physical fitness by walking on beaches and in parks with his female companion, Catherine Elizabeth

Greig. Bulger and Greig love animals and may frequent animal shelters. Bulger has been known to alter his appearance through the use of disguises. He has traveled extensively throughout the United States, Europe, Canada, and Mexico.

CAUTION

JAMES J. BULGER IS BEING SOUGHT FOR HIS ROLE IN NUMEROUS MURDERS COMMITTED FROM THE EARLY 1970S THROUGH THE MID-1980S IN CONNECTION WITH HIS LEADERSHIP OF AN ORGANIZED CRIME GROUP THAT ALLEGEDLY CONTROLLED EXTORTION, DRUG DEALS, AND OTHER ILLEGAL ACTIVITIES IN THE BOSTON, MASSACHUSETTS, AREA. HE HAS A VIOLENT TEMPER AND IS KNOWN TO CARRY A KNIFE AT ALL TIMES.

CONSIDERED ARMED AND EXTREMELY DANGEROUS

IF YOU HAVE ANY INFORMATION CONCERNING THIS PERSON, PLEASE CONTACT YOUR <u>LOCAL FBI OFFICE</u> OR THE NEAREST <u>U.S. EMBASSY OR CONSULATE.</u>

REWARD

The FBI is offering a $1,000,000 reward for information leading directly to the arrest of James J. Bulger.

August 1999
Poster Revised November 2000

From http://www.fbi.gov/mostwant/topten/fugitives/bulger.htm

Appendix C
18 U.S.C. 2510 and 18 U.S.C. 2518

18 U.S.C. 2510

As used in this chapter—

(1) "wire communication" means any aural transfer made in whole or in part through the use of facilities for the transmission of communications by the aid of wire, cable, or other like connection between the point of origin and the point of reception (including the use of such connection in a switching station) furnished or operated by any person engaged in providing or operating such facilities for the transmission of interstate or foreign communications or communications affecting interstate or foreign commerce and such term includes any electronic storage of such communication;

(2) "oral communication" means any oral communication uttered by a person exhibiting an expectation that such communication is not subject to interception under circumstances justifying such expectation, but such term does not include any electronic communication;

(3) "State" means any State of the United States, the District of Columbia, the Commonwealth of Puerto Rico, and any territory or possession of the United States;

(4) "intercept" means the aural or other acquisition of the contents of any wire, electronic, or oral communication through the use of any electronic, mechanical, or other device;

(5) "electronic, mechanical, or other device" means any device or apparatus which can be used to intercept a wire, oral, or electronic communication other than—

    (a) any telephone or telegraph instrument, equipment or facility, or any component thereof,

        (i) furnished to the subscriber or user by a provider of wire or electronic communication service in the ordinary course of its business and being used by the subscriber or user in the ordinary course of its business or furnished by such subscriber or user for connection to the facilities of such service and used in the ordinary course of its business; or (ii) being used by a provider of wire or electronic communication service in the ordinary course of its business, or by an investigative or law enforcement officer in the ordinary course of his duties;

(b) a hearing aid or similar device being used to correct subnormal hearing to not better than normal;

(6) "person" means any employee, or agent of the United States or any State or political subdivision thereof, and any individual, partnership, association, joint stock company, trust, or corporation;

(7) "Investigative or law enforcement officer" means any officer of the United States or of a State or political subdivision thereof, who is empowered by law to conduct investigations of or to make arrests for offenses enumerated in this chapter, and any attorney authorized by law to prosecute or participate in the prosecution of such offenses;

(8) "contents", when used with respect to any wire, oral, or electronic communication, includes any information concerning the substance, purport, or meaning of that communication;

(9) "Judge of competent jurisdiction" means—

(a) a judge of a United States district court or a United States court of appeals; and

(b) a judge of any court of general criminal jurisdiction of a State who is authorized by a statute of that State to enter orders authorizing interceptions of wire, oral, or electronic communications;

(10) "communication common carrier" shall have the same meaning which is given the term "common carrier" by section 153(h) of title 47 of the United States Code;

(11) "aggrieved person" means a person who was a party to any intercepted wire, oral, or electronic communication or a person against whom the interception was directed;

(12) "electronic communication" means any transfer of signs, signals, writing, images, sounds, data, or intelligence of any nature transmitted in whole or in part by a wire, radio, electromagnetic, photoelectronic or photooptical system that affects interstate or foreign commerce, but does not include—

(a) any wire or oral communication;

(b) any communication made through a tone-only paging device;

(c) any communication from a tracking device (as defined in section 3117 of this title); or

(d) electronic funds transfer information stored by a financial institution in a communications system used for the electronic storage and transfer of funds;

(13) "user" means any person or entity who—

(a) uses an electronic communication service; and

(b) is duly authorized by the provider of such service to engage in such use;

(14) "electronic communications system" means any wire, radio, electromagnetic, photooptical or photoelectronic facilities for the transmission of electronic communications, and any computer facilities or related electronic equipment for the electronic storage of such communications;

(15) "electronic communication service" means any service which provides to users thereof the ability to send or receive wire or electronic communications;

(16) "readily accessible to the general public" means, with respect to a radio communication, that such communication is not—

(a) scrambled or encrypted;

(b) transmitted using modulation techniques whose essential parameters have been withheld from the public with the intention of preserving the privacy of such communication;

(c) carried on a subcarrier or other signal subsidiary to a radio transmission;

(d) transmitted over a communication system provided by a common carrier, unless the communication is a tone only paging system communication; or

(e) transmitted on frequencies allocated under part 25, subpart D, E, or F of part 74, or part 94 of the Rules of the Federal Communications Commission, unless, in the case of a communication transmitted on a frequency allocated under part 74 that is not exclusively allocated to broadcast auxiliary services, the communication is a two-way voice communication by radio;

(17) "electronic storage" means—

    (A) any temporary, intermediate storage of a wire or electronic communication incidental to the electronic transmission thereof; and

    (B) any storage of such communication by an electronic communication service for purposes of backup protection of such communication; and

(18) "aural transfer" means a transfer containing the human voice at any point between and including the point of origin and the point of reception.

18 U.S.C. 2518

(1) Each application for an order authorizing or approving the interception of a wire, oral, or electronic communication under this chapter shall be made in writing upon oath or affirmation to a judge of competent jurisdiction and shall state the applicant's authority to make such application. Each application shall include the following information:

    (a) the identity of the investigative or law enforcement officer making the application, and the officer authorizing the application;

    (b) a full and complete statement of the facts and circumstances relied upon by the applicant, to justify his belief that an order should be issued, including (i) details as to the particular offense that has been, is being, or is about to be committed, (ii) except as provided in subsection (11), a particular description of the nature and location of the facilities from which or the place where the communication is to be intercepted, (iii) a particular description of the type of communications sought to be intercepted, (iv) the identity of the person, if known, committing the offense and whose communications are to be intercepted;

    (c) a full and complete statement as to whether or not other investigative procedures have been tried and failed or why they reasonably appear to be unlikely to succeed if tried or to be too dangerous;

    (d) a statement of the period of time for which the interception is required to be maintained. If the nature of the investigation is such that the authorization for interception should not automatically terminate when the described type of communication has been first obtained, a particular description of facts establishing probable cause to believe that additional communications of the same type will occur thereafter;

(e) a full and complete statement of the facts concerning all previous applications known to the individual authorizing and making the application, made to any judge for authorization to intercept, or for approval of interceptions of, wire, oral, or electronic communications involving any of the same persons, facilities or places specified in the application, and the action taken by the judge on each such application; and

(f) where the application is for the extension of an order, a statement setting forth the results thus far obtained from the interception, or a reasonable explanation of the failure to obtain such results.

(2) The judge may require the applicant to furnish additional testimony or documentary evidence in support of the application.

(3) Upon such application the judge may enter an ex parte order, as requested or as modified, authorizing or approving interception of wire, oral, or electronic communications within the territorial jurisdiction of the court in which the judge is sitting (and outside that jurisdiction but within the United States in the case of a mobile interception device authorized by a Federal court within such jurisdiction), if the judge determines on the basis of the facts submitted by the applicant that—

(a) there is probable cause for belief that an individual is committing, has committed, or is about to commit a particular offense enumerated in section 2516 of this chapter;

(b) there is probable cause for belief that particular communications concerning that offense will be obtained through such interception;

(c) normal investigative procedures have been tried and have failed or reasonably appear to be unlikely to succeed if tried or to be too dangerous;

(d) except as provided in subsection (11), there is probable cause for belief that the facilities from which, or the place where, the wire, oral, or electronic communications are to be intercepted are being used, or are about to be used, in connection with the commission of such offense, or are leased to, listed in the name of, or commonly used by such person.

(4) Each order authorizing or approving the interception of any wire, oral, or electronic communication under this chapter shall specify—

    (a) the identity of the person, if known, whose communications are to be intercepted;

    (b) the nature and location of the communications facilities as to which, or the place where, authority to intercept is granted;

    (c) a particular description of the type of communication sought to be intercepted, and a statement of the particular offense to which it relates;

    (d) the identity of the agency authorized to intercept the communications, and of the person authorizing the application; and

    (e) the period of time during which such interception is authorized, including a statement as to whether or not the interception shall automatically terminate when the described communication has been first obtained.

An order authorizing the interception of a wire, oral, or electronic communication under this chapter shall, upon request of the applicant, direct that a provider of wire or electronic communication service, landlord, custodian or other person shall furnish the applicant forthwith all information, facilities, and technical assistance necessary to accomplish the interception unobtrusively and with a minimum of interference with the services that such service provider, landlord, custodian, or person is according the person whose communications are to be intercepted. Any provider of wire or electronic communication service, landlord, custodian or other person furnishing such facilities or technical assistance shall be compensated therefor by the applicant for reasonable expenses incurred in providing such facilities or assistance. Pursuant to section 2522 of this chapter, an order may also be issued to enforce the assistance capability and capacity requirements under the Communications Assistance for Law Enforcement Act.

(5) No order entered under this section may authorize or approve the interception of any wire, oral, or electronic communication for any period longer than is necessary to achieve the objective of the authorization, nor in any event longer than thirty days. Such thirty-day period begins on the earlier of the day on which the investigative or law enforcement officer first begins to conduct an interception under the order or ten days after the order is entered. Extensions of an order may be granted, but only upon application for an extension made in accordance with subsection (1) of this section and the court making the findings required by subsection (3) of this

section. The period of extension shall be no longer than the authorizing judge deems necessary to achieve the purposes for which it was granted and in no event for longer than thirty days. Every order and extension thereof shall contain a provision that the authorization to intercept shall be executed as soon as practicable, shall be conducted in such a way as to minimize the interception of communications not otherwise subject to interception under this chapter, and must terminate upon attainment of the authorized objective, or in any event in thirty days. In the event the intercepted communication is in a code or foreign language, and an expert in that foreign language or code is not reasonably available during the interception period, minimization may be accomplished as soon as practicable after such interception. An interception under this chapter may be conducted in whole or in part by Government personnel, or by an individual operating under a contract with the Government, acting under the supervision of an investigative or law enforcement officer authorized to conduct the interception.

(6) Whenever an order authorizing interception is entered pursuant to this chapter, the order may require reports to be made to the judge who issued the order showing what progress has been made toward achievement of the authorized objective and the need for continued interception. Such reports shall be made at such intervals as the judge may require.

(7) Notwithstanding any other provision of this chapter, any investigative or law enforcement officer, specially designated by the Attorney General, the Deputy Attorney General, the Associate Attorney General, or by the principal prosecuting attorney of any State or subdivision thereof acting pursuant to a statute of that State, who reasonably determines that

(a) an emergency situation exists that involves—

(i) immediate danger of death or serious physical injury to any person,

(ii) conspiratorial activities threatening the national security interest, or

(iii) conspiratorial activities characteristic of organized crime, that requires a wire, oral, or electronic communication to be intercepted before an order authorizing such interception can, with due diligence, be obtained, and

(b) there are grounds upon which an order could be entered under this chapter to authorize such interception, may intercept such wire, oral, or electronic communication if an application for an order approving the interception is made in accordance with this section within forty-eight hours after the interception has occurred, or begins to occur. In the absence of an order, such interception shall immediately terminate when the communication sought is obtained or when the application for the order is denied, whichever is earlier. In the event such application for approval is denied, or in any other case where the interception is terminated without an order having been issued, the contents of any wire, oral, or electronic communication intercepted shall be treated as having been obtained in violation of this chapter, and an inventory shall be served as provided for in subsection (d) of this section on the person named in the application.

(8)   (a)   The contents of any wire, oral, or electronic communication intercepted by any means authorized by this chapter shall, if possible, be recorded on tape or wire or other comparable device. The recording of the contents of any wire, oral, or electronic communication under this subsection shall be done in such way as will protect the recording from editing or other alterations. Immediately upon the expiration of the period of the order, or extensions thereof, such recordings shall be made available to the judge issuing such order and sealed under his directions. Custody of the recordings shall be wherever the judge orders. They shall not be destroyed except upon an order of the issuing or denying judge and in any event shall be kept for ten years. Duplicate recordings may be made for use or disclosure pursuant to the provisions of subsections (1) and (2) of section 2517 of this chapter for investigations. The presence of the seal provided for by this subsection, or a satisfactory explanation for the absence thereof, shall be a prerequisite for the use or disclosure of the contents of any wire, oral, or electronic communication or evidence derived therefrom under subsection (3) of section 2517.

(b)   Applications made and orders granted under this chapter shall be sealed by the judge. Custody of the applications and orders shall be wherever the judge directs. Such applications and orders shall be disclosed only upon a showing of good cause before a judge of competent jurisdiction and shall not be destroyed except on order of the issuing or denying judge, and in any event shall be kept for ten years.

(c)   Any violation of the provisions of this subsection may be punished as contempt of the issuing or denying judge.

(d) Within a reasonable time but not later than ninety days after the filing of an application for an order of approval under section 2518(7)(b) which is denied or the termination of the period of an order or extensions thereof, the issuing or denying judge shall cause to be served, on the persons named in the order or the application, and such other parties to intercepted communications as the judge may determine in his discretion that is in the interest of justice, an inventory which shall include notice of—

(1) the fact of the entry of the order or the application;

(2) the date of the entry and the period of authorized, approved or disapproved interception, or the denial of the application; and

(3) the fact that during the period wire, oral, or electronic communications were or were not intercepted. The judge, upon the filing of a motion, may in his discretion make available to such person or his counsel for inspection such portions of the intercepted communications, applications and orders as the judge determines to be in the interest of justice. On an ex parte showing of good cause to a judge of competent jurisdiction the serving of the inventory required by this subsection may be postponed.

(9) The contents of any wire, oral, or electronic communication intercepted pursuant to this chapter or evidence derived therefrom shall not be received in evidence or otherwise disclosed in any trial, hearing, or other proceeding in a Federal or State court unless each party, not less than ten days before the trial, hearing, or proceeding, has been furnished with a copy of the court order, and accompanying application, under which the interception was authorized or approved. This ten-day period may be waived by the judge if he finds that it was not possible to furnish the party with the above information ten days before the trial, hearing, or proceeding and that the party will not be prejudiced by the delay in receiving such information.

(10) (a) Any aggrieved person in any trial, hearing, or proceeding in or before any court, department, officer, agency, regulatory body, or other authority of the United States, a State, or a political subdivision thereof, may move to suppress the contents of any wire or oral communication intercepted pursuant to this chapter, or evidence derived therefrom, on the grounds that—

(i) the communication was unlawfully intercepted;

(ii) the order of authorization or approval under which it was intercepted is insufficient on its face; or

(iii) the interception was not made in conformity with the order of authorization or approval.

Such motion shall be made before the trial, hearing, or proceeding unless there was no opportunity to make such motion or the person was not aware of the grounds of the motion. If the motion is granted, the contents of the intercepted wire or oral communication, or evidence derived therefrom, shall be treated as having been obtained in violation of this chapter. The judge, upon the filing of such motion by the aggrieved person, may in his discretion make available to the aggrieved person or his counsel for inspection such portions of the intercepted communication or evidence derived therefrom as the judge determines to be in the interests of justice.

(b) In addition to any other right to appeal, the United States shall have the right to appeal from an order granting a motion to suppress made under paragraph (a) of this subsection, or the denial of an application for an order of approval, if the United States attorney shall certify to the judge or other official granting such motion or denying such application that the appeal is not taken for purposes of delay. Such appeal shall be taken within thirty days after the date the order was entered and shall be diligently prosecuted.

(c) The remedies and sanctions described in this chapter with respect to the interception of electronic communications are the only judicial remedies and sanctions for nonconstitutional violations of this chapter involving such communications.

(11) The requirements of subsections (1)(b)(ii) and (3)(d) of this section relating to the specification of the facilities from which, or the place where, the communication is to be intercepted do not apply if—

(a) in the case of an application with respect to the interception of an oral communication—

(i) the application is by a Federal investigative or law enforcement officer and is approved by the Attorney General, the Deputy Attorney General, the Associate Attorney General, an Assistant Attorney General, or an acting Assistant Attorney General;

(ii) the application contains a full and complete statement as to why such specification is not practical and identifies the person committing the offense and whose communications are to be intercepted; and

   (iii) the judge finds that such specification is not practical; and

(b) in the case of an application with respect to a wire or electronic communication—

   (i) the application is by a Federal investigative or law enforcement officer and is approved by the Attorney General, the Deputy Attorney General, the Associate Attorney General, an Assistant Attorney General, or an acting Assistant Attorney General;

   (ii) the application identifies the person believed to be committing the offense and whose communications are to be intercepted and the applicant makes a showing that there is probable cause to believe that the person's actions could have the effect of thwarting interception from a specified facility;

   (iii) the judge finds that such showing has been adequately made; and

   (iv) the order authorizing or approving the interception is limited to interception only for such time as it is reasonable to presume that the person identified in the application is or was reasonably proximate to the instrument through which such communication will be or was transmitted.

(12) An interception of a communication under an order with respect to which the requirements of subsections (1)(b)(ii) and (3)(d) of this section do not apply by reason of subsection (11)(a) shall not begin until the place where the communication is to be intercepted is ascertained by the person implementing the interception order. A provider of wire or electronic communications service that has received an order as provided for in subsection (11)(b) may move the court to modify or quash the order on the ground that its assistance with respect to the interception cannot be performed in a timely or reasonable fashion. The court, upon notice to the government, shall decide such a motion expeditiously.

APPENDIX D
DEPARTMENT OF JUSTICE GUIDELINES
REGARDING THE USE OF CONFIDENTIAL INFORMANTS

January 8, 2001

TABLE OF CONTENTS

I. GENERAL PROVISIONS

A. PURPOSE AND SCOPE

1. The purpose of these Guidelines is to set policy regarding the use of Confidential Informants, as defined below, in criminal investigations and prosecutions by all Department of Justice Law Enforcement Agencies and Federal Prosecuting Offices, as defined below.

2. These Guidelines do not apply to the use of Cooperating Defendants/ Witnesses or Sources of Information, as defined below, unless a Department of Justice Law Enforcement Agency, in its discretion, chooses to apply these Guidelines to such persons.

3. These Guidelines are mandatory and supersede the Attorney General's Guidelines on the Use of Informants in Domestic Security, Organized Crime, and Other Criminal Investigations (December 15, 1976); the Attorney General's Guidelines on FBI Use of Informants and Confidential Sources (December 2, 1980); Resolution 18 of the Office of Investigative Agency Policies (August 15, 1996); and any other guidelines or policies that are inconsistent with these Guidelines. These Guidelines do not supersede otherwise applicable ethical obligations of Department of Justice attorneys, which can, in certain circumstances (for example, with respect to contacts with represented persons), have an impact on law enforcement agents' conduct.

4. These Guidelines do not limit the ability of a Department of Justice Law Enforcement Agency to impose additional restrictions on the use of Confidential Informants.

5. These Guidelines apply to the use of a Confidential Informant in a foreign country only to the extent that the Confidential Informant is reasonably likely to be called to testify in a domestic case.

6. These Guidelines do not apply to the use of Confidential Informants in foreign intelligence or foreign counterintelligence investigations.

B. DEFINITIONS

1. "Department of Justice Law Enforcement Agency" or "JLEA"—

   a. The Drug Enforcement Administration;

   b. The Federal Bureau of Investigation;

    c. The Immigration and Naturalization Service;

    d. The United States Marshals Service; and

    e. The Department of Justice Office of the Inspector General.

2. "Field Manager"—a JLEA's first-line supervisor, as defined by the JLEA (typically, GS-14 rank or higher).

3. "Senior Field Manager"—a JLEA's second-line supervisor, as defined by the JLEA (typically, GS-15 rank or higher).

4. "Federal Prosecuting Office" or "FPO"—

    a. The United States Attorneys' Offices;

    b. The Criminal Division, Tax Division, Civil Rights Division, Antitrust Division, and Environmental and Natural Resources Division of the Department of Justice; and

    c. Any other litigating component of the Department of Justice with authority to prosecute federal criminal offenses.

5. "Chief Federal Prosecutor"—the head of a FPO.

6. "Confidential Informant" or "CI"—any individual who provides useful and credible information to a JLEA regarding felonious criminal activities, and from whom the JLEA expects or intends to obtain additional useful and credible information regarding such activities in the future.

7. "Cooperating Defendant/Witness"—any individual who:

    a. meets the definition of a CI;

    b. has agreed to testify in a proceeding as a result of having provided information to the JLEA; and

    c. (i) is a defendant or potential witness who has a written agreement with a FPO, pursuant to which the individual has an expectation of future judicial or prosecutive consideration or assistance as a result of having provided information to the JLEA, or

       (ii) is a potential witness who has had a FPO concur in all material aspects of his or her use by the JLEA.

8. "Source of Information"—any individual who:

   a. meets the definition of a CI;

   b. provides information to a JLEA solely as a result of legitimate routine access to information or records, such as an employee of the military, a law enforcement agency, or a legitimate business (e.g., phone company, banks, airlines), and not as a result of criminal association with persons of investigative interest to the JLEA; and

   c. provides such information in a manner consistent with applicable law.

9. "High Level Confidential Informant"—a CI who is part of the senior leadership of an enterprise that

   a. has: (i) a national or international sphere of activities, or (ii) high significance to the JLEA's national objectives, even if the enterprise's sphere of activities is local or regional; and

   b. engages in, or uses others to commit, any of the conduct described below in paragraph (I)(B)(10)(b)(i)–(iv)

10. "Tier 1 Otherwise Illegal Activity"—any activity that:

    a. would constitute a misdemeanor or felony under federal, state, or local law if engaged in by a person acting without authorization; and

    b. that involves

       (i)   the commission or the significant risk of the commission, of any act of violence by a person or persons other than the Confidential Informant;[1]

       (ii) corrupt conduct, or the significant risk of corrupt conduct, by senior federal, state, or local public officials;

       (iii) the manufacturing, importing, exporting, possession, or trafficking of controlled substances in a quantity equal to or

---

[1] Bookmaking that is significantly associated with, or substantially controlled by, organized crime ordinarily will be within the scope of paragraph (I)(B)(10)(b)(i). Thus, for example, where bookmakers have a financial relationship with members or associates of organized crime, and/or use members or associates of organized crime to collect their debts, the conduct of those bookmakers would create a significant risk of violence, and would therefore fall within the definition of Tier 1 Otherwise Illegal Activity.

exceeding those quantities specified in United States Sentencing Guidelines § 2D1.1(c)(1);

(iv) financial loss, or the significant risk of financial loss, in an amount equal to or exceeding those amounts specified in United States Sentencing Guidelines § 2F1.1 (b)(1)(M);[2]

(v) a Confidential Informant providing to any person (other than a JLEA agent) any item, service, or expertise that is necessary for the commission of a federal, state, or local offense, which the person otherwise would have difficulty obtaining; or

(vi) a Confidential Informant providing to any person (other than a JLEA agent) any quantity of a controlled substance, with little or no expectation of its recovery by the JLEA.

11. "Tier 2 Otherwise Illegal Activity"—any other activity that would constitute a misdemeanor or felony under federal, state, or local law if engaged in by a person acting without authorization.

12. "Fugitive"—an individual:

a. for whom a federal, state, or local law enforcement agency has placed a wanted record in the NCIC (other than for a traffic or petty offense);

b. who is located either within the United States or in a country with which the United States has an extradition treaty; and

c. whom the law enforcement agency that has placed the wanted record in the NCIC is willing to take into custody upon his or her arrest and, if necessary, seek his or her extradition to its jurisdiction.

13. "Confidential Informant Review Committee" or "CIRC"—a committee, created by a JLEA for purposes of reviewing certain

---

[2] The citations to the United States Sentencing Guidelines (USSG) Manual are to the 2000 Edition. The references herein to particular USSG Sections are intended to remain applicable to the most closely corresponding USSG level in subsequent editions of the USSG Manual in the event that the cited USSG provisions are amended. Thus, it is intended that subsection (iii) of this paragraph will remain applicable to the highest offense level in the Drug Quantity Table in future editions of the USSG Manual, and that subsection (iv) of the paragraph will remain applicable to dollar amounts that, in future editions of the USSG Manual, trigger sentencing enhancements similar to that set forth in the current section 2F1.1(b)(1)(M). Any ambiguities in this regard should be resolved by the Assistant Attorney General for the Criminal Division.

decisions relating to the registration and utilization of CI's, the chair of which is a JLEA official at or above the level of Deputy Assistant Director (or its equivalent) and the membership of which includes the following two representatives designated by the Assistant Attorney General for the Criminal Division of the Department of Justice (each of whom shall be considered a "Criminal Division representative"): (i) a Deputy Assistant Attorney General for the Criminal Division; and (ii) an Assistant United States Attorney.

C. PROHIBITION ON COMMITMENTS OF IMMUNITY BY FEDERAL LAW ENFORCEMENT AGENCIES

A JLEA agent does not have any authority to make any promise or commitment that would prevent the government from prosecuting an individual for criminal activity that is not authorized pursuant to paragraph (III)(C) below, or that would limit the use of any evidence by the government, without the prior written approval of the FPO that has primary jurisdiction to prosecute the CI for such criminal activity. A JLEA agent must take the utmost care to avoid giving any person the erroneous impression that he or she has any such authority.

D. REVEALING A CONFIDENTIAL INFORMANT'S TRUE IDENTITY

Except in the case of approvals and reviews described below in paragraphs (II)(A)(3) (review of long-term CIs), (III)(B)(8) (coordination concerning payments to CIs), (IV)(D)(1) (notification that CI has obtained privileged information), and (V)(D) (coordination concerning deactivation of CI, but only with respect to a CI whose identity was not previously disclosed), whenever a JLEA is required to make contact of any kind with a FPO pursuant to these Guidelines regarding a CI, the JLEA may not withhold the true identity of the CI from the FPO.

E. DUTY OF CANDOR

Employees of the entities to which these Guidelines apply have a duty of candor in the discharge of their responsibilities pursuant to these Guidelines.

F. MAINTAINING CONFIDENTIALITY

1. A JLEA agent must take the utmost care to avoid conveying any confidential investigative information to a CI (e.g., information relating to electronic surveillance, search warrants, or the identity of other actual or potential informants), other than what is necessary and appropriate for operational reasons.

2. The Chief Federal Prosecutor and his or her designee are required to maintain as confidential the identity of any CI and the information the CI

has provided, unless obligated to disclose it by law or Court order. If a JLEA provides the Chief Federal Prosecutor or his or her designee with written material containing such information:

a. Such individual is obligated to keep it confidential by placing it into a locked file cabinet when not in his or her direct care and custody;

b. Access to the information shall be restricted to the Chief Federal Prosecutor or his or her designee and personnel deemed necessary to carry out the official duties related to the case;

c. The Chief Federal Prosecutor or his or her designee is responsible for assuring that each person permitted access to the information is made aware of the need to preserve the security and confidentiality of the information, as provided in this policy;

d. Prior to disclosure of the information to defense counsel or in open Court, the Chief Federal Prosecutor or his or her designee must give the JLEA an opportunity to discuss such disclosure and must comply with any other applicable provision of 28 C.F.R. §§ 16.21–16.29; and

e. At the conclusion of a case or investigation, all written materials containing the information that have not been disclosed shall be forwarded to the JLEA that provided them.[3]

3. Employees of a JLEA and employees of a FPO have a continuing obligation after leaving employment with the Department of Justice and its constituent components to maintain as confidential the identity of any CI and the information he or she provided, unless the employee is obligated to disclose it by law or Court order. See 28 C.F.R. §§ 16.21–16.29.

G. EXCEPTIONS AND DISPUTE RESOLUTION

1. Whenever any of the entities to which these Guidelines apply believes that an exception to any provision of these Guidelines is justified, or whenever there is a dispute between or among any such entities (other than a dispute with the Criminal Division of the Department of Justice) regarding these Guidelines, an exception must be sought from, or the

---

[3] This requirement shall not prevent the Chief Federal Prosecutor or his or her designee from keeping in the relevant case file materials such as motions, responses, legal memoranda, Court orders, and internal office memoranda and correspondence. If any such materials contain information revealing a CI's true identity, the Chief Federal Prosecutor or his or her designee shall maintain the materials in accordance with the provisions of paragraph I (F)(2)(a)–(d), above.

dispute shall be resolved by, the Assistant Attorney General (AAG) for the Criminal Division or his or her designee. The Deputy Attorney General or his or her designee shall hear appeals, if any, from decisions of the AAG.

2. Whenever there is a dispute between the Criminal Division and any of the other entities to which these Guidelines apply, such dispute shall be resolved by the Deputy Attorney General or his or her designee.

3. Any exception granted or dispute resolved pursuant to this paragraph shall be documented in the JLEA's files.

H. RIGHTS OF THIRD PARTIES

Nothing in these Guidelines is intended to create or does create an enforceable legal right or private right of action by a CI or any other person.

I. COMPLIANCE

1. Within 120 days of the approval of these Guidelines by the Attorney General, each JLEA shall develop agency-specific guidelines that comply with these Guidelines, and submit such agency-specific guidelines to the AAG for the Criminal Division for review. The agency-specific guidelines must ensure, at a minimum, that the JLEA's agents receive sufficient initial and in-service training in the use of CIs consistent with these Guidelines, and that compliance with these Guidelines is considered in the annual performance appraisal of its agents. As part of such compliance the JLEA shall designate a senior official to oversee all aspects of its CI program, including the training of agents; registration, review and termination of CIs; and notifications to outside entities.

2. Within 30 days of the approval of these Guidelines, each JLEA shall establish a Confidential Informant Review Committee (CIRC) for the purpose of conducting the review procedures specified in paragraphs (II) (A) (3), (II) (D) (1), and (II) (D) (2).

II. REGISTERING A CONFIDENTIAL INFORMANT

A. SUITABILITY DETERMINATION

1. Initial Suitability Determination

Prior to utilizing a person as a CI, a case agent of a JLEA shall complete and sign a written Initial Suitability Report and Recommendation, which shall be forwarded to a Field Manager for his or her written approval. In completing the Initial, Suitability Report and Recommendation, the case agent must x. address the following factors (or indicate that a particular factor is not applicable):

a. the person's age;

b. the person's alien status;

c. whether the person is a public official, law enforcement officer, union official, employee of a financial institution or school, member of the military services, a representative or affiliate of the media, or a party to, or in a position to be a party to, privileged communications (e.g., a member of the clergy, a physician, or a lawyer);

d. the extent to which the person would make use of his or her affiliations with legitimate organizations in order to provide information or assistance to the JLEA, and the ability of the JLEA to ensure that the person's information or assistance is limited to criminal matters;

e. the extent to which the person's information or assistance would be relevant to a present or potential investigation or prosecution and the importance of such investigation or prosecution;

f. the nature of any relationship between the CI and the subject or target of an existing or potential investigation or prosecution, including but not limited to a current or former spousal relationship or other family tie, and any current or former employment or financial relationship;

g. the person's motivation in providing information or assistance, including any consideration sought from the government for this assistance;

h. the risk that the person might adversely affect a present or potential investigation or prosecution;

i. the extent to which the person's information or assistance can be corroborated;

j. the person's reliability and truthfulness;

k. the person's prior record as a witness in any proceeding;

l. whether the person has a criminal history, is reasonably believed to be the subject or target of a pending criminal investigation, is under arrest, or has been charged in a pending prosecution;

m. whether the person is reasonably believed to pose a danger to the public or other criminal threat, or is reasonably believed to pose a risk of flight;

n. whether the person is a substance abuser or has a history of substance abuse;

o. whether the person is a relative of an employee of any law enforcement agency;

p. the risk of physical harm that may occur to the person or his or her immediate family or close associates as a result of providing information or assistance to the JLEA; and

q. the record of the JLEA and the record of any other law enforcement agency (if available to the JLEA) regarding the person's prior or current service as a CI, Cooperating Defendant/Witness, or Source of Information, including, but not limited to, any information regarding whether the person was at any time terminated for cause.

2. Continuing Suitability Review

a. Each CI's file shall be reviewed by the case agent at least annually. The case agent shall complete and sign a written Continuing Suitability Report and Recommendation, which shall be forwarded to a Field Manager for his or her written approval. In completing the Continuing Suitability Report and Recommendation, the case agent must address the factors set forth above in paragraph (II)(A)(1) (or indicate that a particular factor is not applicable) and, in addition, the length of time that the individual has been registered as a CI and the length of time that the individual has been handled by the same agent or agents.

b. Each JLEA shall establish systems to ensure that all available information that might materially alter a prior suitability determination, including, but not limited to, information pertaining to unauthorized illegal activity by the CI, is promptly reported to a Field Manager and then recorded and maintained in the CI's file. See (IV)(B)(2) below. Upon receipt of any such information, the Field Manager shall ensure that a new Continuing Suitability Report and Recommendation is promptly prepared in light of such new information.

3. Review of Long-Term Confidential Informants[4]

a. When a CI has been registered for more than six consecutive years, and, to the extent such a CI remains open, every six years thereafter, the CIRC shall review the CI's completed Initial and Continuing Suitability Reports and Recommendations and decide whether, and under what conditions, the individual should continue to be utilized as a CI. A Criminal Division representative on the CIRC who disagrees with the decision to approve the continued use of such an individual as a Confidential Informant may seek review of that decision pursuant to paragraph (I)(G).

b. Every three years after a CI's file is reviewed pursuant to the provisions of paragraph (II)(A)(3)(a), if the CI remains registered, the Agency shall conduct an internal review, including review by a designated senior headquarters official, of the CI's completed Initial and Continuing Suitability Reports and Recommendations. If the designated senior headquarters official decides that there are any apparent or potential problems that may warrant any change in the use of the CI, the official shall (i) consult the appropriate Senior Field Manager and (ii) provide the Initial and Continuing Suitability Reports and Recommendations to the CIRC for review in accord with paragraph (II)(A)(3)(a).

B. REGISTRATION

After a Field Manager has approved an individual as suitable to be a CI, the individual shall be registered with that JLEA as a CI. In registering a CI, the JLEA shall, at a minimum, document or include the following in the CI's files:

1. a photograph of the CI;

2. the JLEA's efforts to establish the CI's true identity;

3. the results of a criminal history check for the CI;

4. the Initial Suitability Report and Recommendation;

---

[4] This provision does not apply until one year after the effective date of these Guidelines, when the first set of Continuing Suitability Reports and Recommendations are completed. Further, during the first three years that this provision is in effect, each CIRC may stagger the review of some long-term CIs in order to even out the number of files that must initially be reviewed. However, no later than four years after the effective date of these Guidelines, all of the CIs who have been registered for more than six consecutive years as of the effective date of these Guidelines must be reviewed pursuant to this provision.

5. any promises or benefits, and the terms of such promises or benefits, that are given a CI by a JLEA or any other law enforcement agency (if available to the JLEA);

6. any promises or benefits, and the terms of such promises or benefits, that are given a CI by any FPO or any state or local prosecuting office (if available to the JLEA); and

7. all information that is required to be documented in the CI's files pursuant to these Guidelines (e.g., the provision of the instructions set forth in the next paragraph).

C. INSTRUCTIONS

1. In registering a CI, at least one agent of the JLEA, along with one additional agent or other law enforcement official present as a witness, shall read verbatim the following instructions:

    a. you must provide truthful information to the [JLEA] at all times;

    b. your assistance and the statements you make to the [JLEA] are entirely voluntary;

    c. the United States Government will strive to protect your identity, but cannot promise or guarantee either that your identity will not be divulged as a result of legal or other compelling considerations, or that you will not be called to testify in a proceeding as a witness;

    d. the [JLEA] on its own cannot promise or agree to any consideration by a Federal Prosecutor's Office or a Court in exchange for your cooperation, since the decision to confer any such benefit lies within the exclusive discretion of the Federal Prosecutor's Office and the Court. However, the [JLEA] will consider (but not necessarily act upon) a request by you to advise the appropriate Federal Prosecutor's Office or Court of the nature and extent of your assistance to the [JLEA];

    e. you have no immunity or protection from investigation, arrest or prosecution for anything you say or do, and the [JLEA] cannot promise or agree to such immunity or protection, unless and until you have been granted such immunity or protection in writing by a United States Attorney or his or her designee; and

    f. you have not been authorized to engage in any criminal activity and could be prosecuted for any unauthorized criminal activity in which you have engaged or engage in the future.[5]

2. The agent shall also contemporaneously review with the CI written instructions that state, at a minimum, that:

    a. the CI must abide by the instructions of the JLEA and must not take or seek to take any independent action on behalf of the United States Government;

    b. the CI is not an employee of the United States Government and may not represent himself or herself as such;

    c. the CI may not enter into any contract or incur any obligation on behalf of the United States Government, except as specifically instructed and approved by the JLEA;

    d. the JLEA cannot guarantee any rewards, payments, or other compensation to the CI;

    e. in the event that the CI receives any rewards, payments, or other compensation from the JLEA, the CI is liable for any taxes that may be owed; and

    f. no premises or commitments can be made, except by the Immigration and Naturalization Service, regarding the alien status of any person or the right of any person to enter or remain in the United States.

3. Immediately after these instructions have been given, the agent shall ensure that the CI acknowledges and understands them. The agent shall decide whether to require the CI to sign or initial, and date, a written acknowledgment of the instructions.[6] If, for operational reasons, the agent decides against requiring the CI to sign or initial a written acknowledgment, the agent and the other law enforcement official shall document that the instructions in paragraph 1(a)–(f) above were read

---

[5] This instruction should be provided to any CI who is not authorized to engage in otherwise illegal activity. See paragraph (III)(C)(4) for instructions that must be provided to a CI who is, in fact, authorized to engage in otherwise illegal conduct.

[6] The CI may sign or initial the written acknowledgment by using a pseudonym which has been previously approved and documented in the CI's files and designated for use by only one CI.

verbatim to the CI, and that the remaining instructions were also communicated to the CI, and that the CI orally acknowledged the instructions. In either case, as soon as practicable thereafter, a Field Manager shall review and, if warranted, approve the documentation.

4. These instruction and documentation procedures shall be repeated whenever it appears necessary or prudent to do so, and in any event at least every twelve months.

D. SPECIAL APPROVAL REQUIREMENTS

1. High Level Confidential Informants

a. Prior to utilizing an individual as a High Level Confidential Informant, a case agent of a JLEA shall first obtain the written approval of the CIRC. A Criminal Division representative on the CIRC who disagrees with a decision to approve the use of an individual as a High Level Confidential Informant may seek review of that decision pursuant to paragraph (I) (G).

b. In deciding whether to approve the use of a High Level Confidential Informant, the CIRC shall have access to any Initial or Completed Suitability Reports and Recommendations for the individual in question.

c. After a final decision has been made to approve the use of a High Level Confidential Informant, the CIRC shall consider whether to notify the Chief Federal Prosecutor of any FPO that is participating in the conduct of an investigation that is, or would be, utilizing the High Level Confidential Informant, or any FPO that has been, or would be, working with that individual in connection with a prosecution, of the decision to approve that individual as a High Level Confidential Informant. If the CIRC determines that no such notification shall be made, the reason or reasons for the determination shall be provided to the Criminal Division representatives on the CIRC. A Criminal Division representative on the CIRC who disagrees with a decision not to provide such notification may seek review of that decision pursuant to paragraph (I)(G).

2. Individuals Under the Obligation of a Legal Privilege of Confidentiality or Affiliated with the Media

a. Prior to utilizing as a Confidential Informant an individual who is under the obligation of a legal privilege of confidentiality or affiliated with the media, a case agent of a JLEA shall first obtain the written approval of the CIRC. A Criminal Division representative on the CIRC who disagrees with a decision to approve the use of such an individual as a Confidential Informant may seek review of that decision pursuant to paragraph (I)(G).

b. In deciding whether to approve the use as a Confidential Informant of an individual who is under the obligation of a legal privilege of confidentiality or affiliated with the media, the CIRC shall have access to any Initial or Completed Suitability Reports and Recommendations for the individual in question.

c. After a final decision has been made to approve the use of an individual who is under the obligation of a legal privilege of confidentiality or affiliated with the media as a Confidential Informant, the CIRC shall consider whether to notify the Chief Federal Prosecutor of any FPO that is participating in the conduct of an investigation that is, or would be, utilizing the individual, or any FPO that has been, or would be, working with that individual in connection with a prosecution, of the decision to approve that individual as a Confidential Informant. If the CIRC determines that no such notification shall be made, the reason or reasons for the determination shall be provided to the Criminal Division representatives on the CIRC. A Criminal Division representative on the CIRC who disagrees with a decision not to provide such notification may seek review of that decision pursuant to paragraph (I)(G).

3. **Federal Prisoners, Probationers, Parolees, Detainees, and Supervised Releasees**

a. Consistent with extant Department of Justice requirements, a JLEA must receive the approval of the Criminal Division's Office of Enforcement Operations ("OEO") prior to utilizing as a CI an individual who is in the custody of the United States Marshals Service or the Bureau of Prisons, or who is under Bureau of Prisons supervision. See U.S.A.M. § 9-21.050.

b. Prior to utilizing a federal probationer, parolee, or supervised releasee as a CI, a Field Manager of a JLEA shall determine if the use of that person in such a capacity would violate the terms and conditions of the person's probation, parole, or supervised release. If the Field Manager has reason to believe that it would violate such terms and conditions, prior to using the person as a CI, the Field Manager or his or her designee must obtain the permission of a federal probation, parole, or supervised release official with authority to grant such permission, which permission shall be documented in the CI's files. If such permission is denied or it is inappropriate for operational reasons to contact the appropriate federal official, the JLEA may seek to obtain authorization for the use of such individual as a CI from the Court then responsible for the individual's probation, parole, or supervised release, provided that the JLEA first consults with the FPO for that District.

c. In situations where a FPO is either participating in the conduct of an investigation by a JLEA in which a federal probationer, parolee, or supervised releasee would be utilized as a CI, or where a FPO would be working with a federal probationer, parolee, or supervised releasee in connection with a prosecution, the JLEA shall notify the attorney assigned to the matter prior to using the person as a CI.

4. Current or Former Participants in the Witness Security Program

a. Consistent with extant Department of Justice requirements, a JLEA must receive the approval of OEO and the sponsoring prosecutor (or his or her successor) prior to utilizing as a CI a current or former participant in the Federal Witness Security Program, provided further that the OEO will coordinate such matters with the United States Marshals Service. See U.S. A.M. § 9-21.800.

b. In situations where a FPO is either participating in the conduct of an investigation by a JLEA in which a current or former participant in the Witness Security Program would be utilized as a CI, or where a FPO would be working with a current or former participant in the Witness Security Program in connection with a prosecution, the JLEA shall notify the attorney assigned to the matter prior to using the person as a CI.

5. State or Local Prisoners, Probationers, Parolees, or Supervised Releasees

a. Prior to utilizing a state or local prisoner, probationer, parolee, or supervised releasee as a CI, a Field Manager of a JLEA shall determine if the use of that person in such a capacity would violate the terms and conditions of the person's incarceration, probation, parole, or supervised release. If the Field Manger has reason to believe that it would violate such terms and conditions, prior to using the person as a CI, the Field Manager or his or her designee must obtain the permission of a state or local prison, probation, parole, or supervised release official with authority to grant such permission, which permission shall be documented in the CI's files. If such permission is denied or it is inappropriate for operational reasons to contact the appropriate state or local official, the JLEA may seek to obtain authorization for the use of such individual as a CI from the state or local Court then responsible for the individual's incarceration, probation, parole, or supervised release.

b. In situations where a FPO is either participating in the conduct of an investigation by a JLEA in which a state or local prisoner, probationer, parolee, or supervised releasee would be utilized as a CI, or where a FPO would be working with a state or local prisoner, probationer, parolee, or supervised releasee in connection with a prosecution, the JLEA shall notify the attorney assigned to the matter prior to using the person as a CI.

6. Fugitives

a. Except as provided below, a JLEA shall have no communication with a current or former CI who is a fugitive.

b. A JLEA is permitted to have communication with a current or former CI who is a fugitive:

   (i) if the communication is part of a legitimate effort by that JLEA to arrest the fugitive; or

   (ii) if approved, in advance whenever possible, by a Senior Field Manager of any federal, state, or local law enforcement agency that has a wanted record for the individual in the NCIC and, in the case of a federal warrant, by the FPO for the issuing District.

c. A JLEA that has communication with a fugitive must promptly report such, communication to all federal, state, and local law enforcement agencies and other law enforcement agencies having a wanted record for the individual in the NCIC, and document those communications in the CI's files.

III. RESPONSIBILITIES REGARDING REGISTERED CONFIDENTIAL INFORMANTS

A. GENERAL PROVISIONS

1. No Interference With an Investigation of a Confidential Informant

A JLEA agent must take the utmost care to avoid interfering with or impeding any criminal investigation or arrest of a CI. No agent shall reveal to a CI any information relating to an investigation of the CI. An agent shall not confirm or deny the existence of any investigation of the CI, unless authorized to do so by the Chief Federal Prosecutor; nor shall an agent agree to a request from a CI to determine whether the CI is the subject of any investigation.

2. Prohibited Transactions and Relationships

a. A JLEA agent shall not: (i) exchange gifts with a CI; (ii) provide the CI with any thing of more than nominal value; (iii) receive any thing of more than nominal value from a CI; or (iv) engage in any business or financial transactions with a CI. Except as authorized pursuant to paragraph (III)(B) below, any exception to this provision requires the written approval of a Field Manager, in advance whenever possible, based on a written finding by the Field Manager that the event or transaction in question is necessary and appropriate for operational reasons. This written finding shall be maintained in the CI's files.

b. A Federal Law Enforcement agent shall not socialize with a CI except to the extent necessary and appropriate for operational reasons.

c. In situations where a FPO is either participating in the conduct of an investigation by a JLEA that is utilizing a CI, or working with a CI in connection with a prosecution, the JLEA shall notify the attorney assigned to the matter, in advance whenever possible, if the JLEA approves an exception under paragraph (III)(A)(2)(a) or if a Federal Law Enforcement aunt socializes with a CI in a manner not permitted under paragraph (III)(A)(2)(b).

B. MONETARY PAYMENTS

1. General

Monies that a JLEA pays to a CI in the form of fees and rewards, shall be commensurate with the value, as determined by the JLEA, of the information he or she provided or the assistance he or she rendered to that JLEA. A JLEA's reimbursement of expenses incurred by a CI shall be based upon actual expenses incurred.

2. Prohibition Against Contingent Payments

Under no circumstances shall any payments to a CI be contingent upon the conviction or punishment of any individual.

3. Approval for a Single Payment

A single payment of between $2,500 and $25,000 per case to a CI must be authorized, at a minimum, by a JLEA's Senior Field Manager. A single payment in excess of $25,000 per case shall be made only with the authorization of the Senior Field Manager and the express approval of a designated senior headquarters official.

4. Approval for Annual Payments

Consistent with paragraph (III)(B)(3) above, payments by a JLEA to a CI that exceed an aggregate of $100,000 within a one-year period, as that period is defined by the JLEA, shall be made only with the authorization of the Senior Field Manager and the express approval of a designated senior headquarters official. The headquarters official may authorize additional aggregate annual payments in increments of $50,000 or less.

5. Approval for Aggregate Payments

Consistent with paragraphs (III)(B)(3)(4), and regardless of the time frame, any payments by a JLEA to a CI that exceed an aggregate of $200,000 shall be made only with the authorization of the Senior Field Manager and the express approval of a designated senior headquarters official. After the headquarters official has approved payments to a CI that exceed an aggregate of $200,000, the headquarters official may authorize, subject to paragraph (III)(B)(4) above, additional aggregate payments in increments of $100,000 or less.

6. Documentation of Payment

The payment of any monies to a CI shall be witnessed by at least two law enforcement representatives. Immediately after receiving a payment, the CI shall be required to sign or initial, and date, a written receipt.[7] At the time of the payment, the representatives shall advise the CI that the monies may be taxable income that must be reported to appropriate tax authorities. Thereafter, those representatives shall document the payment and the advice of taxability in the JLEA's files. The documentation of payment shall specify whether the payment is for information, services, or expenses.

7. Accounting and Reconciliation Procedures

Each JLEA shall establish accounting and reconciliation procedures to comply with these Guidelines. Among other things, these procedures shall

---

[7] The CI may sign or initial the written receipt by using a pseudonym which has been previously approved and documented in the CI's files and designated for use by only one CI.

reflect all monies paid to a CI subsequent to the issuance of these Guidelines.

8. Coordination with Prosecution

In situations where a FPO is either participating in the conduct of an investigation by a JLEA that is utilizing a CI, or working with a CI in connection with a prosecution, the JLEA shall coordinate with the attorney assigned to the matter, in advance whenever possible, the payment of monies to the CI pursuant to paragraphs (III)(B)(3)–(5) above.

C. AUTHORIZATION OF OTHERWISE ILLEGAL ACTIVITY

1. General Provisions

a. A JLEA shall not authorize a CI to engage, in any activity that otherwise would constitute a misdemeanor or felony under federal, state, or local law if engaged in by a person acting without authorization, except as provided in the authorization provisions in paragraph (III)(C)(2) below.

b. A JLEA is never permitted to authorize a CI to:

(i)   participate in an act of violence;

(ii) participate in an act that constitutes obstruction of justice (e.g., perjury, witness tampering, witness intimidation, entrapment, or the fabrication, alteration, or destruction of evidence);

(iii) participate in an act designed to obtain information for the JLEA that would be unlawful if conducted by a law enforcement agent (e.g., breaking and entering, illegal wiretapping, illegal opening or tampering with the mail, or trespass amounting to an illegal search); or

(iv) initiate or instigate a plan or strategy to commit a federal, state, or local offense.

2. Authorization

a. Tier 1 Otherwise Illegal Activity must be authorized in advance and in writing for a specified period, not to exceed 90 days, by:

(i)   a JLEA's Special Agent in Charge (or the equivalent); and

(ii) the appropriate Chief Federal Prosecutor.[8]

b. Tier 2 Otherwise Illegal Activity must be authorized in advance and in writing for a specified period, not to exceed 90 days, by a JLEA's Senior Field Manager.

c. For purposes of this paragraph, the "appropriate Chief Federal Prosecutor" is the Chief Federal Prosecutor that: (i) is participating in the conduct of an investigation by a JLEA that is utilizing that active CI, or is working with that active CI in connection with a prosecution; (ii) with respect to Otherwise Illegal Activity that would constitute a violation of federal law, would have primary jurisdiction to prosecute the Otherwise Illegal Activity; or (iii) with respect to Otherwise Illegal Activity that would constitute a violation only of state or local law, is located where the otherwise criminal activity is to occur.

3. Findings

a. The JLEA official who authorizes Tier 1 or 2 Otherwise Illegal Activity must make a finding, which shall be documented in the CI's files, that authorization for the CI to engage in the Tier 1 or 2 Otherwise Illegal Activity is

   (i) necessary either to

   (A) obtain information or evidence essential for the success of an investigation that is not reasonably available without such authorization, or

   (B) prevent death, serious bodily injury, or significant damage to property; and

   (ii) that in either case the benefits to be obtained from the CI's participation in the Tier 1 or 2 Otherwise Illegal Activity outweigh the risks.

b. In making these findings, the JLEA shall consider, among other things:

---

[8] Even without an express act of Congress authorizing the conduct at issue, it is within the power and the duty of federal prosecutors, as executive branch officers, to take reasonable measures to discharge the duties imposed on them as executive branch officers, and they will be immune from state action if they take such measures under color of federal law and in good faith.

(i)   the importance of the investigation;

(ii) the likelihood that the information or evidence sought will be
      obtained;

(iii) the risk that the CI might misunderstand or exceed the scope of
      his authorization;

(iv) the extent of the CI's participation in the Otherwise Illegal
      Activity;

(v)   the risk that the JLEA will not be able to supervise closely the CI's
      participation in the Otherwise Illegal Activity;

(vi) the risk of violence, physical injury, property damage, and
      financial loss to the CI or others; and

(vii) the risk that the JLEA will not be able to ensure that the CI does
      not profit from his or her participation in the authorized
      Otherwise Illegal Activity.

4. Instructions

a. After a CI is authorized to engage in Tier 1 or 2 Otherwise Illegal
    Activity, at least one agent of the JLEA, along with one additional
    agent or other law enforcement official present as a witness, shall
    review with the CI written instructions that state, at a minimum,
    that:

    (i)   the CI is authorized only to engage in the specific conduct set
          forth in the written authorization described above and not in any
          other illegal activity;

    (ii) the CI's authorization is limited to the time period specified in the
          written authorization;

    (iii) under no circumstance may the CI:

          (A) participate in an act of violence;

          (B) participate in an act that constitutes obstruction of justice
               (e.g., perjury, witness tampering, witness intimidation,
               entrapment, or the fabrication, alteration, or destruction of
               evidence);

(C) participate in an act designed to obtain information for the JLEA that would be unlawful if conducted by a law enforcement agent (e.g., breaking and entering, illegal wiretapping, illegal opening or tampering with the mail, or trespass amounting to an illegal search); or

(D) initiate or instigate a plan or strategy to commit a federal, state, or local offense;

(iv) if the CI is asked by any person to participate in any such prohibited conduct, or if he or she learns of plans to engage in such conduct, he or she must immediately report the matter to his or her contact agent; and

(v) participation in any prohibited conduct could subject the CI to full criminal prosecution.

b. Immediately after these instructions have been given, the CI shall be required to sign or initial, and date, a written acknowledgment of the instructions.[9] As soon as practicable thereafter, a Field Manager shall review and, if warranted, approve the written acknowledgment.

5. Precautionary Measures

Whenever a JLEA has authorized a CI to engage in Tier 1 or 2 Otherwise Illegal Activity, it must take all reasonable steps to: (a) supervise closely the illegal activities of the CI; (b) minimize the adverse effect of the authorized Otherwise Illegal Activity on innocent individuals; and (c) ensure that the CI does not profit from his or her participation in the authorized Otherwise Illegal Activity.

6. Suspension of Authorization

Whenever a JLEA cannot, for legitimate reasons unrelated to the CI's conduct (e.g., unavailability of the case agent), comply with the precautionary measures described above, it shall immediately: (a) suspend the CI's authorization to engage in Otherwise illegal Activity until such time as the precautionary measures can be complied with; (b) inform the CI that his or her authorization to engage in any Otherwise Illegal Activity has been suspended until that time; and (c) document these actions in the CI's files.

---

[9] The CI may sign or initial the written acknowledgment by using a pseudonym which has been previously approved and documented in the CI's files and designated for use by only one CI.

7. Revocation of Authorization

a. If a JLEA has reason to believe that a CI has failed to comply with the specific terms of the authorization of Tier 1 or 2 Otherwise Illegal Activity, it shall immediately: (i) revoke the CI's authorization to engage in Otherwise Illegal Activity; (ii) inform the CI that he or she is no longer authorized to engage in any Otherwise Illegal Activity; (iii) comply with the notification requirement of paragraph (IV)(B) below; (iv) make a determination whether the CI should be deactivated pursuant to paragraph (V); and (v) document these actions in the CI's files.

b. Immediately after the CI has been informed that he or she is no longer authorized to engage in any Otherwise Illegal Activity, the CI shall be required to sign or initial; and date, a written acknowledgment that he or she has been informed of this fact.[10] As soon as practicable thereafter, a Field Manager shall review and, if warranted, approve the written acknowledgment.

8. Renewal and Expansion of Authorization

a. A JLEA that seeks to re-authorize any CI to engage in Tier 1 or 2 Otherwise Illegal Activity after the expiration of the authorized time period, or after revocation of authorization, must first comply with the procedures set forth above in paragraphs in (III)(C)(2)—(5).

b. JLEA that seeks to expand in any material way a CI's authorization to engage in Tier 1 or 2 Otherwise Illegal Activity by the JLEA must first comply with the procedures set forth above in paragraphs (III)(C)(2)–(5).

9. Emergency Authorization

a. In exceptional circumstances, a JLEA's Special Agent in Charge (or the equivalent) and the appropriate Chief Federal Prosecutor may orally authorize a CI to engage in Tier 1 Otherwise Illegal Activity without complying with the documentation requirements of paragraphs

---

[10] The CI may sign or initial the written acknowledgment by using a pseudonym which has been previously approved and documented in the CI's files and designated for use by only one CI. If the CI refuses to sign or initial the written acknowledgment, the JLEA agent who informed the CI of the revocation of authorization shall document that the CI has orally acknowledged being so informed and the Field Manager shall, as soon as practicable thereafter, review and, if warranted, approve the written documentation.

(III)(C)(2)–(4) above when they each determine that a highly significant and unanticipated investigative opportunity would be lost were the time taken to comply with these requirements. In such an event, the documentation requirements, as well as a written justification for the oral authorization, shall be completed within 48 hours of the oral approval and maintained in the CI's files.

b. In exceptional circumstances, a JLEA's Senior Field Manager may orally authorize a CI to engage in Tier 2 Otherwise Illegal Activity without complying with the documentation requirements of paragraphs (III)(C)(2)–(4) above when he or she determines that a highly significant and unanticipated investigative opportunity would be lost were the time taken to comply with these requirements. In such an event, the documentation requirements, as well as a written justification for the oral authorization, shall be completed within 48 hours of the oral approval and maintained in the CI's files.

10. Designees

A JLEA's Special Agent in Charge (or the equivalent) and the appropriate Chief Federal Prosecutor may, with the concurrence of each other, agree to designate particular individuals in their respective offices to carry out the approval functions assigned to them above in paragraphs (III)(C)(2)–(9).

D. LISTING A CONFIDENTIAL INFORMANT IN AN ELECTRONIC SURVEILLANCE APPLICATION

1. A JLEA shall not name a CI as a named interceptee or a violator in an affidavit in support of an application made, pursuant to 18 U.S.C. § 2516 for an electronic surveillance order unless the JLEA believes that: (a) omitting the name of the CI from the affidavit would endanger that person's life or otherwise jeopardize an ongoing investigation; or (b) the CI is a bona fide subject of the investigation based on his or her suspected involvement in unauthorized criminal activity.

2. In the event that a CI is named in an electronic surveillance affidavit under paragraph (III)(D)(1) above, the JLEA must inform the Federal prosecutor making the application and the Court to which the application is made of the actual status of the CI.

IV. SPECIAL NOTIFICATION REQUIREMENTS

A. NOTIFICATION OF INVESTIGATION OR PROSECUTION

1. When a JLEA has reasonable grounds to believe that a current or former CI is being prosecuted by, is the target of an investigation by, or is expected to become a target of an investigation by a FPO for engaging in alleged felonious criminal activity, a Special Agent in Charge (or the equivalent) of the JLEA must immediately notify the Chief Federal Prosecutor of that individual's status as a current or former CI.[11]

2. Whenever such a notification is provided, the Chief Federal Prosecutor and Special Agent in Charge (or the equivalent), with the concurrence of each other, shall notify any other federal, state or local prosecutor's offices or law enforcement agencies that are participating in the investigation or prosecution of the CI.

B. NOTIFICATION OF UNAUTHORIZED ILLEGAL ACTIVITY

1. Whenever a JLEA has reasonable grounds to believe that a CI who is currently authorized to engage in specific Tier 1 or 2 Otherwise Illegal Activity has engaged in unauthorized criminal activity, or whenever a JLEA knows that a CI who has no current authorization to engage in any Tier 1 or 2 Otherwise Illegal Activity has engaged in any criminal activity, a Special Agent in Charge of the JLEA (or the equivalent) shall immediately notify the following Chief Federal Prosecutors of the CI's criminal activity and his or her status as a CI:

   a. the Chief Federal Prosecutor whose District is located where the criminal activity primarily occurred, unless a state or local prosecuting office in that District has filed charges against the CI for the criminal activity and there clearly is no basis for federal prosecution in that District by the Chief Federal Prosecutor;

   b. the Chief Federal Prosecutor, if any, whose District is participating in the conduct of an investigation that is utilizing that active CI, or is working with that active CI in connection with a prosecution; and

---

[11] A target is "a person as to whom the prosecutor or the grand jury has substantial evidence linking him or her to the commission of a crime and who, in the judgment of the prosecutor, is a putative defendant." United States Attorney's Manual § 9-11.151.

   c. the Chief Federal Prosecutor, if any, who authorized the CI to engage in Tier 1 Otherwise Illegal Activity pursuant to paragraph (III) (C) (2) (a) above.[12]

2. Whenever such notifications are provided, the Chief Federal Prosecutor(s) of the FPOs and the Special Agent in Charge (or the equivalent), with the concurrence of each other, shall notify any state or local prosecutor's office that has jurisdiction over the CI's criminal activity, and that has not already filed charges against the CI for the criminal activity, of the fact that the CI has engaged in such criminal activity. The Chief Federal Prosecutor(s) and the Special Agent in Charge (or the equivalent) are not required, but may with the concurrence of each other, also notify the state and local prosecutor's office of the person's status as a CI.

C. NOTIFICATION REGARDING CERTAIN FEDERAL JUDICIAL PROCEEDINGS

Whenever a JLEA has reasonable grounds to believe that: (1) a current or former CI has been called to testify by the prosecution in any federal grand jury or judicial proceeding; (2) the statements of a current or former CI have been, or will be, utilized by the prosecution in any federal judicial proceeding; or (3) a federal prosecutor intends to represent to a Court or jury that a current or former CI is or was a coconspirator or other criminally culpable participant in any criminal activity, a Special Agent in Charge (or the equivalent) of the JLEA shall immediately notify the Chief Federal Prosecutor for that proceeding of the individual's status as a current or former CI.

D. PRIVILEGED OR EXCULPATORY INFORMATION

1. In situations where a FPO is either participating in the conduct of an investigation by a JLEA that is utilizing a CI, or working with a CI in connection with a prosecution, the JLEA shall notify the attorney assigned to the matter, in advance whenever possible, if the JLEA has reasonable grounds to believe that a CI will obtain or provide information that is subject to, or arguably subject to, a legal privilege of confidentiality belonging to someone other than the CI.

2. If the JLEA has reasonable grounds to believe that a current or former CI has information that is exculpatory as to a person who is expected to

---

[12] Whenever such notifications to FPOs are provided, the JLEA must also comply with the Continuing Suitability requirements described above in paragraph (II)(A)(2).

become a target of an investigation, or as to a target of an investigation, or as to a defendant (including a convicted defendant), the JLEA shall notify the Chief Federal Prosecutor responsible for the investigation or prosecution of such exculpatory information.

E. RESPONDING TO REQUESTS FROM CHIEF FEDERAL PROSECUTORS REGARDING A CONFIDENTIAL INFORMANT

If a Chief Federal Prosecutor seeks information from a Special Agent in Charge (or the equivalent) as to whether a particular individual is a current or former CI, and states the specific basis for his or her request, the Special Agent in Charge (or the equivalent) shall provide such information promptly. If the Special Agent in Charge (or the equivalent) has an objection to providing such information based on specific circumstances of the case, he or she shall explain the objection to the Chief Federal Prosecutor making the request and any remaining disagreement as to whether the information should be provided shall be resolved pursuant to paragraph (I)(G).

F. FILE REVIEWS

Whenever a JLEA discloses any information about a CI to a FPO pursuant to paragraphs (IV)(A)–(E), the Special Agent in Charge (or the equivalent) and the Chief Federal Prosecutor shall consult to facilitate any review and copying of the CI's files by the Chief Federal Prosecutor that might be necessary for the Chief Federal Prosecutor to fulfill his or her office's disclosure obligations.

G. DESIGNEES

A Special Agent in Charge (or the equivalent) and a Chief Federal Prosecutor may, with the concurrence of each other, agree to designate particular individuals in their respective offices to carry out the functions assigned to them in paragraphs (IV)(A)–(F).

V. DEACTIVATION OF CONFIDENTIAL INFORMANTS

A. GENERAL PROVISIONS

A JLEA that determines that a CI should be deactivated for cause or for any other reason shall immediately:

1. deactivate the individual;

2. document the reasons for the decision to deactivate the individual as a CI in the CI's files;

3. if the CI can be located, notify the CI that he or she has been deactivated as a CI and obtain documentation that such notification was provided in the same manner as set forth in paragraph (II)(C)(2); and

4. if the CI was authorized to engage in Tier 1 or Tier 2 Otherwise Illegal Activity pursuant to paragraph (III)(C)(2)(a)–(b), revoke that authorization under the provisions of paragraph (III)(C)(7).

B. DELAYED NOTIFICATION TO A CONFIDENTIAL INFORMANT

A JLEA may delay providing the notification to the CI described above in Paragraph (V)(A)(3) during the time such notification might jeopardize an ongoing investigation or prosecution or might cause the flight from prosecution of any person. Whenever a decision is made to delay providing a notification, that decision, and the reasons supporting it, must be documented in the CI's files.

C. CONTACTS WITH FORMER CONFIDENTIAL INFORMANTS DEACTIVATE FOR CAUSE

Absent exceptional circumstances that are approved by a Senior Field Manager, in advance whenever possible, an agent of a JLEA shall not initiate contacts with, or respond to contacts from, a former CI who has been deactivated for cause. When granted, such approval shall be documented in the CI's files.

D. COORDINATION WITH PROSECUTORS

In situations where a FPO is either participating in the conduct of an investigation by a JLEA that is utilizing a CI, or working with a CI in connection with a prosecution, the JLEA shall coordinate with the attorney assigned to the matter, in advance whenever possible, regarding any of the decisions described in paragraphs (V)(A)–(C).

* * * * * * * * * *

The foregoing guidelines regarding the use of confidential informants are issued under the authority of the Attorney General pursuant to 28 U.S.C. §§ 509, 510, and 533.

Date: January 8, 2001

Janet Reno
Attorney General

Chapter 6

The End of the Story

Informants are needed to solve certain types of crimes, usually those with no victims and, therefore, without witnesses or victims to report them. Such invisible crimes include dealing in narcotics, vice, gambling, and tax evasion. In addition, crimes with reluctant victims such as extortion, blackmail, or loan-sharking also require informants. The fundamental question raised by the previous chapters is whether the benefits to society in solving these crimes outweigh the cost associated with the use of informants. Numerous significant costs have been shown to result from the informant structure in our country.

The system of criminal justice in the United States is often referred to as an accusatory system. In such a system the state has a heavy burden (beyond a reasonable doubt) to prove the guilt of the accused. The corollary to this principle is to ensure that the innocent are not convicted. The informant system creates an interesting anomaly. Although needed by the state to meet its heavy burden, the informant system rewards guilty informants and sometimes, because of the character of the informants and their incentive to provide information, results in the conviction of innocent people.

Justice Louis Brandeis, in his famous dissenting opinion in *Olmstead v. United States*, 277 U.S. 438, 471 (1928) (Brandeis, J. dissenting), was concerned about the government benefiting from the results of its illegal activities. *Olmstead* involved wiretapping to obtain evidence. Brandeis said the following:

> In a government of laws, existence of the government will be imper-
> iled if it fails to observe the law scrupulously. Our Government is the
> potent, the omnipresent teacher. For good or for ill, it teaches the
> whole people by its example. Crime is contagious. If the Govern-
> ment becomes a lawbreaker, it breeds contempt for law; it invites
> every man to become a law unto himself; it invites anarchy. To de-
> clare that in the administration of the criminal law the end justifies
> the means—to declare that the Government may commit crimes in
> order to secure the conviction of a private criminal—would bring
> terrible retribution. Against that pernicious doctrine this Court
> should resolutely set its face.[1]

Brandeis's major concern was the symbolic appearance of the judiciary
participating in sanctioning government lawbreakers. In *Olmstead,* the
judiciary was an indirect participant by allowing the use of evidence illegally obtained by the executive branch. However, as we learned from
previous chapters that addressed high-echelon informants as well as jailhouse informants, the involvement of the judiciary is often more direct.
Courts grant rewards and concessions for these informants. Given the
participation of the executive and the judiciary, the appearance of sanctioning law-breaking permeates the criminal justice system.

An excellent example where the cost of using an informant outweighs the crime-solving benefits is the story of Whitey Bulger (Chapter
5). The U.S. Attorney for Boston, Donald Stern, characterized the FBI's
relationship with Bulger as "a deep stain on the FBI." He frankly admitted that this relationship was a mistake, too great a cost to society.
"They were at least as bad and at least as violent as the Mafia . . . certainly based upon what we know, it was a horrible mistake for these
guys [Bulger and Flemmi] to be used as informants."[2]

Since the jailhouse informant and the high-echelon informant were
involved in criminal activity, it would probably be fair to characterize
them as criminals. Their motivation for informing was self-interest,
whether to get a reduced sentence or promote their own criminal enterprise. Judas and Linda Tripp, noncriminal citizens, present a more complicated and less apparent reason for informing. In these two instances it is at
least arguable that their informing could have been motivated by altruisitic
reasons. Nevertheless, with political informing, a person is always subject
to the accusation of being motivated by political consideration, either fa-
voring the government in power (Rome) as in the case of Judas, or disfa-
voring the existing power structure as in the case of Linda Tripp.

The issue that needs to be addressed regarding the criminal informant is how we can ensure that the informant's relationship does not get

so out of hand that societal costs of sanctioning illegal activity begin to outweigh the societal benefits of crime solving? To put it more graphically, "Everybody in this business knows that you have to make deals with bad guys . . . but at some point, you have to cut them off when they are no bigger than the people they have given you."[3] In analyzing an informant relationship a prosecutor usually weighs the benefits the informant will provide in the investigation and ultimate prosecution with the costs to society (i.e., how much the informant has been involved in criminal activity). In addition, the possibility that the informant is lying must be part of the equation.

This is a complicated proposition. For many years the FBI encouraged the development of high-level informants. An agent was rewarded with advancement, commendations, and favorable treatment because of his success in developing informants. The success of FBI agent John Connolly, as discussed in Chapter 5, is a good example of this reward system. As illustrated, close relationships and alliances with informants have often made it difficult for the law enforcement agent to discern the good guy from the bad guy. In addition, getting good informants requires special skill, including the ability of the police to be con men.[4] Thus, the crime-solving aspect of the relationship between the informant and the police can be dominant while the societal costs are largely ignored.

In considering the responsibility of the informant, law enforcement, as indicated by the story of Leslie White in Chapter 4, must be vigilant concerning the reward system that creates incentives to commit perjury and implicate innocent people. When one considers that the informant's culpability and responsibility are assessed by the same law enforcement agent and/or agency that benefits from the informant's relationship, the agency's assessment of the informant's character is likely to be biased.

The story of Carlos Luna (Chapter 3) demonstrated how easily the nature of the informant's relationship can be hidden from the public's attention. Often only when something awful or unexpected happens do we learn of this underbelly of the criminal justice system. Thus, our analysis that highlighted the problems resulting from the use and abuse of informants has not shed much light on the effectiveness of informants when the benefits associated with their use greatly outweighed the costs. A typical example of a beneficial informant relationship is a drug crime. Often the police nab a user who is in possession of drugs to feed his habit. A concession to the user who is situated at the low end of the illegal drug chain might result in information implicating the distributor of drugs who is located higher up on the drug chain.

It should be pointed out that often there are good standards and guidelines in place to monitor the informant relationship, but given the clandestine nature associated with these relationships, monitoring whether law enforcement has adhered to these guidelines is often ineffective. For example, in the *Attorney General: Guidelines on FBI Use of Informants and Confidential Sources* (December 1, 1980), the introduction states: "but special care must be taken to carefully evaluate and closely supervise their use, and to insure that individual rights are not infringed and that the government itself does not become a violator of law." Despite the good intentions evident in these guidelines, more is needed to ensure against informant abuses. The primary responsibility for monitoring informant relationships has been left with the police, who, as Justice Benjamin Cardozo once observed, are engaged in the competitive enterprise of fettering out crime.

The situation of the political informant is substantially different: The prosecuting attorney has direct involvement with the informant from the beginning, and for the most part the informant is not involved in criminal activity. The decision to use the informant depends on the importance of the evidence the informant can provide coupled with the credibility of the informant. In weighing the evidence, the prosecutor must be cognizant of the effect prosecution of the official's malfeasance may have on the function of the government. The Tripp case presents a unique situation. Kenneth Starr was appointed as special prosecutor pursuant to the Independent Counsel Act to eliminate the appearance of political influence. It would simply not look good for the U.S. Attorney, who is appointed by the president, to investigate the president. Despite an intensive, costly, and time-consuming investigation, Starr did not have anything to show for his labor. Then along came Linda Tripp with her story of President Clinton's relationship with a former White House intern. Starr's use of Tripp raises an obvious question. Did Starr use Tripp to save face, or did he indeed go through an appropriate evaluation in his decision to use Tripp? Did he really consider her credibility, the quality of her information, and the costs of prosecuting the president?

Although the preceding chapters have elaborated on many of the problems resulting from the use of informants, they do not recognize the intrinsic worth of informants in solving crimes that otherwise cannot be solved. Thus, informants remain a necessary evil. Former Director of the FBI William Webster said, "The informant is the single most important tool in law enforcement." In his turn, former Director Clarence Kelly said, "Without informants there is nothing."[5] Mechanisms need to be put in place that will help deal with the issues raised by this book. In developing these safeguards one must understand that they can never be naively regarded as foolproof because they ultimately depend on the integrity of law enforcement personnel, prosecutors, and police. In addition, the nature of the informant's relationship requires great secrecy. Attempting to exercise greater control over the relationship between informants and law enforcement will necessarily compromise the concern for secrecy and make it much harder to cultivate effective informants. Nevertheless, my suggestions for change do include greater public awareness and closer scrutiny of the informant relationship. This can be accomplished in a number of ways. The so-called fourth estate—the press—through its investigative reporting has often shed light on the problems associated with informants. Once public attention has been drawn to the problem, political pressure can begin to build. Such political pressure often results in official inquiry by a governmental body and so that ultimately reform comes about.

Each scenario presented in this book shows in some way how public scrutiny can lead to reform. In Chapter 4 the series of articles involving jailhouse informants written by investigative reporter Ted Rohrlich and published in *The Los Angeles Times* resulted in the convening of an independent grand jury. Ultimately, the grand jury's recommendations for reform were instituted. As mentioned in Chapter 3, the Boston Police instituted guidelines to deal with the issue of a nonexistent informant once public attention had been focused on it.

Still another example of the positive influence of public scrutiny is the chapter on Bulger. On *60 Minutes*, on April 8, 2001, Ed Bradley introduced the segment "FBI and the Mob" as follows:

> As if the FBI didn't have enough on its hands trying to explain that one of its top agents has been arrested and charged with spying for the Russians, the bureau may have an even bigger problem trying to explain its 25-year relationship with the notorious boss of the Irish mob in Boston, James "Whitey" Bulger, whom the FBI recruited as a secret informant to get information about Bulger's archrivals in the Italian Mafia.
>
> In exchange for that information, the FBI, in effect, gave Bulger *carte blanche*, which allowed him to get away with robbery, drug dealing, and extortion and, according to a federal indictment, the murders of at least 19 people. What's more, one FBI agent has been charged with tipping off Bulger six years ago that he was about to be arrested, and that let him get away.

As some of these facts have come to light, the federal government has taken affirmative steps to deal with some of the problems associated with informants. For example, on May 3, 2001, the House Committee on Government Reform focused on FBI informant practices in Boston. They looked at the case of Joseph Salvati who spent almost thirty years in prison because the FBI covered up information that Salvati was framed to protect an informant. According to Salvati's attorney, Victor Garo, "The federal government determined that it was more important for them to protect informants than it was for innocent people to be framed. The federal government determined that Joe Salvati's life was expendable.[6] In addition, as mentioned in Chapter 5, on January 8, 2001, U.S. Attorney General Janet Reno issued *Department of Justice Guidelines Regarding the Use of Confidential Informants*.

Public exposure is also a crucial factor in the Linda Tripp situation. Unfavorable publicity associated first with Kenneth Starr's five-year, $40 million investigation of a land deal in Arkansas eventually expanded to public concern about his manipulation of the president's affair with an intern. As a result of the increased public scrutiny of Starr's actions, Congress decided not to renew the Independent Counsel Act when it expired in June, 1999.

Shedding light on the problem leaves open the question of how to address the problem once it has been exposed. Although the situation involving political informants is substantially different from that of the typical criminal informant, the solution, which I will discuss, focuses on the prosecutor. In making the prosecutor the point person, I am assuming that the prosecutor is answerable to the public either because she is an elected official or because she is working for an elected official. Many of the reforms that we have already discussed take this approach.

The law enforcement system in this country is not monolithic. Police departments, prosecutors, prison officials, and the judiciary are each independent and contribute in different yet interrelated ways to the system. Given the independence of the different elements of the law enforcement system, it is difficult for a prosecutor's office to deal with informant abuses by the police or by jailers. Nevertheless, since information always ends up with the prosecutor, who decides whether to use the information, she is the best person to oversee informant operations. In addition, as an officer of the court she is under ethical obligation "to seek justice not merely to convict."[7] "A prosecutor has the responsibility of a minister of justice and not simply that of an advocate."[8] A prosecutor is responsible for ensuring that the gigantic forces and power of the state are exercised fairly and to further the administration of justice. Justice George Sutherland, in his decision in *Berger v. United States*, 295 U.S. 78 at 88 (1935), described the role of a prosecutor as follows:

The United States Attorney is the representative not of an ordinary party to a controversy, but to a sovereignty whose obligation to govern impartially is as compelling as its obligation to govern at all; and whose interest therefore, in a criminal prosecution is not that it shall win a case, but that justice shall be done. As such, he is in a peculiar and very definite sense the servant of the law, the twofold aim of which is that guilt shall not escape or innocence suffer. He may prosecute with earnestness and vigor indeed, he should do so. But, while he may strike hard blows, he is not at liberty to strike foul ones. It is as much his duty to retrain from improper methods calculated to produce a wrongful conviction as it is to use every legitimate means to bring a just one.

In our legal analysis in the previous chapters, we pointed out the ways in which the Constitution protects individual criminal defendants when informant issues arise. These protections are often difficult to utilize, however, since the law places a heavy burden on the defendant in court to gain the identities of informants and to prove that the police are lying. The cases we discussed placed a great deal of responsibility on the prosecutor to disclose information that might have been useful to the defense. This duty to disclose certainly includes informant abuses. The new reforms attempt to make the prosecutor more responsible for the acts of the police and jailers in their use of informants. The *Department of Justice Guidelines Regarding the Use of Confidential Informants* significantly interject the U.S. Attorney into the operation and maintenance of informants. In addition, both the Los Angeles County grand jury and the ensuing publicity mentioned in Chapter 4 made the District Attorney's Office assume more responsibility for the fabrication of the jailhouse informants. One significant change was to require that the three top officials in the District Attorney's Office approve any use of jailhouse informants. Such approval was dependent on concrete evidence that the informant was telling the truth. These innovations put more direct responsibility on the prosecution and in some instances on its supervisors. Now that it has been given direct responsibility, the prosecution can no longer turn a blind eye to informant abuses. In addition, more responsibility in the hands of the prosecutor will result in closer monitoring of law enforcement officers in the field. Closer monitoring of field officers is indeed very sensible because their desire to gain evidence for a particular crime may cause them to lose sight of the bigger picture. In this way, zeal for crime-solving makes abusing the system more likely. Assigning more responsibility to the prosecutor would go a long way toward ameliorating this problem as well as the problem of a fabricated (nonexistent) informant discussed in Chapter 3.

I should point out that prosecutors, despite their aspirations and hopes to conduct themselves ethically, often get so involved in proving their cases that they turn a blind eye to their ethical responsibilities. A prosecutor also is involved in the so-called competitive enterprise of ferreting out crime and often has a close relationship with the law enforcement officer in charge of the particular informant. This relationship is essential for the prosecutor to successfully prosecute crimes. The grand jury investigation of Los Angeles specifically found "very little effort was expanded by the District Attorney's office to investigate the background and motivation of most jail house informants in order to assess their credibility prior to presenting them in court as witnesses."[9] Ethical constraints and insulation from direct dealings with an informant make the monitoring by a prosecutor a step in the right direction. Nevertheless, there are still some systemic concerns, given the nature of our adversary system. As much as prosecutors like to put vandals in jail, they also like to keep their jobs. Most state prosecutors must rely on the ballot box. Being answerable to the electorate and having the responsibility enumerated in the *Guidelines* squarely on their shoulders, prosecutors have political incentives, as well as moral and ethical ones, to deal with informant abuses.

A prosecutor has a great deal of power and much discretion in exercising that power. The situation discussed in Chapter 2 involving the special prosecutor, Kenneth Starr, highlights this problem. The fundamental problem was how a prosecutor could pursue high elected officials, including the President of the United States, without becoming overzealous. Maintaining public confidence in the investigation, while staying removed from politics, was a difficult task.

Over sixty years ago, in 1940, Supreme Court Justice Robert Jackson, in a speech to U.S. Attorneys, captured the problem with the Starr investigation:

> If the prosecutor is obliged to choose his case, it follows that he can choose his defendants. Therein is the most dangerous power of the prosecutor: that he will pick people that he thinks he should get, rather than cases that need to be prosecuted. With the law books filled with a great assortment of crimes, a prosecutor stands a fair chance of finding at least a technical violation of some act on the part of almost anyone. In such a case, it is not a question of discovering the commission of a crime and then looking for the man who has committed it, it is a question of picking the man and then searching the law books, or putting investigators to work, to pin some offense on him. It is in this realm—in which the prosecutor

picks some person whom he dislikes or desires to embarrass, or selects some group of unpopular persons and then looks for an offense, that the greatest danger of abuse of prosecuting power lies.[10]

Justice Antonin Scalia, dissenting in *Morrison v. Olson*, 487 U.S. 654 (1988), a case upholding the Independent Counsel Act, was concerned that there were no checks on the power of the independent counsel. Unlike the Attorney General or U.S. Attorney who were answerable to an elected official—the president—there were no checks and balances on the significant power of the independent counsel. Thus, the electorate did not have any direct power over the independent counsel. Unlike the situation involving an elected prosecutor, the independent counsel had unfettered discretion. A check on the power of the prosecutor is essential in ensuring that the prosecutor keeps his zealousness in tow.

Informants are needed in this society to solve certain crimes. It is important that the problems associated with informants come to the public attention so that methods can be devised to address these problems. Grand jury investigations, criminal indictments, media attention, and legislative investigations all play a role in shedding a light on what has been a dark secret of law enforcement techniques. Public attention and solutions placing responsibility squarely on the shoulders of the prosecutor should begin to deal with the informant issues raised in this book.

Notes

CHAPTER 1. A HISTORICAL OVERVIEW OF INFORMANTS

1. Gary T. Marx, "Thoughts on a Neglected Category of Social Movement Participant: The Agent Provocateur and the Informant," *American Journal of Sociology* 402 (September 1974): 80–82.

2. *Black's Law Dictionary* (6th ed., 1990) defines "informer" or "informant" as "an undisclosed person who confidentially discloses material information of a law violation, thereby supplying a lead to officers for their investigation of a crime. This does not include persons who supply information only after being interviewed by police officers, or who give information as witnesses during the course of investigation. Rewards for information obtained from informers is provided by 18 U.S.C.A. §3059."

3. Russell L. Bintliff, *Police Procedural: A Writer's Guide to Police and How They Work* (1993), 80.

4. See Michael Gagarin, *Early Greek Law* (1986), 63–64; Andocides, *On the Mysteries* 36.43 ff.2o; Jacob Burckhardt, *The Greeks and Greek Civilization* (1998), 281; John E. Stambaugh, *The Ancient Roman City* (1988), 126–127; Clifford S. Zimmerman, "Toward a New Vision of Informants: A History of Abuses and Suggestions for Reform," *Hastings Constitutional Law Quarterly* 81, no. 165 (fall 1994): 22.

5. Gagarin, ibid.

6. Douglas M. MacDowell, *The Law in Classical Athens* (1978), 181.

7. Matthew R. Christ, *The Litigious Athenian* (1998), 143. According to MacDowell (ibid.) the act of informing is referred to as *menysis*.

8. MacDowell, ibid.

9. See *The Columbia Encyclopedia* (5th ed, 1993); and Burckhardt, *The Greeks and Greek Civilization*, 281.

10. Burckhardt, ibid.

11. Stambaugh, *The Ancient Roman City*, 125–127.

12. Martyn Percy, "Arguments for Easter: The Day When Even God Needs a Scapegoat; Poor Judas. The Tendency to Lay the Blame for the Sin of the World at the Feet of One Man Is Not Restricted to Gospel Writers. Look Around," *The Independent* (London), April 2, 1999, 7.

13. *United States v. Frost*, 914 F.2d 756, 770 (6th Cir. 1990).

14. Raymond E. Brown, *The Death of the Messiah: From Gethsemane to the Grave* (1994), 1399–1404.

15. See W.H. Kent, "Judas Iscariot," in *The Catholic Encyclopedia*, vol. 8. Available: <http://www.newadvent.org/cathen/08539a.htm> (visited July 17, 2000).

16. See Hyam Maccoby, *The Myth of Jewish Evil* (1992), 79.

17. Larry B. Stammer, "New Look at Ancient Betrayer; For Centuries, Judas Iscariot Has Been the Archetype of the Traitor. But Some Scholars Are Beginning to Wonder If He Was a Villain at All," *Los Angeles Times*, April 21, 2000, Al.

18. See ibid., 104

19. W.W. Story, *A Roman Lawyer in Jerusalem in the First Century* (1908).

20. Warren W. Wiersbe, *Classic Sermons on Judas Iscariot* (1995).

21. See Gregg Zoroya, "Monica Does D.C. Touring the Favourite Haunts of the World's Most Famous Intern," *The Toronto Sun*, March 28, 1999, T6.

22. See Stammer, "New Look at Ancient Betrayer."

23. Zimmerman, "Toward a New Vision of Informants," 152–156.

24. Ibid., 155–156.

25. Leon Radzinowicz, *A History of English Criminal Law and Its Administration from 1750* (1981), 2:138.

26. Zimmerman, "Toward a New Vision of Informants," 157–166.

27. Douglas Hay, Peter Linebaugh, John G. Rule, E. P. Thompson, and Cal Winslow, *Albion's Fatal Tree: Crime and Society in Eighteenth–Century England* (1975), 198.

28. See ibid.; and Zimmerman, "Toward a New Vision of Informants," 157–166.

29. Gary T. Marx, *Undercover: Police Surveillance in America* (1988), 18–19; and John Briggs, Christopher Harrison, Angus McInnes, and David Vincent, *Crime and Punishment in England: An Introductory History* (1996), 216–217.

30. Marx, *Undercover*, 18–19.

31. Briggs, *Crime and Punishment in England*, 216.

32. See Andrew Boyd, *The Informers: A Chilling Account of the Supergrasses in Northern Ireland* (1984), 7–24.

33. Charles A. Wright and Kenneth W. Graham Jr., *Federal Practice and Procedure*, §5702 (1992).

34. Michael Tonry, ed. *The Handbook of Crime and Punishment* (1998), 444–445.

35. Marx, *Undercover*, 405–409.

36. Federal Bureau of Investigation, *Avoiding the Informant Trap: A Blueprint for Control*, FBI Law Enforcement Bulletin (November 1998).

CHAPTER 2. THE POLITICAL INFORMANT

1. Linda Tripp's self-description of her pet peeve in her 1967 high school yearbook.

2. See *In Re Grand Jury Proceedings (Linda R. Tripp)*, 1998 WL 754889, pt. 1, *5 (D.D.C. June 30, 1998). All facts in this chapter, unless otherwise noted, originate from this source.

3. See Michael Isikoff and Evan Thomas, "Clinton and the Intern," *Newsweek*, February 2, 1998, 30.

4. See Elaine Sciolino and Don Van Natta Jr., "Testing of a President: The Confidant," *New York Times*, March 15, 1998, sec. 1, p. 1.

5. See Michael Isikoff, "A Twist in *Jones v. Clinton*: Her Lawyers Subpoena Another Woman," *Newsweek*, August 11, 1997, 30.

6. See Sciolino and Van Natta Jr., "Testing of a President."

7. See Jane Mayer, "Portrait of a Whistleblower," *New Yorker*, March 23, 1998, 46; and *Newsweek*, April 13, 1998, 26.

8. See Francis X. Clines, "Impeachment: The Scene—Capitol Sketchbook; A Stealthy Tripp, More Cat Than Canary," *New York Times*, December 22, 1998, A29.

9. See Don Van Natta Jr., "The President's Trial: The Betrayer," *New York Times*, February 12, 1999, A1.

10. See *In Re Grand Jury Proceedings,* 1998 WL 754889, pt. 5, *2.

11. See William Safire, "Essay: The Supervictim," *New York Times*, March 11, 1999, A31.

12. Andrew Morton, *Monica's Story* (1999), 178.

13. Van Natta Jr., "The President's Trial."

14. See Sciolino and Van Natta Jr., "Testing of a President."

15. See Evan Thomas and Michael Isikoff, with Daniel Klaidman, "The Tripp Trap?" *Newsweek*, July 13, 1998, 22, 24.

16. See ibid.

17. See Stephen Labaton, "Linda Tripp Is Focus of Maryland Criminal Inquiry Over Taped Calls," *New York Times*, July 8, 1998, A18.

18. See Stephen Labaton, Don Van Natta Jr., and Jill Abramson, "The President under Fire: The Investigation," *New York Times*, January 25, 1998, A1; and Labaton, "Linda Tripp."

19. See ibid.

20. Sciolino and Van Natta Jr., "Testing of a President."

21. See Jamie Gangel, "Linda Tripp Speaks about Her Motives in Recording Monica Lewinsky's Phone Conversation," *Today* (NBC television broadcast, February 12, 1999), available in Lexis-Nexis Transcripts database.

22. See Van Natta Jr., "The President's Trial."

23. See Isikoff, "Clinton and the Intern," 31.

24. Ibid.

25. Sciolino and Van Natta Jr., "Testing of a President."

26. *In Re Grand Jury Proceeding,* 1998 WL 754889, pt. 3, 10.

27. Ibid.

28. "The President under Fire: Linda Tripp's Statement on Role in Case," *New York Times*, January 31, 1998, A8.

29. See Mayer, "Portrait of a Whistleblower," *New Yorker*, 47.

30. See Sciolino and Van Natta Jr., "Testing of a President."

31. See ibid.

32. *In Re Grand Jury Proceedings*, 1998 WL 754889, pt. 3, *7.

33. Ibid.

34. *In Re Grand Jury Proceedings*, 1998 WL 754889, pt. 3, 5. Tony Snow is currently a conservative columnist and a frequent stand-in on Rush Limbaugh's radio talk show.

35. See Thomas and Isikoff, with Klaidman, "The Tripp Trap?" 23.

36. Gangel, "Linda Tripp Speaks."

37. Labaton, Van Natta Jr., and Abramson, "The President under Fire."

38. Ibid.

39. See ibid.

40. Gangel, "Linda Tripp Speaks."

41. Ibid.

42. Sciolino and Van Natta Jr., "Testing of a President."

43. Jane Mayer suggests this theory in her profile of Linda Tripp, "Portrait of a Whistleblower" (p. 34). She indicates that in interviews Tripp's friends described her as being "slightly obsessive about marital infidelity."

44. Labaton, "Linda Tripp."

45. See Justice William Brennan, "State Constitutions and the Protection of Individual Rights," *Harvard Law Review* 90 (1977): 489, 491. Observing the cut back in individual rights in Supreme Court decisions, he wrote: "[S]tate courts no less than federal are and ought to be guardians of our liberties. But the point I want to stress here is that state courts cannot rest when they have afforded their citizens the full protections of the federal Constitution. State constitutions, too, are a font of individual liberties, their protections often extending beyond those required by the Supreme Court's interpretation of federal law. The legal revolution which has brought federal law to the fore must not be allowed to inhibit the independent protective force of state law—for without it, the full realization of our liberties cannot be guaranteed."

46. Md. Code Ann., Cts. & Jud. Pro. §10-402 (a)(1).

47. Ibid. §10-401 (3) (1998).

48. See ibid.

49. See David Johnston, "Jurors in Maryland Indict Linda Tripp in Lewinsky Tapes," *New York Times*, July 31, 1999, A1.

50. See Md. Code. Ann. Cts. & Jud. Pro., §10-401 (3) (1998).

51. Ibid. §10-402 (c)(3).

52. On January 26, 1998, Maryland's state attorney general, Marna L. McLendon, announced she would not pursue criminal charges against Linda Tripp. See *Newschannel 2 First At Five* (WMAR-TV television broadcast, January 27, 1998) (transcript on file on Lexis-Nexis).

53. See Jerry Seper, "State Indicts Tripp for Taping; Maryland Jurors Hand Up 2 Counts," *Washington Times*, July 31, 1999, A1.

54. Ibid.

55. It should be pointed out that Julie Hyatt Steele was indicted for lying to the grand jury during the Lewinsky investigation; she went to trial, the jury hung, and the Office of the Independent Counsel decided not to retry. See Eric Lichtblau, "Starr Won't Seek to Retry McDougal, Steele; Whitewater: Prosecutor Failed to Win Convictions in Obstruction Cases, Charges Are Now Pending Against Only Webster Hubbell," *Los Angeles Times*, May 26, 1999, A10.

56. Johnston, "Jurors in Maryland."

57. See Saundra Torry and Raja Mishra, "Tripp Indicted on Charges of Wiretapping: Maryland Law Prohibits Taping without Consent," *Washington Post*, July 31, 1999, A01.

58. U.S. Constitution, Amendment 10: "The powers not delegated to the United States by the Constitution, nor prohibited by it to the States, are reserved to the States respectively, or to the people."

59. The statute, in pertinent part, reads "Such investigative and prosecutorial functions and powers shall include—making applications to any Federal court for a grant of immunity to any witness, consistent with applicable statutory requirements, or for warrants, subpoenas, or other court orders, and for purposes of sections 6003, 6004, and 6005 of Title 18, exercising the authority vested in a United States attorney or the Attorney General."

60. See Paul W. Valentine, "Tripp Knowingly Violated Md. Wiretap Law; Immunity Deal with Starr May Put Her Case Beyond Reach of State," *Washington Post*, October 6, 1998, B1.

61. U.S. Constitution art. VI, sec. 3, cl. 2: "This Constitution, and the Laws of the United States which shall be made in Pursuance thereof; and all

Treaties made, or which shall be made, under the Authority of the United States, shall be the supreme Law of the Land; and the Judges in every State shall be bound thereby, any Thing in the Constitution or Laws of any State to the Contrary notwithstanding."

62. See James A. Strazzella and William W. Taylor III, "Federalizing Crime: Examining the Congressional Trend to Duplicate State Laws," *Criminal Justice* 14, no. 1 (Spring 1999): 4–9.

63. See Eric Lichtblau, "Pledge of Immunity Doesn't Shield Tripp, Judge Rules Scandal: The Former Friend of Monica S. Lewinsky Failed to Block Her Trial on State Charges in the Taping of Conversations with Former Intern," *Los Angeles Times*, December 15, 1999, A18.

64. *Maryland v. Tripp*, Memorandum Opinion of Judge Diane Leasure, May 5, 2000, page 28.

65. See Associated Press, "Tripp's Attorney Accuses Lewinsky of Lying During Pretrial Hearing," *Associated Press Newswires*, March 21, 2000. See also *Maryland v. Tripp*.

66. See *Maryland v. Tripp*, page 7.

67. See Mary Otto, "Md. Judge Dismisses Tripp Wiretap Case," *Washington Post*, June 1, 2000, A10.

68. Bob Hohler, "Wiretapping Case is Dropped Move Follows Curbs on Lewinsky Data," *Boston Globe*, May 25, 2000, A3.

69. See Christopher Thorne, "U.S. Tripp Wiretap," *Associated Press Newswires*, May 25, 2000, 12:20:00.

CHAPTER 3. THE NONEXISTENT INFORMANT

1. See Mark Curriden, "Secret Threat to Justice: There Are Few Controls Over the Hidden Alliance of Agents and Informers," *National Law Journal*, February 20, 1995, A1.

2. See Appendix B. The Boston Police Department informant policy dated June 10, 1996, lists the motivations for an informant as follows: "a. personal gratification, which may include collecting rewards; b. revenge; c. rivalry; d. avoiding criminal prosecution."

3. See Doris Sue Wong, "Informant Is Not the Right One, Defense in Officer's Slaying Says," *Boston Globe*, March 1, 1989, Metro/Region, 1; see also Mark Curriden, "Behind the Affidavits, Some Informants Are Fiction," *National Law Journal*, February 20, 1995, A29.

4. In an unrelated decision of the U.S. Supreme Court, *Maryland v. Buie*, the court authorized a protective sweep when the police have a reasonable basis to believe that they are in danger. The scope of this search is limited to the justification, such as finding people lurking on the premises who could do harm to the officers, that necessitated the search in the first place. 494 U.S. 325, 327–328 (1990).

5. See Harvey Silverglate, "*In Re Commonwealth v. Lewin*: The Making of a Crooked Case," *Boston Phoenix*, March 10–16, 1989.

6. See Doris Sue Wong, "Suffolk DA's Homicide Chief Goes Today," *Boston Globe*, August 31, 1992, Metro/Region.

7. See Appendix A. In the affidavit, the informant is described as one "who has proven reliable in the past by providing your affiant with information that led to the arrest and now pending case in Suffolk Superior Court of one Miguel Sarracent for Trafficking in Cocaine, Possession of Class D with Intent to Distribute and unlawful Possession of a firearm, also for the conviction in Suffolk Superior Court of one June Samaniego for Possession of Class B with Intent to Distribute." Probably as a result of this case, the Supreme Judicial Court in *Commonwealth v. Amral*, 407 Mass. 511 (1990), approved the practice of not naming in a search warrant affidavit the person previously arrested and convicted as a result of the informant's information.

8. See Jerome H. Skolnick, "Deception by Police," *Criminal Justice Ethics* (summer/fall 1982): 40, 43.

9. Mark Curriden conducted interviews with more than fifty judges and magistrates in Alabama, Georgia, and Tennessee. He found than none of them had ever required an officer to disclose or produce the identity of an informant. (See Mark Curriden, "The Informant Trap," *National Law Journal*, March 20, 1995.)

10. In *Commonwealth v. Amral*, the Massachusetts court allowed for a lesser showing to determine the veracity of the affidavit. The court recognized that since a defendant lacks access to the necessary information to make a *Franks* showing the trial judge should hold an in camera hearing when the defendant by affidavit casts reasonable doubt on the truth of the affidavit.

11. See Christopher Slobogin, "Reform: The Police: Testilying: Police Perjury and What to Do about It," *University of Colorado Law Review* 67 (1996): 1037, 1046–1048.

12. See Slobogin, "Reform," 1047 (citing Myron W. Orfield Jr., "Deterrence, Perjury, and the Heater Factor: An Exclusionary Rule in the Chicago Criminal Courts," *University of Colorado Law Review* 63 [1992]: 75, 112).

13. See ibid., 1047 and n. 47.

14. See ibid., 1047–1048 (referring to Morgan Cloud, "The Dirty Little Secret," *Emory Law Journal* 43 [1994]: 1311, 1323–1324).

15. See ibid., 1040 n. 11. Slobogin cites the Commission to Investigate Allegations of Police Corruption and the Anti-Corruption Procedures of the Police Department, City of New York, Commission Report 36 (1994) (Milton Mollen, Chair) [hereinafter "Mollen Report"].

16. Doris Sue Wong, "Luna Convicted of Perjury, Filing False Reports," *Boston Globe*, June 6, 1991, Metro/Region, 1.

17. See Patricia Nealon, "Extortion Trial Witness Tells of Police Abuses," *Boston Globe*, April 8, 1998, A1.

18. See ibid.

19. "Mollen Report," 36.

20. See Morgan Cloud, "*People v. Simpson*: Perspectives on the Implications for the Criminal Justice System: Judges, 'Testilying,' and the Constitution," *Southern California Law Review* 69 (1996): 1341, 1350–1351.

    Nearly a quarter century ago, the Knapp Commission was at least the fifth in a series of public committees appointed since 1844 to investigate corruption in the New York Police Department. In addition to detailing various forms of police corruption, the Knapp Commission documented how corruption could induce officers to prepare false investigative reports and offer false testimony. In the wake of the highly publicized Rodney King incident, the Christopher Commission was appointed to study violence by Los Angeles police officers. It documented the use of excessive force, concluded that this is a national problem, and revealed how attempts to cover up the use of violence can lead officers to file false reports and testify untruthfully about their conduct. The Christopher Commission explained that affirmative lies were only part of the problem: "Perhaps the greatest single barrier to the effective investigation and adjudication of complaints is the officers' unwritten code of silence" (ibid., quoting *Report of the Independent Commission on the Los Angeles Police Department* [1991], xx).

21. See Irving Younger, "The Perjury Routine," *The Nation*, May 8, 1967, 96–97.

22. See Orfield, "Deterrence, Perjury, and the Heater Factor," 75.

23. Ibid., 104.

24. See generally, "Mollen Report."

25. See ibid., 36. See also Cloud, "*People v. Simpson*," 1354–1355.

26. Curriden, "The Informant Trap," A29.

27. See Cloud, "*People v. Simpson*," 1356.

28. "Mollen Report," 38.

29. Ibid., 41.

30. See Slobogin, "Reform," 1043.

31. See Eric Blumenson and Eva Nilsen, "Policing for Profit: The Drug War's Hidden Economic Agenda," *University of Chicago Law Review* 65 (1998): 35.

32. See notes in "Plea Bargaining and the Transformation of the Criminal Process," *Harvard Law Review* 90 (1977): 564, 569.

33. See "Mollen Report," 36–37.

34. See Cloud, "*People v. Simpson*," 1351.

35. See Slobogin, "Reform," 1045.

36. See Cloud, "*People v. Simpson*," 1353.

37. See Slobogin, "Reform," 1047–1048.

38. See Sean P. Murphy, "Rush to Misjudgment: Fumbling the Lewin Case," *Boston Globe*, November 4, 1990, Metro/Region, 29.

39. Peter Reuter, "Licensing Criminals: Police and Informants," *Rand Paper Series* (October 1982).

40. Ibid., 3–7.

CHAPTER 4. JAILHOUSE INFORMANTS

1. Hugo Adam Bedau and Michael L. Radelet, "Miscarriages of Justice in Potentially Capital Cases," *Stanford law Review* 40 (November 1987): 21, 56–64. This article documents 117 cases in which criminal defendants were convicted based on perjured testimony of prosecution witnesses. Some of these convictions involved death sentences.

2. A slang term derived from the phrase, "Book 'em, Danno," used in the old television series *Hawaii Five*-O. See Ted Rohrlich and Robert Stewart, "Jailhouse Snitches: Trading Lies for Freedom," *Los Angeles Times*, April 16, 1989.

3. "Report of the 1989–90 Los Angeles County Grand Jury: Investigation of Jail House Informants in the Criminal Justice System in Los Angeles County," June 26, 1990 [hereinafter "Grand Jury Report"].

4. Ted Rohrlich, "Jail Informant Had Allies on Side of the Law," *Los Angeles Times*, November 20, 1988.

5. Ted Rohrlich, "Jail Informant Owns Up to Perjury in a Dozen Cases," *Los Angeles Times*, January 4, 1990, A1.

6. "Grand Jury Report," 2–5.

7. Ibid., 11, 12, 19.

8. Ibid., 16.

9. Ibid., 90.

10. *The Commission on Proceedings Involving Guy Paul Morin, Before The Honourable Fred Kaufman, C.M., Q.C.,* (1998); Recommendation 36, p. 602. A commission was appointed by Attorney General Charles Harnick of Canada to look into the wrongful murder conviction of Guy Paul Morin. Harnick appointed Fred Kaufman, a former justice of the Quebec Court of Appeal. Thirty of Kaufman's 119 recommendations were aimed at restricting the testimony of jailhouse informants.

11. "Grand Jury Report," 39.

12. Ted Rohrlich, "Perjurer Sentenced to 3 Years; Crime: Informant Blew the Whistle on Use of Jailhouse Liars-for-Hire, but No Law Officers Were Charged for Conspiring with Him," *Los Angeles Times*, May 20, 1992, B1 (quoting Douglas Dalton, special counsel to the Los Angeles County Grand Jury).

13. Ted Rohrlich, "Authorities Go Fishing for Jailhouse Confessions," *Los Angeles Times*, March 4, 1990, A1.

14. "Grand Jury Report," 68, 121.

15. Rohrlich, "Jail Informant Owns Up."

16. Rohrlich, "Perjurer Sentenced to 3 Years."

17. "Grand Jury Report," 90.

18. Rohrlich, "Perjurer Sentenced to 3 Years."

19. "Grand Jury Report," 121. Testimony of senior management official in the District Attorney's Office.

20. Mass. Rules of Prof'l Conduct, Rule 3.8, cmt. [1].

21. See Stanley Z. Fisher, "The Prosecutor's Ethical Duty to Seek Exculpatory Evidence in Police Hands: Lessons from England," *Fordham Law Review* 68 (2000): 1379, 1382.

22. William Bastone, "Tony Limo's Wild Ride," *Village Voice*, December 27, 1994, 25.

23. From the trial transcript of Sarivola on December 11, 1985, in the case of *Arizona v. Fulminante* in the Superior Court of the State of Arizona in

and for the County of Maricopa before Judge Stephen Gerst [hereinafter "Fulminante Trial Transcript"].

24. "Fulminante Trial Transcript." Sarivola described it as follows: "Loan sharking is when you lend money to somebody for a higher rate of interest than they would pay at a bank, and should they not pay the loan, you use violence or threats to collect the money."

25. "Fulminante Trial Transcript," December 12, 1985. Testimony of Walter Ticano, special agent, Federal Bureau of Investigation.

26. Ibid. Ticano testified that Sarivola provided information on the Colombo, Gambino, Genovese, and Luchese organized crime families.

27. "Fulminante Trial Transcript," December 11, 1985. Testimony of Sarivola.

28. Brent Whiting, "Prosecutor Asks Court for New Judge; Says Ruling Out Murder-Trial Witness Is 'Bias,'" *Arizona Republic*, April 7, 1994, B1. Donna Sarivola's reasons included complications from oral surgery, a back injury from bowling, and finally fear for her safety in Arizona. The prosecution did not subpoena her because they anticipated she would voluntarily appear. (By way of aside, the trial judge got into a bit of a controversy with the Arizona Association of Chiropractic when he demeaned a note from a chiropractor with regard to Donna's back injury. See Brent Whiting, "Chiropractor's Note Fails to Impress Skeptical Judge," *Arizona Republic*, September 8, 1993, B3.)

29. Brent Whiting, "No-Shows Rule Out Witness," *Arizona Republic*, October 14, 1993, B6.

30. Brent Whiting, "Man Guilty of Killing Stepdaughter 1st Conviction Was Tossed Out over Confessions," *Arizona Republic*, June 22, 1994, B2.

31. William Bastone, "Tony Limo's Wild Ride."

CHAPTER 5. HIGH-LEVEL INFORMANTS

1. Peter Reuter, "Licensing Criminals: Police and Informants," *Rand Paper Series* (October 1982), 8–9. "Top Echelon informants were . . . members of an organized crime group who could furnish information on the highest levels of organized crime groups of national significance." *United States v. Salemme*, 91 F.Supp.2d 141, 187 (D.Mass. 1999). (All facts, unless otherwise noted, are from this court decision).

2. See Clifford L. Karchmer, "Keeping Informants under Control," *New York Times*, August 3, 1981, A15.

3. *United States v. Francis P. Salemme* et al.; and *United States v. John Martorano*, 91 F.Supp.2d 141 (1999).

4. Paul Sullivan, "Shooting Latest Chapter in Hub's Gory Legacy," *Boston Herald*, November 7, 1995, 6.

5. Some sixty people were killed during this gang war. Kevin Cullen, "Code of Silence Intact, Winter Gets 10 Years," *Boston Globe*, May 18, 1993, 1.

6. "Boston Mobster Joins Elite Group on FBI List," *Chicago Tribune*, November 30, 2000, Evening Update Edition, 2.

7. "The Rise, Fall, and Escape of Whitey Bulger," *Boston Globe*, March 5, 1995, 25.

8. Sean Flynn, "Good Guy, Bad Guy," *Boston Magazine*, November 1998, 64, 106.

9. "The Key Players; Winter Hill Gang; James J. (Whitey) Bulger"; Spotlight, *Boston Globe*, March 5, 1995, 24.

10. Gerald O'Neill, Christine Chenlund, Dick Lehr, Kevin Cullen, and Mary Elizabeth Knox, "The Bulger Mystique; Law Enforcement Officials' Lament about an Elusive Foe: Where Was Whitey?" *Boston Globe*, September 20, 1988, 1. By 1983, when the Angiulo brothers were convicted and incarcerated, Bulger became the most powerful mobster in Boston.

11. Kevin Cullen, "Focus Turns to Fugitive Bulger's FBI Ties; Lawyers, Officers Await Answers from Agency Files," *Boston Globe*, May 29, 1997, B1.

12. See Jack Kelly, "How America Met the Mob," *American Heritage*, July/August 2000, 76, 85.

13. Kevin Cullen, "Mobster's Charges Put the FBI on the Defensive; Many Demanding Answers on the Handling of Bulger, Flemmi," *Boston Globe*, July 5, 1999, B1. Bulger and Flemmi were informants from 1971 until December 1990.

14. Shelley Murphy, "Informants: Handle with Care; FBI Work with Flemmi, Bulger Proves Messy," *Boston Globe*, June 30, 1997, B1.

15. Patricia Nealon, "U.S. Says Flemmi Turned Informant to Torpedo Rivals, Immunity Disputed as Hearings Begin," *Boston Globe*, January 7, 1998, B2.

16. Cullen, "Mobster's Charges Put the FBI on the Defensive."

17. Gerald O'Neill, Dick Lehr, and Kevin Cullen, "New Team, Tactics Hastened Whitey Bulger's Fall; Spotlight," *Boston Globe*, March 5, 1995, 1.

18. National Public Radio, "All Things Considered," December 24, 1999 (available on Lexis). Comment of Mike Barnicle to host Robert Siegel.

19. Andrea Estes, "Feds Detail Bulger, Inc.," *Boston Herald*, September 30, 2000, 1.

20. Patricia Nealon, "FBI Trusted 2 Gangsters, Ex-Agent Says; Offers More Details of Cozy Relationship," *Boston Globe*, April 21, 1998, B4 (quoting former FBI agent Nicholas Gianturco).

21. "Married to the Mob?; Story of Informer and How His Relationship with the FBI Helped Him Build Criminal Empire," *Dateline NBC News*, March 17, 2000 (transcript available on Lexis). Comments by John Connolly, former FBI agent and the handler for Bulger.

22. Shelley Murphy, "Informants."

23. Cullen, "Mobster's Charges Put the FBI on the Defensive."

24. Ralph Ranalli, "Lawyer: Irish Feds Targeted Italians," *Boston Herald*, June 25, 1997, 6.

25. Ibid.

26. See Nealon, "FBI Trusted 2 Gangsters."

27. Ralph Ranalli, "Allegations Paint Ugly Picture of a Gang's License to Kill," *Boston Globe*, September 29, 2000, A24.

28. Dick Lehr and Gerald O'Neill, *Black Mass: The Irish Mob, the FBI, and a Devil's Deal* (2000), 17–18.

29. See Lehr and O'Neill, *Black Mass*, 5.

30. Flynn, "Good Guy, Bad Guy," 65.

31. Lehr and O'Neill, *Black Mass*, 14.

32. Michael Patrick MacDonald, *All Souls: A Family Story from Southie* (1999). In this book, MacDonald describes himself and his family members growing up in Southie.

33. William Bulger, *While the Music Lasts: My Life in Politics* (1996), 4.

34. Lehr and O'Neill, *Black Mass*, 15.

35. Ibid., x.

36. Flynn, "Good Guy, Bad Guy," 64, 68–69.

37. "Married to the Mob?"

38. Ralph Ranalli and Andy Dabilis, "Case Mounts Against Ex-FBI Agent Connolly Allegedly Tipped Informants," *Boston Globe*, October 12, 2000, B1.

39. O'Neill, Chenlund, Lehr, Cullen, and Knox, "The Bulger Mystique."

40. Maggie Mulvihill, "Ex-Fed Attorney Weld: I Didn't Know," *Boston Herald*, June 7, 1997, 8.

41. Ibid.

42. See Patricia Nealon, "Ex-Agent Says FBI Knew of Drug Role of Bulger, Flemmi," *Boston Globe*, April 15, 1998, B5.

43. Ralph Ranalli, "Kin Say Slain Executive Feared Jai Alai Operation," *Boston Herald*, March 11, 1996, 4.

44. Ralph Ranalli, "FBI Official Feared Agent Would Leak Info to Mob," *Boston Herald*, April 17, 1998, 17.

45. Shelley Murphy, "Gangster Implicates Bulger in Plea Deal," *Boston Globe*, July 13, 2000, A1.

46. See Fred Bayles, "Bodies May Add to Boston Mob Case," *USA Today*, January 17, 2000, 3A. *The Boston Globe* obtained a transcript of a debriefing with him six weeks before his death. Dick Lehr, "Mob Underling's Tale of Guns, Drugs, Fear Weeks before His Death, Mcintyre Felt 'Trapped,'" *Boston Globe*, February 27, 2000, A1.

47. Ralph Ranalli, "Bulger Aide Admits Crimes in Plea Deal," *Boston Globe*, July 21, 2000, B3.

48. Shelley Murphy, "Dorchester Body Is Id'd as Woman with Ties to Flemmi," *Boston Globe*, June 22, 2000, B4. See also Andrea Estes, "Third Body in Mob Grave Identified," *Boston Herald*, June 22, 2000, 4.

49. Shelley Murphy, "Deal with Bulger Cohort May be Near," *Boston Globe*, May 16, 2000, B1. See also Murphy, "Gangster Implicates Bulger."

50. Jonathan Wells, Jack Meyers, and Maggie Mulvihill, "Special Report: Eyewitness To Evil; Ex-Agent Details Widespread Teachery in Hub FBI Office," *Boston Herald*, April 11, 2001, 1.

51. David Weber, "Reports Reveal FBI Knew of Pair's Crime," *Boston Herald*, May 8, 1998, 4.

52. Wells, Meyers, Mulvihill, "Eyewitness to Evil."

53. *Sixty Minutes*, CBS, April 8, 2001.

54. Kevin Cullen, "Checkmate Move in Gangsters Game," *Boston Globe*, June 19, 1997, A25.

55. Ralph Ranalli, "Mighty Whitey–Witness: Feds Rallied to Protect Bulger," *Boston Herald*, January 8, 1998, 1.

56. See Kevin Cullen and Shelley Murphy, "FBI to Keep Control of Bulger Manhunt; Some Other Agencies See Conflict of Interest," *Boston Globe*, June 13, 1997, B1.

57. Lehr and O'Neill, *Black Mass*, 129.

58. Patricia Nealon, "Evidence Portrays Flemmi, Bulger as Great Help to FBI," *Boston Globe*, January 8, 1998, A1.

59. Ibid.

60. "Rivera Live: Release of FBI Audiotapes Gained from Undercover Informants Which Now Threaten Two Cases Pending against Alleged Mafia Members," *CNBC News Transcripts*, June 17, 1997 (available on Lexis).

61. Ralph Ranalli, "Ex-Fed Agent Offered Deal for Testimony," *Boston Herald*, January 21, 1998, 6.

62. Nealon, "Evidence Portrays."

63. See also the statement by U.S. Attorney Donald Stern quoted in Mitchell Zuckoff, "Bulger Case Sparks Probe in U.S. House; Meehan Questions Informant Use," *Boston Globe*, July 24, 1998, A1.

64. Cullen, "Mobster's Charges Put the FBI on the Defensive."

65. Cullen, "Checkmate Move in Gangsters' Game."

66. Andrea Estes, "Bulger, Flemmi Charged with 21 Slayings," *Boston Herald*, September 29, 2000, 1.

67. Shelley Murphy, "Flemmi Guilty Plea on Rackets Expected," *Boston Globe*, May 15, 2001, A1.

68. Shelley Murphy and Judy Rakowsky, "Former Star FBI Agent Is Charged: Connolly Alerted Bulger, Indictment Says," *Boston Globe*, December 23, 1999, A1.

69. Edmund Mahony, "3 Bodies Uncovered in Boston; A Former Mobster's Tip Leads FBI Agents Thursday to the Remains of a Woman and Two Men, One of Whom Is Believed to Have Been Murdered for Being an Informant," *Hartford Courant*, January 15, 2000, A12.

70. Andrea Estes, "Lawyer: FBI Man Followed Rules; Agent Had OK to Ignore Mobsters' Crimes," *Boston Herald*, June 27, 2000, 5.

71. Shelley Murphy, "Connolly Denounces Charges. He and Flemmi Both Arraigned," *Boston Globe*, October 20, 2000, B2.

72. See Shelley Murphy, "Informants."

73. See Patricia Nealon, "Flemmi's Role as Informant Outlined; He Is Tied to Applications for Bugs and Wiretaps, Judge Says," *Boston Globe*, December 19, 1997, B2.

74. Since Bulger is still a fugitive, he did not testify and there is no ruling with regard to him. Since the nature of Flemmi's relationship is identical to that of Bulger, I am attributing the finding of facts to be logically applicable to each.

75. See Robert M. Bloom, "Judicial Integrity: A Call for Its Reemergence in the Adjudication of Criminal Cases," *Journal of Criminal Law and Criminology* 84 (1993): 462.

76. Robert M. Bloom and Mark S. Brodin, *Constitutional Criminal Procedure: Examples and Explanations* (1992), 103.

77. See Patricia Nealon, "FBI Makes Admission on Bulger; Confirms 'Whitey' Was an Informant," *Boston Globe*, June 7, 1997, A1 (quoting from a statement by Judge Wolf).

78. See Robert Suro and Christopher P. Daly, "Alleged Mob Chief's Work as FBI Informant Puts Cases in Doubt," *Washington Post*, June 22, 1997, A1; see also Patricia Nealon, "Informant Listed in Application for 1989 Bugging Revelation Could Hurt Case Against Mob Surveillance," *Boston Globe*, June 28, 1997, B2.

79. See "Rivera Live: Analysis: Mobster Angelo Mercurio's Courtroom Admission That He Was a Snitch for the US Government," *CNBC News Transcripts*, June 18, 1997 (available on Lexis).

80. Shelley Murphy, "Mobster Pleads Guilty to Murders; Judge Considers Martorano Deal," *Boston Globe*, October 1, 1999, B1.

81. Judy Rakowsky, "Director Says FBI Erred in Bulger Case," *Boston Globe*, August 5, 1999, A1.

82. Shelley Murphy, "Kevin Weeks Was Eager to Cut a Deal Implicating Longtime Mentor James 'Whitey' Bulger in Murder after the Fugitive Crime Boss Hung Him Out to Dry," *Boston Globe*, January 29, 2000, B1.

83. See Patricia Nealon, "Informer Crimes Allegedly Ignored; Report Cites Acts by Bulger, Flemmi," *Boston Globe*, September 13, 1997, B1; see also Ralph Ranalli, "Did FBI Get Help 'Flipping' Mob Killer Barboza?" *Boston Herald*, August 5, 1997, 4.

84. See Nealon, "FBI Makes Admission on Bulger."

85. See Kevin Cullen, "Maverick Judge Stands Firm in Informant Case," *Boston Globe*, June 17, 1997, A1.

86. See Ralph Ranalli, "Mob Pair Paid Agent; Flemi Affidavit: $5G Loan to FBI Man Wasn't Returned," *Boston Herald*, January 6, 1998, 1.

87. See Ranalli, "Ex-Fed Agent Offered Deal."

88. See Ralph Ranalli, "Ex-FBI Man to Testify at Mob Trial," *Boston Herald*, August 4, 1997, 4.

89. Lehr and O'Neill, *Black Mass*, 319–320.

90. Ibid. See also Ranalli, "Did FBI Help?"

91. See Ranalli, "Mob Pair Paid Agent."

92. See Ralph Ranalli, "Ex-FBI Agent: Flemmi Only Gave 'Weak' Info," *Boston Herald*, January 10, 1998, 14.

93. Lehr and O'Neill, *Black Mass*, 294–295.

94. See Patricia Nealon and Shelley Murphy, "Ex-FBI Agent Describes Warm Ties with Flemmi, Bulger; Retiree Tells of Wines, Christmas Gifts," *Boston Globe*, January 16, 1998, B1.

95. See ibid.

96. See "Ex-Agent Sorry He Took Gifts," *Patriot Ledger* (Concord, MA), January 16, 1998, 9.

97. See Ralph Ranalli, "Ills Keep Former Mob-buster from Trial," *Boston Herald*, March 25, 1998, 18.

98. Lehr and O'Neill, *Black Mass*, 238. Throughout the rest of this appendix, numbers in parentheses are page number(s) references to this book.

CHAPTER 6. THE END OF THE STORY

1. *Olmstead v. United States* 277 U.S. 438, 485 (1928).

2. Ralph Ranalli, "Allegations Paint Ugly Picture of a Gang's License to Kill," *Boston Globe*, September 29, 2000, A24.

3. Kevin Cullen, "Mobster's Charges Put the FBI on the Defensive; Many Demanding Answers in the Handling of Bulger and Flemmi," *Boston Globe*, July 5, 1999, B1.

4. See Sanford J. Unger, *FBI* (1975), 403.

5. Gary Katzman, *Inside the Criminal Process* (1990), 39.

6. Shelly Cohen, "No Apology from Agent in Salvati Case but He Acknowledged a Man's Innocence," *Boston Globe*, May 4, 2001, B1.

7. ABA Standard for the Prosecution Function and the Model Rules-Standard 3-1.2(c).

8. *Id.* Comment 1 to Model Rule 3.8.

9. "Grand Jury Report" at 74.

10. Jackson, "The Federal Prosecutor." Address delivered at the Second Annual Conference of United States Attorneys, April 1, 1940.

Bibliography

CASES

Aguilar v. State of Texas, 378 U.S. 108 (1964)

Alcorta v. Texas, 355 U.S. 28 (1957)

Alderman v. United States, 394 U.S. 165 (1969)

Arizona v. Fulminante, 499 U.S. 279 (1991)

Arizona v. Fulminante, 975 P.2d 75 (Ariz. 1999)

Bartkus v. Illinois, 359 U.S. 121 (1959)

Bemis v. United States, 30 F.3d 220 (1st Cir. 1994)

Berger v. United States, 295 U.S. 78 (1935)

Brady v. Maryland, 373 U.S. 83 (1963)

Brewer v. Williams, 430 U.S. 387, 398 (1977)

Brown v. Walker, 161 U.S. 591 (1896)

California v. Greenwood, 486 U.S. 35 (1988)

Carter v. United States, 417 F.2d 384 (9th Cir. 1969); cert. denied, 399 U.S. 935, reh'g denied, 400 U.S. 855

Chapman v. California, 386 U.S. 18 (1967)

Commonwealth v. Amral, 407 Mass. 511 (1990)

Commonwealth v. Lewin, 405 Mass. 566 (1989)

Commonwealth v. Lewin, 407 Mass. 617 (1990)

Commonwealth v. Upton, 394 Mass. 363 (1985)

Counselman v. Hitchcock, 142 U.S. 547 (1892)

Earley v. Smoot, 846 F.Supp. 451 (D. Md. 1994)

Escobedo v. Illinois, 378 U.S. 478 (1964)

Fearnow v. C. & P. Telephone Co., et al., 104 Md. App. 1, 655 A.2d 1 (1995)

Feldman v. United States, 322 U.S. 487 (1944)

Franks v. Delaware, 438 U.S. 154 (1978)

Gerstein v. Pugh, 420 U.S. 103 (1975)

Gideon v. Wainswight, 372 U.S. 335 (1963)

Giglio v. United States, 405 U.S. 150 (1972)

Hawes v. Carberry, 103 Md. App. 214, 653 A.2d 479 (1995)

Heath v. Alabama, 474 U.S. 82 (1985)

Hoffa v. United States, 385 U.S. 293 (1966)

Illinois v. Gates, 462 U.S. 213 (1983)

Illinois v. Perkins, 496 U.S. 292 (1990)

In Re Bianchi, 542 F.2d 98 (1st Cir. 1976)

In Re Grand Jury Proceedings: United States v. Buckley, 860 F.2d 11 (2nd Cir. 1988)

In Re Grand Jury Proceedings (Linda R. Tripp), 1998 WL 754889, pt. 1 (D.D.C. June 30, 1998)

In Re Groban, 352 U.S. 330 (1957)

Kastigar v. United States, 406 U.S. 441 (1972)

Katz v. United States, 369 F.2d 130 (9th Cir. 1966)

Katz v. United States, 389 U.S. 347 (1967)

Kirby v. Illinois, 406 U.S. 682 (1972)

Knapp v. Schweitzer, 357 U.S. 371 (1958)

Kuhlman v. Wilson, 477 U.S. 436 (1986)

Kyles v. Whitley, 514 U.S. 419 (1995)

Lewis v. United States, 385 U.S. 206 (1966)

Malloy v. Hogan, 378 U.S. 7 (1964)

Mapp v. Ohio, 367 U.S. 643 (1961)

Marron v. United States, 275 U.S. 192 (1927)

Maryland v. Buie, 494 U.S. 325 (1990)

Massiah v. United States, 377 U.S. 201 (1964)

McCray v. Illinois, 386 U.S. 300 (1967)

Minnesota v. Carter, 525 U.S. 83 (1998)

Minnesota v. Olson, 495 U.S. 91 (1990)

Miranda v. Arizona, 384 U.S. 436 (1996)

Mooney v. Holohan, 294 U.S. 103 (1935)

Moulton v. Maine, 474 U.S. 159 (1985)

Murphy v. Waterfront Comm'n of New York Harbor, 378 U.S. 52 (1964)

Napue v. Illinois, 360 U.S. 264 (1959)

Olmstead v. United States, 277 U.S. 438, 471 (1928)

Petric v. State, 66 Md. App. 470, 504 A.2d 1168 (1986)

Rakas v. Illinois, 439 U.S. 128 (1978)

Reina v. United States, 364 U.S. 507 (1960)

Rochin v. California, 342 U.S. 165 (1952)

Roviaro v. United States, 353 U.S. 53 (1957)

Rowe v. Griffin, 497 F.Supp. 610 (M.D. Ala. 1980), aff'd, 676 F.2d 524

Roy v. United States, 38 Fed. Cl. 184 (Fed. Cl. 1997)

Santobello v. New York, 404 U.S. 257 (1971)

Smith v. Maryland, 442 U.S. 735 (1979)

Spinelli v. United States, 393 U.S. 410 (1969)

State v. Burnett, 42 N.J. 377 (1964)

State v. Fulminante, 161 Ariz. 237 (1988)

United States v. Agurs, 427 U.S. 97 (1976)

United States v. Bagley, 473 U.S. 667 (1985)

United States v. Baptista-Rodriguez, 17 F.3d 1354 (11th Cir. 1994)

United States v. Ceccolini, 435 U.S. 268 (1978)

United States v. Cervantes-Pacheco, 826 F.2d 310 (5th Cir. 1987)

United States v. Crow Dog, 532 F.2d 1182 (8th Cir. 1976)

United States v. Flemmi, 255 F.3d 78 (1st Cir. 2000)

United States v. Frost, 914 F.2d 756 (6th Cir. 1990)

United States v. Giordano, 416 U.S. 505 (1974)

United States v. Harvey, 869 F.2d 1439 (11th Cir. 1989)

United States v. Henry, 447 U.S. 264 (1980)

United States v. Leon, 468 U.S. 897 (1984)

United States v. Levy, 577 F.2d 200 (3d Cir. 1978)

United States v. Mastroianni, 749 F.2d 900 (1st Cir. 1984)

United States v. McCown, 711 F.2d 1441 (9th Cir. 1983)

United States v. Miller, 425 U.S. 435 (1976)

United States v. Morrison, 449 U.S. 361 (1981)

United States v. Murdock, 284 U.S. 141 (1931)

United States v. North, 920 F.2d 940 (D.C. Cir. 1990)

United States v. Patrick, 542 F.2d 381 (7th Cir. 1976)

United States v. Payner, 447 U.S. 727 (1980)

United States v. Raddatz, 447 U.S. 667 (1980)

United States v. Rice, 421 F.Supp. 871 (E.D. IL, 1976)

United States v. Rodman, 519 F.2d 1058 (1st Cir. 1975)

United States v. Ruggiero, 928 F.2d 1289 (2d Cir. 1991)

United States v. Salemme, 91 F.Supp.2d 141 (D.Mass. 1999)

United States v. Schmidgall, 25 F.3d 1533 (11th Cir. 1994)

United States v. Trammel, 583 F.2d 1166 (10th Cir. 1978) aff'd 445 U.S. 40 (1980)

United States v. Valencia, 541 F.2d 618 (6th Cir. 1976)

United States v. White, 401 U.S. 745 (1971)

Weeks v. United States, 232 U.S. 383 (1914)

Wong Sun v. United States, 371 U.S. 471 (1963)

WORKS CITED

"All Things Considered." *National Public Radio*. December 24, 1999. Available on Lexis.

Andocides. *On the Mysteries* 36.43 ff.2o.

Associated Press. "Tripp's Attorney Accuses Lewinsky of Lying During Pretrial Hearing." *Associated Press Newswires*, March 21, 2000.

Bastone, William. "Tony Limo's Wild Ride." *Village Voice*, December 27, 1994, 25.

Bayles, Fred. "Bodies May Add to Boston Mob Case." *USA Today*, January 17, 2000, 3A.

Bedau, Hugo Adam, and Michael L. Radelat. "Miscarriage of Justice in Potentially Capital Cases." *Stanford Law Review* 40.

Bintliff, Russell L. *Police Procedural: A Writer's Guide to Police and How They Work*. 1993.

Black's Law Dictionary. 6th ed. 1990.

Bloom, Robert M. "Judicial Integrity: A Call for Its Reemergence in the Adjudication of Criminal Cases." *Journal of Criminal Law and Criminology* 84 (1993): 462.

Bloom, Robert M., and Mark S. Brodin. *Constitutional Criminal Procedure: Examples and Explanations*. 1992.

"Boston Mobster Joins Elite Group on FBI List." *Chicago Tribune*, November 30, 2000, Evening Update Edition, 2.

Boyd, Andrew. *The Informers: A Chilling Account of the Supergrasses in Northern Ireland*. 1984.

Briggs, John, Christopher Harrison, Angus McInnes, and David Vincent. *Crime and Punishment in England: An Introductory History*. 1996.

Brennan, William. "State Constitutions and the Protection of Individual Rights." *Harvard Law Review* 90 (1997): 489, 491.

Brown, Raymond E. *The Death of the Messiah: From Gethsemane to the Grave*. 1994.

Bulger, William. *While the Music Lasts: My Life in Politics*. 1996.

Burckhardt, Jacob. *The Greeks and Greek Civilization*. 1998.

Christ, Matthew R. *The Litigious Athenian*. 1998.

Clines, Francis X. "Impeachment: The Scene—Capitol Sketchbook; A Stealthy Tripp, More Cat Than Canary." *New York Times*, December 22, 1998, A29.

Cohen, Shelly. "No Apology from Agent in Salvati Case but He Acknowledged a Man's Innocence." *Boston Globe*, May 4, 2002, B1.

The Columbia Encyclopedia. 5th ed. 1993.

Cullen, Kevin. "Code of Silence Intact, Winter Gets 10 Years." *Boston Globe*, May 18, 1993, 1.

———. "Focus Turns to Fugitive Bulger's FBI Ties; Lawyers, Officers Await Answers from Agency Files." *Boston Globe*, May 29, 1997, at B1.

———. "Maverick Judge Stands Firm in Informant Case." *Boston Globe*, June 17, 1997, A1.

———. "Checkmate Move in Gangsters Game." *Boston Globe*, June 19, 1997, A25.

———. "Mobster's Charges Put the FBI on the Defensive; Many Demanding Answers in the Handling of Bulger and Flemmi." *Boston Globe*, July 5, 1999, B1.

Cullen, Kevin, and Shelley Murphy. "FBI to Keep Control of Bulger Manhunt; Some Other Agencies See Conflict of Interest." *Boston Globe*, June 13, 1997, B1.

Estes, Andrea. "Third Body in Mob Grave Identified." *Boston Herald*, June 22, 2000, 4.

———. "Lawyer: FBI Man Followed Rules; Agent Had OK to Ignore Mobsters' Crimes." *Boston Herald*, June 27, 2000, 5.

———. "Bulger, Flemmi Charged with 21 Slayings." *Boston Herald*, September 29, 2000, 1.

———. "Feds Detail Bulger, Inc." *Boston Herald*, September 30, 2000, 1.

"Ex-Agent Sorry He Took Gifts." *Patriot Ledger* (Concord, MA), January 16, 1998, 9.

Federal Bureau of Investigation. *Avoiding the Informant Trap: A Blueprint for Control.* FBI Law Enforcement Bulletin. November 1998.

Fisher, Stanley Z. "The Prosecutor's Ethical Duty to Seek Exculpatory Evidence in Police Hands: Lessons from England." *Fordham Law Review* 68 (2000): 1279, 1382.

Flynn, Sean. "Good Guy, Bad Guy." *Boston Magazine*, November 1998, 64, 68–69, 106.

Gagarin, Michael. *Early Greek Law.* 1986.

Hay, Douglas, Peter Lindbaugh, John G. Rule, E. P. Thompson, and Cal Winslow. *Albion's Fatal Tree: Crime and Society in Eighteenth-Century England.* 1975.

Hohler, Bob. "Wiretapping Case Is Dropped; Move Follows Curbs on Lewinsky Data." *Boston Globe*, May 25, 2000, A3.

Isikoff, Michael. "A Twist in *Jones v. Clinton*: Her Lawyers Subpoena Another Woman." *Newsweek*, August 11, 1997, 30.

Isikoff, Michael, and Evan Thomas. "Clinton and the Intern." *Newsweek*, February 2, 1998, 30.

Johnston, David. "Jurors in Maryland Indict Linda Tripp in Lewinsky Tapes." *New York Times*, July 31, 1999, A1.

Karchmer, Clifford L. "Keeping Informants under Control." *New York Times*, August 3, 1981, A15.

Katzman, Gary. *Inside the Criminal Process*. 1990.

Kelly, Jack. "How America Met the Mob." *American Heritage*, July/August 2000, 76, 85.

Kent, W.H. "Judas Iscariot." In *The Catholic Encyclopedia*. Vol. 8. Available: <http://www.newadvent.org/cathen/08539a.htm> (visited July 17, 2000).

"The Key Players; Winter Hill Gang; James J. (Whitey) Bulger; Spotlight." *Boston Globe*, March 5, 1995, 24.

Labaton, Stephen. "Linda Tripp Is Focus of Maryland Criminal Inquiry over Taped Calls." *New York Times*, July 8, 1998, A18.

Labaton, Stephen, Don Van Natta Jr., and Jill Abramson. "The President under Fire: The Investigation." *New York Times*, January 25, 1998, A1.

Lehr, Dick. "Mob Underling's Tale of Guns, Drugs, Fear Weeks before his Death, McIntyre Felt 'Trapped.'" *Boston Globe*, February 27, 2000, A1.

Lehr, Dick, and Gerald O'Neill. *Black Mass: The Irish Mob, the FBI, and a Devil's Deal*. 2000.

Lichtblau, Eric. "Starr Won't Seek to Retry McDougal, Steele; Whitewater: Prosecutor Failed to Win Convictions in Obstruction Cases, Charges Are Now Pending against Only Webster Hubbell." *Los Angeles Times*, May 26, 1999, A10.

———. "Pledge of Immunity Doesn't Shield Tripp, Judge Rules Scandal: The Former Friend of Monica S. Lewinsky Failed to Block Her Trial on State Charges in the Taping of Conversations with Former Intern." *Los Angeles Times*, December 15, 1999, A18.

Maccoby, Hyam. *The Myth of Jewish Evil*. 1992.

MacDonald, Michael Patrick. *All Souls: A Family Story from Southie*. 1999.

Macdowell, Douglas M. *The Law in Classical Athens*. 1978.

Mahony, Edmund. "3 Bodies Uncovered in Boston; A Former Mobster's Tip Leads FBI Agents Thursday to the Remains of a Woman and Two Men, One of Whom Is Believed to Have Been Murdered for Being an Informant." *Hartford Courant*, January 15, 2000, A12.

"Married to the Mob?; Story of Informer and How His Relationship with the FBI Helped Him Build Criminal Empire." *Dateline NBC News*. March 17, 2000. Available on Lexis.

Marx, Gary T. "Thoughts on a Neglected Category of Social Movement Participant: The Agent Provocateur and the Informant." *American Journal of Sociology* 402 (September 1974): 80–82.

———. *Undercover: Police Surveillance in America*. 1988.

Mayer, Jane. "Portrait of a Whistleblower." *New Yorker*, March 23, 1998, 34, 46; and *Newsweek*, April 13, 1998, 47.

Morton, Andrew. *Monica's Story*. 1999.

Mulvihill, Maggie. "Ex-Fed Attorney Weld: I Didn't Know." *Boston Herald*, June 7, 1997, 8.

Murphy, Sean P. "Rush to Misjudgment: Fumbling the Lewin Case." *Boston Globe*, November 4, 1990, Metro/Region, 29.

Murphy, Shelley. "Informants: Handle with Care; FBI Work with Flemmi, Bulger Proves Messy." *Boston Globe*, June 30, 1997, B1.

———. "Mobster Pleads Guilty to Murders; Judge Considers Martorano Deal." *Boston Globe*, October 1, 1999, B1.

———. "Kevin Weeks Was Eager to Cut a Deal Implicating Longtime Mentor James 'Whitey' Bulger in Murder after the Fugitive Crime Boss Hung Him Out to Dry." *Boston Globe*, January 29, 2000, B1.

———. "Flemmi Guilty Plea on Rackets Expected." *Boston Globe*, May 15, 2001, A1.

———. "Deal with Bulger Cohort May Be Near." *Boston Globe*, May 16, 2000, B1.

———. "Dorchester Body Is Id'd as Woman with Ties to Flemmi." *Boston Globe*, June 22, 2000, B4.

———. "Gangster Implicates Bulger in Plea Deal." *Boston Globe*, July 13, 2000, A1.

———. "Connolly Denounces Charges. He and Flemmi Both Arraigned." *Boston Globe*, October 20, 2000, B2.

Murphy, Shelley, and Judy Rakowsky. "Former Star FBI Agent Is Charged: Connolly Alerted Bulger, Indictment Says." *Boston Globe*, December 23, 1999, A1.

Nealon, Patricia. "U.S. Says Flemmi Turned Informant to Torpedo Rivals, Immunity Disputed as Hearings Begin." *Boston Globe*, January 7, 1998, B2.

———. "Evidence Portrays Flemmi, Bulger as Great Help to FBI." *Boston Globe*, January 8, 1998, Al.

———. "Extortion Trial Witness Tells of Police Abuses." *Boston Globe*, April 8, 1998, A1.

———. "Ex-Agent Says FBI Knew of Drug Role of Bulger, Flemmi." *Boston Globe*, April 15, 1998, B5.

———. "FBI Trusted 2 Gangsters, Ex-agent Says; Offers More Details of Cozy Relationship." *Boston Globe*, April 21, 1998, B4.

———. "FBI Makes Admission on Bulger; Confirms 'Whitey' Was an Informant." *Boston Globe*, June 7, 1997, Al.

———. "Informant Listed in Application for 1989 Bugging Revelation Could Hurt Case Against Mob Surveillance." *Boston Globe*, June 28, 1997, B2.

———. "Informer Crimes Allegedly Ignored; Report Cites Acts by Bulger, Flemmi." *Boston Globe*, September 13, 1997, B1.

———. "Flemmi's Role as Informant Outlined; He Is Tied to Applications for Bugs and Wiretaps, Judge Says." *Boston Globe*, December 19, 1997, B2.

Nealon, Patricia, and Shelley Murphy. "Ex-FBI Agent Describes Warm Ties with Flemmi, Bulger; Retiree Tells of Wines, Christmas Gifts." *Boston Globe*, January 16, 1998, B1.

O'Neill, Gerald, Dick Lehr, and Kevin Cullen. "New Team, Tactics Hastened Whitey Bulger's Fall; Spotlight." *Boston Globe*, March 5, 1995, 1.

O'Neill, Gerald, Christine Chenlund, Dick Lehr, Kevin Cullen, and Mary Elizabeth Knox. "The Bulger Mystique; Law Enforcement Officials' Lament about an Elusive Foe: Where was Whitey?" *Boston Globe*, September 20, 1988, 1.

Orfield, Myron W. Jr. "Deterrence, Perjury, and the Heater Factor: An Exclusionary Rule in the Chicago Criminal Courts." *University of Colorado Law Review* 63 (1992): 75, 112.

Otto, Mary. "Md. Judge Dismisses Tripp Wiretap Case." *Washington Post*, June 1, 2000, A10.

Percy, Martyn. "Arguments for Easter: The Day When Even God Needs a Scapegoat; Poor Judas. The Tendency to Lay the Blame for the Sin of the World at the Feet of One Man Is Not Restricted to Gospel Writers. Look Around." *The Independent* (London), April 2, 1999, 7.

"Plea Bargaining and the Transformation of the Criminal Process." *Harvard Law Review* 90 (1977): 564, 569.

"The President under Fire; Linda Tripp's Statement on Role in Case." *New York Times*, January 31, 1998, A8.

Radzinowicz, Leon. *A History of English Criminal Law and Its Administration from 1750*. Vol. 2. 1981.

Rakowsky, Judy. "Director Says FBI Erred in Bulger Case." *Boston Globe*, August 5, 1999, A1.

Ranalli, Ralph, "Kin Say Slain Executive Feared Jai Alai Operation." *Boston Herald*, March 11, 1996, 4.

———. "Lawyer: Irish Feds Targeted Italians." *Boston Herald*, June 25, 1997, 6.

———. "Ex-FBI Man to Testify at Mob Trial." *Boston Herald*, August 4, 1997, 4.

———. "Did FBI Help 'Flipping' Mob Killer Barboza?" *Boston Herald*, August 5, 1997, 4.

———. "Mob Pair Paid Agent; Flemmi Affidavit: $5G Loan to FBI Man Wasn't Returned." *Boston Herald*, January 6, 1998, 1.

———. "Mighty Whitey–Witness: Feds Rallied to Protect Bulger." *Boston Herald*, January 8, 1998, 1.

———. "Ex-FBI Agent: Flemmi Only Gave 'Weak' Info." *Boston Herald*, January 10, 1998, 14.

———. "Ex-Fed Agent Offered Deal for Testimony." *Boston Herald*, January 21, 1998, 6.

———. "Ills Keep Former Mob-buster from Trial." *Boston Herald*, March 25, 1998, 18.

———. "FBI Official Feared Agent Would Leak Info to Mob." *Boston Herald*, April 17, 1998, 17.

———. "Bulger Aide Admits Crimes in Plea Deal." *Boston Globe*, July 21, 2000, B3.

———. "Allegations Paint Ugly Picture of a Gang's License to Kill." *Boston Globe*, September 29, 2000, A24.

Ranalli, Ralph, and Andy Dabilis. "Case Mounts against Ex-FBI Agent Connolly Allegedly Tipped Informants." *Boston Globe*, October 12, 2000, B1.

Reuter, Peter. "Licensing Criminals: Police and Informants." *Rand Paper Series*. October 1982.

"The Rise, Fall, and Escape of Whitey Bulger." *Boston Globe*, March 5, 1995, 25.

"Rivera Live: Analysis: Mobster Angelo Mercurio's Courtroom Admission That He Was a Snitch for the U.S. Government." *CNBC News Transcripts*. June 18, 1997. Available on Lexis.

"Rivera Live: Release of FBI Audiotapes Gained from Undercover Informants Which Now Threaten Two Cases Pending against Alleged Mafia Members." *CNBC News Transcripts*. June 17, 1997. Available on Lexis.

Rohrlich, Ted. "Jail Informant Had Allies on Side of the Law." *Los Angeles Times*, November 20, 1988.

————. "Jail Informant Owns Up to Perjury in a Dozen Cases." *Los Angeles Times*, January 4, 1990, A1.

————. "Authorities Go Fishing for Jailhouse Confessions." *Los Angeles Times*, March 4, 1990, A1.

————. "Perjurer Sentenced to 3 Years; Crime: Informant Blew the Whistle on Use of Jailhouse Liars-for-Hire, but No Law Officers Were Charged for Conspiring with Him." *Los Angeles Times*, May 20, 1992, B1.

Rohrlich, Ted, and Robert Stewart. "Jailhouse Snitches; Trading Lies for Freedom." *Los Angeles Times*, April 16, 1989.

Safire, William. "Essay: The Supervictim." *New York Times*, March 11, 1999, A31.

Sciolino, Elaine, and Don Van Natta Jr. "Testing of a President: The Confidant." *New York Times*, March 15, 1998, sec. 1, p. 1.

Seper, Jerry. "State Indicts Tripp for Taping; Maryland Jurors Hand Up 2 Counts." *Washington Times*, July 31, 1999, A1.

Silverglate, Harvey. "*In Re Commonwealth v. Lewin*: The Making of a Crooked Case." *Boston Phoenix*, March 10–16, 1989.

Skolnick, Jerome H. "Deception by Police." *Criminal Justice Ethics* (summer/fall 1982): 40, 43.

Slobogin, Christopher. "Reform: The Police: Testilying: Police Perjury and What to Do about It." *University of Colorado Law Review* 67 (1996): 1037, 1046–1048.

Stambaugh, John E. *The Ancient Roman City*. 1988.

Stammer, Larry B. "New Look at Ancient Betrayer; For Centuries, Judas Iscariot Has Been the Archetype of the Traitor. But Some Scholars Are Beginning to Wonder If He Was a Villain at All." *Los Angeles Times*, April 21, 2000, A1.

Story, W.W. *A Roman Lawyer in Jerusalem in the First Century*. 1908.

Sullivan, Paul. "Shooting Latest Chapter in Hub's Gory Legacy." *Boston Herald*, November 7, 1995, 6.

Suro, Robert, and Christopher P. Daly. "Alleged Mob Chief's Work As FBI Informant Puts Cases in Doubt." *Washington Post*, June 22, 1997, A1.

Thomas, Evan, and Michael Isikoff, with Daniel Klaidman. "The Tripp Trap?" *Newsweek*, July 13, 1998, 22, 24.

Thorne, Christopher. "US Tripp Wiretap." *Associated Press Newswires*, May 25, 2000, 12:20:00.

Tonry, Michael, ed. *The Handbook of Crime and Punishment*. 1998.

Torry, Saundra, and Raja Mishra. "Tripp Indicted on Charges of Wiretapping: Maryland Law Prohibits Taping without Consent." *Washington Post*, July 31, 1999, A01.

Unger, Sanford J. *FBI*. 1975.

Valentine, Paul W. "Tripp Knowingly Violated Md. Wiretap Law; Immunity Deal with Starr May Put Her Case beyond Reach of State." *Washington Post*, October 6, 1998, B1.

Van Natta Jr., Don. "The President's Trial: The Betrayer." *New York Times*, February 12, 1999, A1.

Weber, David. "Reports Reveal FBI Knew of Pair's Crime." *Boston Herald*, May 8, 1998, 4.

Wells, Jonathan, Jack Meyers, and Maggie Mulvihill. "Eyewitness to Evil: Ex-Agent Details Widespread Treachery in Hub FBI Office." *Boston Herald*, April 11, 2001, 1.

Whiting, Brent. "Chiropractor's Note Fails to Impress Skeptical Judge." *Arizona Republic*, September 8, 1993, B3.

———. "No-Shows Rule Out Witness." *Arizona Republic*, October 14, 1993, B6.

———. "Prosecutor Asks Court for New Judge; Says Ruling Out Murder-Trial Witness Is 'Bias.'" *Arizona Republic*, April 7, 1994, B1.

———. "Man Guilty of Killing Stepdaughter 1st Conviction Was Tossed Out over Confessions." *Arizona Republic*, June 22, 1994, B2.

Wiersbe, Warren W. *Classic Sermons on Judas Iscariot*. 1995.

Wong, Doris Sue. "Informant Is Not the Right One, Defense in Officer's Slaying Says." *Boston Globe*, March 1, 1989, Metro/Region, 1.

———. "Luna Convicted of Perjury, Filing False Reports." *Boston Globe*, June 6, 1991.

———. "Suffolk DA's Homicide Chief Goes Today." *Boston Globe*, August 31, 1992, Metro/Region.

Wright, Charles A, and Kenneth W. Graham Jr. *Federal Practice and Procedure*, §5702.

Younger, Irving. "The Perjury Routine." *The Nation*, May 8, 1967, 96–97.

Zoroya, Gregg. "Monica Does D.C. Touring the Favourite Haunts of the World's Most Famous Intern." *Toronto Sun*, March 28, 1999, T6.

Zuckoff, Mitchell. "Bulger Case Sparks Probe in U.S. House; Meehan Questions Informant Use." *Boston Globe*, July 24, 1998, A1.

Cases Index

Subject Index

ABOUT THE AUTHOR

ROBERT M. BLOOM is Professor of Law at Boston College Law School. He has written extensively in the area of criminal procedure, focusing on police abuses and the Fourth Amendment.